Burnout

for
dummies®
A Wiley Brand

Burnout

by Eva Selhub, MD

Burnout For Dummies®

Published by: **John Wiley & Sons, Inc.**, 111 River Street, Hoboken, NJ 07030-5774, www.wiley.com

Copyright © 2023 by John Wiley & Sons, Inc., Hoboken, New Jersey

Published simultaneously in Canada

For general information on our other products and services, please contact our Customer Care Department within the U.S. at 877-762-2974, outside the U.S. at 317-572-3993, or fax 317-572-4002. For technical support, please visit https://hub.wiley.com/community/support/dummies.

Wiley publishes in a variety of print and electronic formats and by print-on-demand. Some material included with standard print versions of this book may not be included in e-books or in print-on-demand. If this book refers to media such as a CD or DVD that is not included in the version you purchased, you may download this material at http://booksupport.wiley.com. For more information about Wiley products, visit www.wiley.com.

Library of Congress Control Number: 2022947348

ISBN 978-1-119-89493-3 (pbk); ISBN 978-1-119-89494-0 (ebk); ISBN 978-1-119-89495-7 (ebk)

SKY10036910_101422

Contents at a Glance

Table of Contents

Introduction

I f you are feeling burned out, depressed, unmotivated, without purpose or passion, or unproductive at work or at home, you are not alone. Burnout is everywhere and has become especially prevalent since the COVID-19 pandemic, though it was a widespread problem even prior. Whether you are taxed from being overworked, undersupported, or a full-time caregiver or overwhelmed by never-ending responsibilities, the causes and reasons that have led you to burnout are varied, complex, and very real indeed.

In lieu of ongoing uncertainty coming in the form of pandemics, school shootings, job demands, loss of loved ones, illness, or economic instability, it is not surprising that burnout is so prevalent. The question is, does burnout need to happen to so many people? Can it be healed, and better yet, can burnout be prevented?

It's important to remember that you are innately wired to adapt to difficulty and you do have the tools within you to heal. In each and every one of us, there exists a strong and resilient person who can overcome adversity and burnout. The key is to be able to tap into this wiring, this part of you that wants to thrive and live fully, so that you can set the course to flourishing, freedom, and fulfillment. This may not sound possible from your vantage point now, given that you feel exhausted and spent. But know that it is possible.

Your path is unique to you, and this book is intended to help readers embark on their personal journey to discovering their way through healing burnout. You find out what burnout is, the factors involved that get you there, how to identify the role you may have played, the importance of mindful compassion when it comes to healing, and the various other strategies that can help you get out of burnout and back to feeling resilient and flourishing. Hopefully, this book will provide you with wisdom and guidance, helping you uncover more closely who you are, your tendencies, your wants, the job that is right for you, and ways to treat yourself with love and compassion so that you can find your way to enjoying a meaningful and fulfilling life.

About This Book

I just got off a call with a dear friend who I was advising on how to avoid burnout when I received a call from the publishing house asking if I would be willing to write *Burnout For Dummies.* It seemed like it was meant to be, and indeed I was excited to have the opportunity to share my experiences and knowledge with others who could benefit from it.

I have been helping people with burnout for over 25 years, whether they have come to my clinical practice or I work with them currently in my coaching practice. What I have learned is that though no two individuals have the same journey, there are many universal factors that do apply to everybody. This book covers the variety of factors that can lead to burnout, ways in which you can recognize the signs and symptoms, how to examine your job and identify whether it's the right fit for you, how to enhance compassion toward yourself, and how to build a slew of skills and tools to help you through and out of burnout. *Burnout For Dummies* offers insight, easy-to-follow instructions, practical tips, time-honored wisdom, and do-it-yourself exercises that enable you to embody the knowledge so that it becomes reality.

Hopefully, you will find the information in this book to be practical, loving, and applicable to your work and life. Explore the book and feel free to read the chapters that appeal to you or read from cover to cover. Experiment with the exercises and take time to reflect. Read it once or several times. Bring the words into practice as you see fit. You may want to read some of the exercises and record yourself so that you can listen as you keep your eyes closed and mindfully follow the practices. Be sure to listen to the recordings that are offered and check out the cheat sheet. You didn't get to burnout overnight, so the healing process is therefore a journey of discovery, one that hopefully, this book can serve as a guide for.

Foolish Assumptions

When writing this book, I made the assumption that the majority of people with burnout have medical complaints, seeing as how many of the people I have helped had been my patients. The truth is that burnout can happen to anyone with or without medical issues, and the key is to catch the warning signs before physical or psychological problems arise or get worse. I may have foolishly assumed also that you don't want to struggle more than you already are, and that you want to learn how to find ways to thrive instead of dive. Perhaps you are tired and don't have the energy to do it, but I believe that you can, foolishly or not. I believe there is a rich and strong part within you that is eager to read to learn, discover, and do what it takes to move through and out of burnout to find fulfillment and joy. I have not foolishly assumed that this book has all of the answers to burnout. Do know that. Foolish or not, though, I do believe this book will help.

Icons Used in This Book

Throughout this book, I use icons to draw your attention to particular kinds of information, exercises, or opportunities to reflect. Here's what they mean:

This icon alerts you to important insights, clarifications, or ways to do things better.

I use this icon whenever I want your attention. Please read the text associated with it for important information.

This icon lets you know that the exercise you're reading can be found online as an audio track. See the next section for more details.

Beyond the Book

In addition to the material in this printed book, go to www.dummies.com to find a Cheat Sheet with tips that will serve as reminders or quick-access information. Simply type "Burnout For Dummies Cheat Sheet" in the search box on Dummies.com.

But wait! There's more: You can download a dozen audio tracks of some of the best exercises from the book, which are flagged with the Play icon. To access these audio tracks, go to www.dummies.com/go/burnoutfd.

Where to Go from Here

The book is designed in such a way so that you don't have to read the book from cover to cover. Rather, you can open the book to the chapter you're interested in. You get to decide how and what you want to learn. Of course, if you want to understand the basis of burnout and use it as the foundation from which you jump off and learn everything else, go in chronological order and build the knowledge you need as you go along.

Take your pick, enjoy the read, and feel free to let me know how your journey goes at www.drselhub.com!

1

Turning the Tide on the Burnout Epidemic

IN THIS PART . . .

Get an overview of what constitutes burnout to help guide you on your journey.

Take a quiz to evaluate if and how you are burned out.

Find out about the scope of burnout, who it is affecting, and why.

Appreciate the impact burnout has on society, families, relationships, and health.

Chapter **1**

So You Think You're Burned Out

C hances are, whether you have purchased this book or just picked it up to have a look, you are already thinking that you, or someone you care about, is experiencing burnout and you are hoping there is a way out. The good news is there is a way, but it isn't so much an out as a through, back to the part of you that is full of life, joy, and vitality.

Know that there is no quick fix to burnout. Perhaps you're thinking you are too tired or exhausted to even read through this book. But ask yourself this: Who noticed that you were feeling uneasy or tired? Who picked up the book wanting to feel better? Some part of you has become aware that you are tired, lacking motivation, feeling disconnected or irritated, and so forth. Some part of you believes you don't have to feel this way. It's this very part of you that isn't burned out!

There is a part of you that has raised the alarm and essentially nudged you; a little voice inside you that said, "this isn't right" or "you shouldn't have to feel this way" and then motivated you to take action.

Guess what? This part of you, whether big or small, is the part of you that is not burned out and the part of you that this book will connect with and help flourish, similar to the way you might pull weeds from around a beautiful flower so that it can feel the light and grow to its full potential. You have arrived at this point in time with everything you need to live a full and thriving life free of burnout because you have the capacity to notice the current conditions and to respond to them with kindness, warmth, and a sense of purpose. You will discover in these pages how you came to be in this place; how you can navigate more effectively through and beyond it; how you can prevent ending up here again; and even more importantly, how to find a deeply satisfying and meaningful way of being in your work and in your life. Sound okay to you? Great! Time to get started.

What Exactly *Is* Burnout?

If you're like me, your first instinct when authors start talking about defining terms (aside from noticing your eyes glazing over) may be to skip ahead to the "good stuff." After all, what good is a dictionary when you're suffering and in pain? You simply want the pain to go away, and the sooner the better. However, consider indulging me here and being a little bit patient so that we can get started on the right foot and be absolutely sure that we (you and I) are talking about the same thing when we use the word "burnout."

Burnout is a term that gets tossed around a lot these days, not only because it is rampant in our modern lives (more on this later) but also because it has become a label that we have come to apply to a wide range of non-burnout experiences. The word "burnout" seems to be experiencing the same fate as the word "trauma," which was intended to denote a deeply distressing or disturbing experience or a physical injury but has since been applied to everything from torture to rude baristas at Starbucks. I giggle to myself thinking about the reaction of one of my exercise buddies when I mentioned that I would be writing a book on burnout. He said (laughing), "I need that. I'm so burned out I am practically a walking text-book," while going on to do 150 squats. Needless to say, I explained to him that he may be feeling weary about life and "over the [COVID-19] pandemic," but burnout itself actually has a more specific definition. The very mere facts that he had such a positive attitude, had plenty of energy to work out and go hiking that very same day, and enjoyed his work were representative of the likelihood that he actually was *not* burned out, at least, not yet by the looks of it.

The term "burnout" was first coined by the psychologist Herbert Freudenberger in the 1970s. It is defined by the World Health Organization (WHO) as an "occupational phenomenon" that is ". . . a syndrome conceptualized as resulting from chronic workplace stress that has not been successfully managed. It is characterized by three dimensions: 1) feelings of energy depletion or exhaustion; 2) increased mental distance from one's job, or feelings of negativism or cynicism related to one's job; and 3) reduced professional efficacy." I explore these manifestations of burnout much more deeply later in this chapter.

The WHO definition goes on to specifically state that "burnout refers specifically to phenomena in the occupational context and should not be applied to describe experiences in other areas of life." In modern society, however, the line between work and "other areas of life" has sufficiently blurred to the extent that it is really unfair to talk concretely about "work-life balance" or to imply that burnout would only arise from your job, if, for example, you are a parent, the primary caregiver for an aging parent, or a volunteer leader of a community organization. For the purposes of this book, I say that burnout arises out of your attempts to fulfill your obligations of *any* kind. Indeed, burnout is not exclusive to work. It is a stress-related issue, and you can therefore arrive at burnout as a result of the cumulative effect of stress from too many obligations in any area of your life.

What burnout is not

Putting aside this little shift to looking at all your obligations as a potential source of burnout, it can be valuable to focus on figuring out what burnout *is* and also what it *is not*, so you can invest your time and attention in addressing the larger challenge itself and not waste your effort on "Band-Aid fixes." What I'm suggesting here is the equivalent of "work smarter, not harder," and getting a better sense of what you are trying to improve or correct will help you be more effective in reducing burnout and increasing satisfaction in your life. Taking pain medication to address the symptoms of a shoulder injury can certainly help dull the pain, but appreciating that the pain comes from a broken bone will go a lot farther toward long-term relief of the pain. Appreciating the source of burnout versus the symptoms can help you be more effective.

You can see in the earlier WHO definition that the term "burnout" addresses a *syndrome* that results from *chronic* stress from your obligations. It's worthwhile to unpack those two terms a bit further to appreciate both the depth and the seriousness of burnout and begin to highlight some ways to reduce it in your life.

A *syndrome* is defined as a group of symptoms that consistently occur together or a condition characterized by a set of associated symptoms, traits, or distinctive features. Because these traits or symptoms occur in a kind of cluster of unpleasantness, chasing after one or the other of them is not likely to address the true underlying cause, even if relieving one of them could feel good in the moment.

Many people today feel distraught, overwhelmed, and anxious as a result of managing through the COVID-19 pandemic and financial and global uncertainty. You may be one of them. Are you tired and worried, but still have time and energy to enjoy your life; do you feel more or less satisfied at work and feel rejuvenated after a good weekend getaway (that you can afford)?

Or are you are feeling profoundly exhausted? It feels like there isn't enough time in the day to meet all of your obligations. Perhaps your mother is unwell and requires frequent doctor's visits or around-the-clock care, your new boss is extremely demanding and unforgiving, and you feel more and more like a failure and not good enough. Your body aches, you worry about getting COVID-19, and you can't remember when you had a full night's sleep. You want a break but don't see one in sight as your family relies on your income. Will a night out with friends help? Maybe a mani-pedi or a massage?

The real question is whether quick fixes can actually address your deep feelings of exhaustion or cynical attitude in any meaningful way. They may help you feel somewhat better . . . for a while, but in the end you're likely to find (or you've already found) that these are drops in a bucket that is far bigger than a single act can fill. This isn't an argument for not doing these things, but just a way of saying that a complex challenge like burnout calls for a broader approach if you really want to turn the tide.

REMEMBER

Burnout isn't like a headache or a sore muscle that can be treated with a pill or a massage. It isn't something that happens because you have a rough day, nor is it having to do a difficult thing as part of your obligations (even if it is distasteful or downright degrading). Rather, it's more complex and a reflection of something more chronic and insidious that requires deeper care and support.

What makes burnout so complex

The other key word in the WHO definition is *chronic*. A chronic syndrome is one that has persisted for a long time or constantly recurs and is hard to eradicate. What this term *chronic* suggests is that there are no quick fixes to a problem that has been something like a constant (and difficult) companion to you for a while. It's been around for so long, in fact, that it has graced you with a myriad of health issues that may have driven you to seek medical care — when you can get there — and when you can't, to popping pills or self-medicating with food or alcohol.

It's important to note one more aspect of the WHO definition before moving on. It states that burnout "is *not* classified as a medical condition." The significance of this statement is that there is no clear treatment for it, and it is considered a factor ". . . influencing health status or contact with health services." In practical terms, this line points to two important points that are considered later in this book. First, burnout may very well drive you to the doctor (who may or may not recognize your complaints as burnout or know exactly how to treat it), and second, it has very real physical health consequences nonetheless, well beyond the specific symptoms you may experience. The medical consequences of burnout are huge and widespread, and I explore these further a bit later. Note, however, that they are symptoms and add to the complexity of burnout, but they do not constitute burnout in of themselves.

Here's a helpful table to differentiate bad feelings or bad days from true burnout.

Not Burnout	Burnout
You have a bad day.	*Every* day is a bad day.
Caring about things feels hard.	Caring about your life feels like a total waste of energy.
You're tired.	You're exhausted all the time.
You have some dull or difficult tasks to do routinely.	The majority of your day is consumed with mind-numbingly dull or overwhelming tasks.
You wonder if you're making a difference.	You feel like nothing you do makes a difference and nobody appreciates what you do.
You have doubts and are sometimes pessimistic.	You (or your colleagues) find you to be cynical and a "Debbie Downer."

HOW BURNOUT FEELS ON THE INSIDE

Armando took a certain pride and pleasure in being a driver for Amazon. Frankly, he got a little jolt of satisfaction each time he happened to see the face of some happy package recipient mimic the smile logo on the side of the boxes he left on doorsteps all over town. Being a delivery driver can be a demanding job sometimes, but Armando had done it before, and all in all, he appreciated the activity, the challenge, and being able to be outdoors and mobile most of the day.

Of course, nobody anticipated the pandemic, much less the incredible impact it would have on everyone in different ways. For Armando, there were two converging freight trains of reality that collided in his path and made it hard for him to live up to Amazon's slogan of "Work hard. Have fun. Make history." First, as people were unable to go out and purchase much of what they needed, orders placed with the online giant skyrocketed quickly. At the same time, people were quitting their jobs in record numbers, and Armando's co-workers seemed to be dropping like flies.

The company expected Armando to pick up the slack, and he felt that he was being asked to do ten-hour shifts in six hours, without breaks or lunch. While he hadn't done it himself, he'd heard the stories of other drivers feeling compelled to bring a bottle to pee into so they didn't have to stop on their appointed rounds. At the end of each day, Armando came home to his wife and son sore, hungry, and exhausted — eating

(continued)

(continued)

something, falling into bed, and doing it all again the next day. His days off were spent resting, without the energy to do anything he enjoyed, like playing with his son or helping his wife around the house.

For Armando, who was raised to feel a deep responsibility for supporting his family and being self-sufficient, the sheer enormity of his task each day seemed to grow exponentially. He began to feel helpless to manage the demands and even found himself having dreams of being washed away by floods or chased by people with guns. The dreams led him to have fitful sleep and to wake up far from rested. Rather than feeling good about delivering supplies to people in need, he began to question why people were so materialistic and felt they needed so much "stuff." He got impatient on the road when someone cut him off, and he was uncharacteristically irritable with the people he encountered.

Always a healthy person, Armando began to find that he struggled with headaches, lost his appetite, and really kept his distance from his family and his co-workers on a regular basis, feeling detached and generally trapped in a hamster wheel of fruitless activity.

This is one of the many faces of burnout, and I share it here not to discourage or dishearten you, but simply to begin to take a word and give it a face and shape that anyone can relate to. It's also important to point out that burnout happens to people with the best of intentions and all the necessary skills to cope. In other words, burnout is not a reflection of personal weakness or a fatal flaw; it happens to the best of us, and as you find out in these pages, there is a way through it to a life of satisfaction and joy.

Looking for the Signs of Burnout

As with many chronic conditions, burnout is a very sneaky adversary and can slowly but stealthily find its way into your life when you are much too busy to be watching for it. Also, like the proverbial road to hell, the road to burnout is paved with more than a few good intentions. While you may think of yourself as having traveled that road and arrived at the bitter end of it in a state of burnout, it really can be helpful to retrace your steps as a way of helping you extricate yourself and also absolve yourself of some guilt over how you got here.

The point is that psychologists understand the onset of burnout as being a slow, steady progress that may be virtually undetectable at first but slowly grows over time through a series of fairly predictable stages that are worth reviewing here.

Using the Three R approach

I suggest that dealing with burnout requires the "Three R" approach that most healthcare providers follow:

>> **Recognition:** Watch for and take note of early stages and warning signs of burnout.

>> **Restabilize:** Aim to reestablish some semblance of stability in any way that you can by seeking support and managing stress.

>> **Resilience:** Build your ability to respond productively to stress by cultivating better physical health, emotional balance, mental clarity, healthy relationships, spiritual connection, and leadership qualities — what I call the six pillars of resilience. For more on this topic, check out one of my other titles, *Resilience For Dummies,* also published by Wiley.

It's helpful to get to know burnout and its early stages in particular, so you can start on the road to attending to the first R of recognizing the signs.

Step 1: Honeymoon phase

Do you remember being in love in that first phase of a new relationship? Your new partner (or job) can do no wrong. Their quirks are cute, and they seem to walk on water. You feel like you are also walking on water, full of energy, creative, and optimistic (there is a biological reason for this that we explore later). You take on more and more responsibilities and find yourself working late hours, going to bed late, and waking up early. You're tired, but you think to yourself, "It's a good tired!"

Step 2: Onset of stress

One day you happen to notice that something has been missing from your life lately: your friends and family! Somehow, you've gotten so immersed in your work and its demands that you've lost touch with important people and activities that used to be your best supports. Your visits to the gym seem less frequent, and you find yourself making some fast (but questionable) food choices to eat on the go because you're skipping breaks to get things done. Every now and then you find that focusing is more challenging, and maybe you're getting headaches, feeling a little creeping anxiety, or even noticing a general sense of not-quite-rightness in your body. Your little errands are not getting done like they used to, and you miss your quiet moments to catch your breath and decompress.

Step 3: Chronic stress

We all have stressful periods in our lives, but at some point your frequent experience of these high-stress times has begun to erode your problem-solving skills, and you notice that the work you are doing isn't quite as good or as accurate as it used to be. You may notice the tiniest of feelings of being out of control or powerless over things around you, and in order to avoid the discomfort of this state of affairs, you start procrastinating a bit more. The praise or recognition that maybe you received before is now not so common, and this just adds to your discomfort. You may find yourself becoming increasingly sensitive to slights by others, and as a result, you may find yourself distancing from others so you can avoid uncomfortable interactions. The distancing can also take the form of binge-watching on streaming services, endless social media scrolling, or over-reliance on alcohol or worse.

Step 4: Burnout

Perhaps you neglected the warning signs in the earlier stages, and you now find yourself at critical exhaustion levels that make it hard to cope with the demands of your obligations. You have a pervasive sense of powerlessness that can easily slip into despair and disillusionment. You may begin to feel betrayed by your job, your boss, your body, or the system you work in. The options for escaping the grip of burnout feel like they are slipping away, and you may be experiencing what psychologists call "learned helplessness." You may be feeling physical symptoms like digestive problems, chronic headaches, or even panic attacks, and you may be feeling like surrendering to it all. If others haven't noticed it before, your pessimism is becoming more obvious, and you are harboring a lot of self-doubt and self-criticism, feeling as if you have failed in some way.

Step 5: Habitual burnout

Many individuals who experience burnout in their lives have done so before, sometimes many times, and one way or the other, they seem to have been able to extricate themselves from it through some combination of self-care, setting limits, taking breaks, and a variety of good coping techniques like meditation, seeking social support or mentorship, or getting out in nature. But with this fifth stage of burnout, you just can't seem to snap out of it or get yourself back on track. It's almost as if burnout has become the "new normal" for you and a part of your everyday life, however unpleasant that may be. This is the critical period when "situational burnout" can very well impact your career, your relationships, and even the things you previously enjoyed and looked forward to. At this stage, you are particularly vulnerable to bouts of depression and may need outside help to overcome what you are facing. This is a dark place to be, but even this difficult experience can be transcended with the tools you can find in these pages.

The steps previously noted may feel familiar, but then again, you may not have noticed any such stages, or your circumstances may be unique. These are just typical examples; they may or may not feel relevant to you. The following sections drill down into each of the three WHO-defined clusters of symptoms. See if you recognize yourself in any of them.

No gas in the tank: Emotional exhaustion

"I feel like I'm wearing those ankle weights from the gym all day, every day," says Chelsey, a police officer in a mid-sized American city. Chelsey joined the force nearly ten years ago and, all in all, has found her job to be interesting, challenging, and rewarding over the years. But over the past 18 months or so, due to budget cuts, increasing anti-policing sentiment, and some recent changes in department leadership, she has found herself slowing down and finding everything to be an effort.

"I used to notice that I was tired at the end of a busy day, but this is definitely different. When I was tired, I could bounce back after a good night's sleep or a weekend off to spend with my dogs and friends . . . mostly my dogs," she says with a laugh. "But lately I almost feel like I wake up tired, my body aches, and it takes a huge effort to just get out of bed, into my uniform, and in to the station."

Exhaustion is a kind of pervasive tiredness that one feels in one's bones sometimes. Other people describe a kind of "emotional exhaustion" where they can't muster up enthusiasm for things they used to enjoy, and when faced with challenges they opt for passivity and surrender over engagement. For example, Chelsey was recently asked to come in and cover for an absent colleague when she had other important plans, but rather than speak up and advocate for herself, she simply gave in and agreed to come in. As you can imagine if you have ever surrendered in a similar situation, this leads to lingering feelings of resentment and irritation that just make things worse.

Exhaustion is not a pretty picture, and when it comes to trying to follow well-meaning advice from friends to "just snap out of it" or "fake it 'til you make it," you just don't have it in you to do even those things when you're in this state, compounding your feelings of failure or helplessness. It's a downward spiral that can be hard to reverse. Hard, but not impossible. Stay tuned: There are ways to re-energize and reverse that spiral.

Not feeling it: Depersonalization

Seven syllables is a lot, and the word "depersonalization" sounds pretty fancy and clinical, but the reality of it (the felt experience of depersonalization) is really quite simple. Malcolm has been a devoted son all his life, especially more recently when he agreed to have his father come to live with him as his father began experiencing symptoms of increasing dementia. In the early days, when the experience was new, it gave Malcolm great satisfaction to support his father, who had been such a powerful figure in his own life over the years. But as the disease advanced and the demands on Malcolm grew, it felt like his father was slipping away. But when he took a moment to really look at the situation, Malcom observed something else as well.

"I had a moment when I almost felt like a robot, where it was like I didn't actually control what I was saying or doing, and I was just going through the motions," Jack reported sheepishly. "Here was this man that I love so deeply, and I was treating him like an object or a stranger. It kind of freaked me out on one level, but another part of me just didn't seem to care."

Feelings of depersonalization can be unsettling and disturbing in some ways and can lead to feelings of emotional numbness for some and a kind of cynical attitude for others. Some people describe it as feeling like they are in a trance or under a spell, and if they are also feeling the exhaustion described previously, it can be a kind of "double-whammy" where they feel disconnected and too tired to care about it. If this feels discouraging and, frankly, a little depressing, you're right.

Not cutting it: Ineffectiveness

Lydia prided herself in the sheer volume of work she could produce as an attorney in a large firm. She went into the legal profession knowing that the demands would be high and her free time would be short. "I like to say that I eat stress for breakfast!" she says. "I love the law and mostly the law loves me back, but lately I would have to say that my love has been unrequited, to say the least." Having faced a number of setbacks in the courtroom and in the office, Lydia has begun noticing that her work is suffering a bit. "I feel like I've lost my edge and I can't seem to find it anywhere. I still love the actual work, but all the hassles of bureaucracy, office politics, and ridiculous expectations are taking a toll."

Having had some periods of low mood and pessimism about her ability to have an impact with her work as a result, Lydia has begun to notice self-doubt creeping into her inner dialogue, and the harder she tries to argue against that self-doubt and the negative voice of her inner critic, the louder it seems to get. In the meantime, she just isn't doing the kind of work she and her bosses have come to expect from her, and it has become a difficult spiral to manage.

The challenge with noticing that you're not performing at your best is that you may feel either too exhausted to do anything about it, or you may muster up a burst of energy to "sprint" a bit in hopes of jump-starting your productivity and the quality of your work. This rarely works and may even compound the problem by further exhausting and disappointing your inner critic. In many ways, ineffectiveness is a symptom of the underlying syndrome of burnout, so only treating the symptom itself is unlikely to be helpful in the long run. What this book helps you do is to get at the roots of the challenge of burnout, which ultimately allows your work to improve and you to thrive.

The Several "Flavors" of Burnout

If someone asked you what burnout is, you would probably offer up an example of someone highly overworked and trying like crazy to keep up with unreasonable demands, with no time to "refill the tank" with rest or relaxation. And you would be absolutely right. But burnout can manifest in a number of different ways and can result from a myriad of different circumstances. It's important to be familiar with the "flavors of burnout" so you can adequately assess whether you are experiencing burnout.

REMEMBER

Please note that I very purposefully said "whether you are experiencing burnout" and not "whether you are burned out." You are feeling anxiety or you are struggling with sadness, but you are *not* those things: *You are not your burnout.* This may seem like an esoteric word game, but it has real implications: When you can actually see that you are separate from your emotional or physical experiences, the possibility of shifting your relationship with those experiences and loosening their grip on you begins to open up. Perhaps you can reflect a bit on how much you identify yourself as a burned-out person. Has it become your identity? Take some time to consider it.

As such, you are not your burnout, but burnout can show up in a slew of different ways in your life or maybe for someone you love. Researchers have identified different types of burnout and each is explored briefly below.

Overload: Burnout by volume

This is the classic form of burnout that we most readily associate with the term. Having too many demands upon you simply grinds you down and wears you out. This is not to say that everyone who is busy suffers from burnout. In fact, many people actually thrive on being super-busy. I know many people who work in the restaurant business, for instance, feel more energized by the hustle and bustle of the kitchen during the busy times. The same is true for many executives I coach who are more motivated by imminent deadlines and the need to multi-task.

The capacity varies from person to person, and even in a busy work environment, there is such a thing as unbalanced busyness. If you add an obnoxious, demanding boss or terrible working conditions, what was once a nirvana can turn into a living hell for many. That is to say, being busy is a relative term, and being busy without some semblance of balance sets the stage for burnout to set in. Higher stress loads that are managed can eventually lead to a big deficit. Sometimes too much of a good thing is literally just too much, and burnout soon follows, even in a job you may have previously loved.

How you might end up with too much work is another matter that we explore further in Part 2 as we begin to move "upstream" to see how we can prevent burnout from happening at all.

Underload: Burnout by boredom

If you fit the category of *burnout by volume,* then you may think to yourself that the idea of *burnout by boredom* seems preposterous. It may be similar to a person who is poor being told that a lot of stress is associated with having too much money. Hard to imagine, huh? But nonetheless, there is a significant risk of burnout for people who are under-challenged in their work, expected to do dull, mindless, repetitive tasks without variety, and those who see their work as meaningless. We can all tolerate a bit of mindlessness in our work from time to time. For example, I have found myself sometimes being willing to sort through a spreadsheet and rearrange data just because it is the kind of mindless activity that allows my brain to rest and recover.

But what if you basically feel uninspired by your life or your work? You may not know where to even begin to make changes and feel stuck or paralyzed in that predicament. And just imagine how that same person would react if you told them, "Hey, you know what? A year from now your life is going to look exactly like it looks right now." What sort of a meltdown might you undergo if you were the one being told that?

Each person has an optimal level of arousal where they function best. Specifically, there is an optimal place, a sweet spot of challenge and arousal that falls somewhere between total inertia and maximum arousal. Scientists refer to this phenomenon as the Yerkes-Dodson Law, which states that there is a relationship between pressure and performance, such that performance increases with physiological or mental arousal, but only up to a point. When arousal becomes too high, performance then decreases. Think of the athlete who needs a certain amount of stimulation to approach peak performance, but at a certain point if they bear down too much or try too hard, their performance actually decreases. The person who experiences burnout by boredom is on the extremely low side of this continuum, and the one who faces burnout by volume is on the high side. Just like Goldilocks and the Three Bears, the key is finding the place in between that is "just right."

Undersupported: Burnout by neglect

Burnout by neglect results from a long history of being overlooked, ignored, or lacking guidance, which over time leads the person to feel increasingly more helpless and inadequate. As expectations are not clearly expressed and support to accomplish tasks isn't given, the person experiences more feelings of insecurity and incompetency.

Have you had this experience? Perhaps you came into the job feeling insecure about your abilities to begin with, or maybe you came in fairly confident, but your boss has never bothered to explain anything to you or given you the support you need to do the tasks required of you. You still aren't sure if you are doing things right, and over time, you have felt more inadequate, less confident, and ulti-mately, less motivated. "Why bother?" you may have asked yourself.

In such a scenario, the more helpless to effect change the person feels, the higher the loss of motivation. The person becomes more passive, feels unable to handle the given responsibilities, and subsequently feels increasingly overwhelmed, use-less, and helpless, when in truth, they are not.

Overpleasing: Burnout by socialization

Do you ever notice that you are unusually concerned about what other people think of you? Do you find yourself craving approval and validation on a regular basis? Do you find that your sense of ease and self-satisfaction hinges largely on whether other people like and approve of you? You may be ripe for experiencing *burnout by socialization*. This form of burnout is a curious combination of aspects of the other factors, either being overloaded and undersupported or underloaded and undersupported. It arises primarily from a tendency to be a people pleaser. This means that *you* would rather be uncomfortable than potentially make some-body *else* uncomfortable. You may think of yourself as a natural "giver" and find yourself saying "yes" to things that, down deep, you know you should say "no" to.

Do you have a hard time saying "no"? Think about how this attitude may have opened doors for you now and then. Perhaps you enjoy the feel-good feelings you experience when you see the joy your saying "yes" brings to someone else. Con-versely, do you say "yes" to avoid seeing someone displeased or unhappy? Has it also left you feeling overburdened with only yourself to blame (or resentfully blaming others)?

Neuroscientists might say that you are getting a hit of dopamine (a pleasure neurotransmitter in the brain) when you get the approval of others or when you see that an action you took brought someone else pleasure or happiness. That feel-good feeling that you get with the dopamine surge can become a bit addictive . . . and habitual.

If you do have the tendency to be motivated largely by seeking the approval of other people, you will find that even the day-to-day challenges of your work are exhausting and unfulfilling when you derive no intrinsic pleasure from doing it. A successful commercial fisherman likely feels a kind of pleasure from pulling a big one out of the deep, but if he is the captain's son and is only doing this work because he is seeking the approval of his father, he may be vulnerable to burnout. This kind of chronic lack of satisfaction can lead you to begin to neglect your work. Over time this obviously can lead to a negative feedback loop where you aren't fulfilled by your work, you don't do it (or don't do it well), and you get negative feedback from supervisors or colleagues, causing you to like the work (and yourself) even less. And the next thing you know, you're experiencing burnout.

Of course, no amount of self-care, time off, or shifting your duties in this circumstance is likely to lead to a change of the underlying dynamics of this situation. But as you can see in this book, there are other, more effective ways of dealing with situations like this that can bring greater satisfaction and reduced burnout over time.

Checking Your Burnout Level

Knowing how much burnout you may be experiencing may begin to give you clues about how to tackle the whole phenomenon of burnout in your life. Shall we see how you fare on the burnout quiz?

Note that whatever you score on this quiz, it is not a representation of you being "good" or "bad" but rather a guide to let you know what you may want to focus on or what sort of support you need to become the thriving and happy person you want to be.

Discovering just how burned out you feel

Take some time to consider the following statements and assign each one a number based upon how well it applies to you, using the following scale:

Not At All: 1 point
Rarely: 2 points
Sometimes: 3 points
Often: 4 points
Very Often: 5 points

Statement	Score (1–5)
I've got a short fuse these days and have a tendency to get irritated or angry quite easily over things that used to not bother me much.	
I've got no gas in the tank. I feel physically and emotionally drained.	
When I think about my work, I feel like a "Debbie Downer" in my negative attitude.	
I wonder how I ended up in this job or role and find myself wishing for something else.	
I find myself being less kind and sympathetic to other people and their issues than I ought to be.	
My co-workers and people in my life tend to tick me off more than they used to.	
I question the purpose and meaning of my work or my profession, longing for another situation or a simpler time.	
The people I work with and for don't seem to appreciate or understand me.	
I would like to be able to talk with others about how I feel, but nobody seems available or interested.	
I feel that I could be achieving more than I am, but I just can't seem to do it.	
I find myself feeling weirdly disconnected from my work and from other people, as if I am going through the motions and not really there.	
I sometimes feel like my work is a pressure-cooker to succeed, and I'm the meal being cooked!	
I feel less satisfied with the work I produce or do.	
I get aggravated with basic aspects of my job or what I am asked to do.	
I feel that I am unable to do the best job because of politics, bureaucracy, or systems outside of my direct control.	
I feel more and more like a square peg in a round hole when it comes to my work. I question whether I fit.	
The amount of work I have to do always seems to come at me faster and heavier than I can manage.	
I think I would like to do a better job, but the time just isn't there to do it.	

Statement	Score (1–5)
I sometimes feel like the tail of the dog, where I get wagged around but don't get to have a role in determining my own future and activities.	
I find myself wondering if I'm burned out, and people give me advice for how to feel better.	

What the results mean . . . and what they don't mean

When you total up your score, see how it compares to the scale below:

20–40	No obvious signs of burnout. Time to find ways to flourish!
41–50	Burnout seems unlikely, unless you have a few 4s or 5s
51–70	The caution light is on. You could be at risk for burnout.
71–90	Time to take some action (keep reading), as burnout is likely.
91–100	The red lights are flashing, and you need to act now.

It is important, first and foremost, not to let this simple, unscientific quiz take on too much importance overall. It's a great way to get a quick snapshot of your experience from all angles and to get a general sense of your concerns and how intense they are. This quiz definitely is an informal assessment of burnout, and while it may feel as if it gets at the heart of burnout, it is not scientifically validated. It is what psychologists call *face valid* in that it appears, on the face of it, to capture burnout, but we can't really say for sure that it truly measures the syndrome of burnout. Use your common sense in interpreting what it means, and if you are seeking a truly rigorous, empirically valid measure of burnout, the *Maslach Burnout Inventory* is the industry standard for such things, and it can be purchased from Mind Garden, its publisher.

Nonetheless, your score may be pointing to where you stand when it comes to burnout symptoms, especially when you pay close attention to which statements rated at 4 or 5. Remember to acknowledge that you have already taken a decisive action toward reducing and eliminating burnout in your life. You may find that knowing your relative score on the quiz helps you determine how you may want to proceed through this book. Specifically, the higher your score, the more likely you are to benefit from more of the content presented in this book, as your burnout is more complex. The lower your score, the more you may be able to focus later in the book on Part 4, which focuses on moving beyond burnout to flourishing and thriving.

BURNOUT FIRST-AID

While there are no quick fixes when it comes to burnout, despite how much well-meaning advice there is floating around to that effect, there are some things you can do right this moment if you are alarmed about your level of burnout or feeling particularly discouraged or depressed by your apparent predicament. Most importantly, if you feel that your burnout feels well beyond your capacity to manage it and you may be clinically depressed or feeling suicidal, drop this book and reach out for professional help immediately. If you have an Employee Assistance Program at work, do not hesitate to take advantage of that resource, and if you don't have that resource, seek out local resources for psychological support and treatment above all else. Burnout is serious, and the impact of burnout can be devastating to the person and the people around them.

Aside from seeking professional assistance to manage the effects of burnout, there is great wisdom in the advice you often get from others about self-care — not as a "treatment" for burnout or a cure-all, but simply as a way of creating the tiniest bit of space and relief from the most painful aspects of burnout for now. Let go of needing that self-care (a pedicure, a good run in the park, a beer with the guys, or a night of binge-watching mindless TV shows on Netflix) to be the be-all, end-all response to burnout. Take the pressure off that simple act of self-kindness to be your savior and allow it to be a simple distraction and a bit of a reset that can help you clear your head, break a downward spiral, and create just enough headspace to chart a course forward.

This moment, however, do consider simply asking yourself a very straightforward question: What do I need? There's no need to make the answer complicated or lofty (for example, a brand new job, a promotion, or a vacation in Fiji); instead, ask yourself what you need *in this moment.* Perhaps it's just five minutes to simply sit and breathe, or a good hot cup of tea, or a walk in the neighborhood. Even simply peeling your attention off the computer screen for a few minutes may be the answer to the question. Offer yourself whatever you need without expectation that it will make anything change, but only because in this moment, you need it. Let it be unconditional and sweet and without obligation. Savor it while you can and move on.

"What do I need?" is the fundamental question of self-compassion, that you can find out more about in chapter 9, but you already have the capacity within yourself to begin giving yourself more of what you need. No special training required. Give it a shot and let it be for now.

You may also discover that you aren't sure what you need, which is okay for now too. Simply honor yourself and how you feel, and see what comes up for you.

Taking a moment to simply acknowledge

Before you do anything else, see if you can just pause for a moment, and notice how you feel right now having calculated and considered your burnout score. Maybe close your eyes and see if you can name what emotion you are feeling right now. Is it fear . . . relief . . . curiosity . . . irritation . . . sadness? Could you, just for the moment, simply acknowledge the feelings that are here, the thoughts that go with those feelings, and maybe even notice how they feel in your body? There's no need to change anything just now about how you feel; simply allow yourself to acknowledge the feelings and to feel what you actually feel. This is the foundation of mindfulness, a key resource you possess that will help you navigate the road ahead.

We live in a society where all of us feel as if we have to be doing, doing, doing all the time. Sharks have to move in order to breathe, and sometimes we feel like we are sharks in that way. Nothing is necessarily wrong with being someone who prioritizes GSD (Getting Stuff Done), but there is such forward momentum in that mode that we often miss out on opportunities for a more easeful and rewarding way of being. This is especially challenging when it comes to burnout, because those feelings of never being caught up cause us to naturally want to try harder and do more to *finally* feel satisfied and happy. But that moment rarely comes and mainly we end up feeling more burned out than we did before!

Pausing to notice is not freezing for eternity; it is simply taking the time to stop the relentless *doing* long enough to simply *be present*, look around, consider your options, acknowledge where you've been and where you actually are, and breathe. In these moments of mindfulness, you begin to create a mini-refuge to reconnect with yourself and your deeper intention to not be burned out, and to hear your own inner wisdom if you can simply slow down and quiet down long enough to hear its quiet voice. You discover more about this powerful practice of paying attention and practicing mindfulness in Chapter 8, but you can do it *right now* if you want to get a taste of it.

TIP

Before wrapping up this first chapter, I want to make an important point about blame and fault. Burnout (as you discover in the next few chapters) is determined by a multitude of different factors, including your own personal "bag of tricks" (personality, history, identities, habits, and skills), the various and sundry demands of your situation or job, and the complex larger system or culture in which you live and work. In short, burnout does not stem from any failing on your part alone and does not suggest that you are at fault or to blame for where you find yourself today. To be sure, you may have (probably unconsciously) contributed to getting yourself into this "mess" of burnout, but you didn't do it singlehandedly. See if you can absolve yourself of any lingering guilty feelings or self-blame, regardless of what your inner critical voice may say (more on that rascal in Chapter 10), because it won't help you and it's painful anyway.

As the psychologist Paul Gilbert likes to say about the features of our personality that we have inherited from previous generations and from circumstances outside our control: "It's not your fault, but it *is* your responsibility." Especially when we talk about the future and finding ways through and out of burnout, it is in your hands to make that journey, but you didn't get here (suffering burnout) on purpose or through a personal failing. You had the best of intentions and things went wrong. The important thing is that you are here now trying to find a different way, and this book can help you do just that.

Chapter **2**

Exploring the Scope and Impact of Burnout

O ne of the challenges of social media these days is that these platforms seem to become "highlight reels" of one's life. In sports, "highlight reels" are the edited assemblage of a team or athlete's best performances all compiled into a tight, impressive, and totally unrealistic package to create a positive impression. Facebook or Instagram, with their photos of amazing food, incredible vacations, and wise or witty observations on life, create a similar impression of you or your so-called friends. Looking at your distant cousin's Facebook feed may give you the impression that they have the perfect life, and they never burn the toast, get frustrated with incompetent co-workers, or have periods of sadness or despair.

I have a colleague who is truly the kind of person who enjoys social gatherings and appreciates beautiful moments, and she also enjoys posting such occasions on social media. Recently, she has been tirelessly taking care of a very sick parent, a 24/7 job in itself, in addition to trying to keep up with her actual extremely demanding job, and feeling like she is failing at both. She is exhausted, sleep deprived, angry with her boss, and has little time or energy to socialize. On the very rare occasion that she does get out, she posts on social media, to discover Facebook "friends" commenting on how "great it is how much you get to go out. I wish I had your life." My colleague was truly upset for feeling so misunderstood when she felt the reality of her life was so different. All is not what it seems!

This mismatch between public persona and private suffering is understandable, but it's also misleading for you when you try to get a sense of what you are experiencing and whether it is "normal" to feel the way that you do. When everyone around you looks happy, well-adjusted, and like they're loving life, it only deepens your own sense of somehow being flawed or uniquely outmatched by life and its demands.

My purpose here is to help you remember that as life is filled with trials and tribulations as well as joy and successes, you are not alone in any of it, even if it feels that way sometimes.

Burnout Feels Lonely, But You Are Far from Alone

The experience of burnout can feel like a very dark place. When you are feeling depleted, self-critical, unable to catch up and stretched beyond your capacity to cope, there is a deep-seated phenomenon that seems to happen for most people. I say "deep-seated" because it probably has its roots in our DNA and in the history of our species. Humans are social animals, which is more than just saying that we like to hang out together and play and dance and drink coffee together at Starbucks. We actually *need each other* from infancy to adulthood, and so our survival has depended upon us being accepted in (and protected by) the family, the herd, or the tribe.

Think about our early ancestors. They could not have survived nor propagated our species alone in the wilderness. There was safety in numbers, and we were able to thrive in community when we had support and could be supportive to others. The same is still true today, but a major issue in modern society is that we do not live in herds or as part of an obvious greater community. Especially during the COVID-19 pandemic, feelings of isolation became more of a rule than an exception.

But if you are a gazelle and you are feeling weak or unable to keep up with your herd, you are vulnerable to being the one the cheetah takes out for lunch (and I don't mean inviting you over for sandwiches . . . in this scenario, you *are* the sandwich). So feeling weak, overwhelmed, or separate from others taps directly into this hardwired system of survival. At this point, your vulnerability no longer feels like a passing mood or idea; it feels very real and dangerous in a primordial way. This, in turn, leads you to want to either fight, flee, or freeze to stay alive. Without the energy you would need for the first two options, you go into freeze mode, which is essentially where you are when you are burned out, holding very still or burying your head in the sand (or under the covers), hoping that the threat will pass so that your life can return to normality, whatever that may mean.

THE HISTORY OF BURNOUT

Have you ever said to yourself, "I feel like I'm suffering through a bout of acedia lately"? Me neither. Because until I started researching burnout, I had never heard of the term. But it's interesting to note that a monk and theologian from the early fifth century, named John Cassian, wrote about it. He described the feeling of acedia to be "such bodily listlessness and yawning hunger as though he were worn by a long journey or a prolonged fast . . . next he glances about and sighs that no one is coming to see him. Constantly in and out of his cell *(Author note: He was a monk, after all),* he looks at the sun as if it were too slow in setting."

This sounds a lot like burnout to me. When Cassian speaks of "listlessness," feeling "worn by a long journey or a prolonged fast," and sighing "that no one is coming to see him," one can really feel the depleted, isolated, and burned-out nature of acedia, and it's all too familiar to those of us who have experienced what we call burnout these days. This experience was described specifically in the context of the constrictions of a solitary monastic lifestyle and was said to entail an odd combination of listlessness, free-floating anxiety, and decreased concentration.

If you're like me, you're thinking about the life of a monk, with its simplicity of a single robe, a small cell with a bed and a table and a chair, and days filled with silence and prayer, and wondering how that compares to being an overworked, underappreciated 24/7 sole caregiver to a demented parent. But who are we to judge what was burnout-worthy in the fifth century? Acedia was actually ultimately subsumed under the category of "sloth" as one of the Seven Deadly Sins. I mention this because it also seems to imply that it was, indeed, some kind of transgression on the part of the person experiencing it. In modern terms, this would be "blaming the victim," and we have much more to talk about in this regard later in the book.

When psychologist Herbert Freudenberger (himself a burnout sufferer) first formally defined the syndrome (especially as it applies to the helping professions), he characterized it as "To deplete oneself. To exhaust one's physical and mental resources. To wear oneself out by excessively striving to reach some unrealistic expectation imposed by one's self or the values of society." Again, quite a case for blaming the victim here in Dr. Freudenberger's definition, but subsequent research and refinement, mainly by social psychologist Christina Maslach, went on to further elaborate on the definition (and remove some of the blaming). She defined it as being "a psychological syndrome involving emotional exhaustion, depersonalization, and a diminished sense of personal accomplishment." It is her name that appears on the most popular, empirically supported burnout questionnaire, the Maslach Burnout Inventory.

It may be both a bit alarming on the one hand and comforting on the other to know that this experience of burnout is actually a fairly common human experience, especially in today's world. Know that whatever the feelings you are experiencing in your body, the emotions that plague you, or the thoughts in your head, burnout is not a reflection on your failings as a person, but a very common human experience that arises from your most basic instinct to survive under threatening or overwhelming circumstances.

REMEMBER

You are not alone.

What the statistics say about the prevalence of burnout

When you are feeling burned out, depleted, utterly alone, and isolated, you are actually sharing the experience of burnout with about half of the working world, if a recent study by Indeed (the giant job aggregator website) is to be believed. Of those surveyed, 52 percent reported experiencing burnout in 2021, which was even more than the 43 percent they found prior to the pandemic. For millennials, the number was even higher at 59 percent, and Gen Z wasn't far behind at 58 percent. (Note that there are a number of surveys of burnout in the literature, and many actually put these numbers even higher than this particular study by Indeed.)

It's important not to get too wrapped up in studying the statistics, because in the end, you are a person and not a statistic. Statistics about prevalence of burnout do nothing to change the fact that you are experiencing it, but understanding how old and widespread the phenomenon *is* can definitely help you feel less alone and perhaps more hopeful about the possibility of a way out of it.

One more note about what the studies say about burnout. The study by Indeed further explored people's thoughts about the sources or causes of burnout. Given that the study was done at the height of the pandemic, it provides a unique glimpse into the new reality that many workers faced with the shift to more remote work, and all indications are that this trend will continue into the future. Most workers reported struggling with finding a balance between work and the rest of life.

Specifically, 27 percent of workers reported feeling unable to unplug from work, and that was compounded by the fact that 53 percent of virtual or work-from-home (WFH) employees reported that their workload became heavier after the onset of the pandemic and their shift to WFH status. Of those who stayed working on-site, 34 percent reported that they were working more too. So people were being expected to do more, under challenging working conditions, and in many cases didn't even have the natural barrier between work and life that a job on-site provides.

My hope is that this information provides small comfort that if you are experiencing burnout, you are not alone, and the causes are much bigger than any individual. The good news is that this data actually helps point the way to how we as individuals (as well as companies and systems) can address the significant problem of burnout by identifying the sources.

Who gets burned out?

"Me" is probably how you answered the question of who gets burned out, and you're right, of course. But it can be super helpful to understand better all the factors that contributed to you becoming burned out as well. This way these factors or causes can be addressed in a way that best assures that you can recover from burnout and prevent it from revisiting you in the future. Not surprisingly, many factors predict who experiences burnout, many of them lift the burden off of you as an individual, and virtually all of them also point to clues for how to find your way out of being burned out over time. You may need to be a bit patient, however, which is perhaps the toughest ask of all!

Jobs that put you at risk of burnout

At a more obvious level, there are some professions that are particularly prone to experiencing burnout. (Please note that stress and burnout are not the same thing, as many jobs involve stress and many people *in* those jobs don't experience burnout. However, of course level of stress by itself is a risk factor for burnout.) Among the most burnout-prone jobs are

>> **Physicians:** The American Medical Association has estimated that almost 50 percent of physicians experience symptoms of serious burnout, mainly due to the demands and stress of patient care. No doubt this has compounded with the onset of COVID-19, but the nature of the job itself seems to pose unique challenges and risks for burnout, particularly in emergency medicine, family practice, and internal medicine.

>> **Nurses:** Long shifts, increasing demands, high patient-to-nurse ratios, and a stressed healthcare system leave nurses at particular risk of burnout. The relatively lower prestige in the healthcare hierarchy doesn't help either.

>> **Teachers and school principals:** Teaching has been reported to have the highest burnout rate of any public service job, especially among younger teachers. Difficult working conditions, limited resources, and performance demands from administration combine to create a particularly rich recipe for burnout for teachers and their supervisors.

>> **Police officers:** Working almost exclusively in high-stress, high-risk situations and being exposed to some of the worst aspects of human nature takes a

grievous toll on our law enforcement personnel. In fact, the most committed officers are often the ones who experience more burnout than their colleagues, setting up an alarming paradox for quality policing.

>> **Fast food and retail workers:** Burnout is by no means limited to high-skill, high-prestige occupations. In fact, low pay, monotonous tasks, and unrewarding working conditions combine to create unusually unstable workplaces where employee turnover is very high. This situation in turn leads management to treat their employees as if they are expendable and interchangeable, further worsening the working environment.

These are just a few obvious examples of the most burnout-prone professions, but clearly burnout can arise in almost any role or obligation. However, it is very important to note that many people who serve in these professions, under the very conditions described previously, seem to be able to thrive and are immune to burnout. So clearly, the job itself is not the only factor in predicting whether someone will experience burnout. Thus, you need to dig a little deeper to help understand who gets burned out and why.

Personality profiles that put you at risk of burnout

Some studies have identified three types of employees that are prone to experiencing burnout: the workaholic, the perfectionist, and the people pleaser. Each style represents another pathway into the swamp of burnout, and also a guide to getting out of it.

>> **The workaholic:** If you typecast yourself as a workaholic, your tendency is to be performance-oriented and to repeatedly make little space in your life for life itself, preferring to prioritize work and achievement above all else (for whatever reason). It may be very clear how this pattern can lead to burnout, but it's important to note that it can arise as a result of multiple factors, like simply working too much, having trouble finding a fulfilling work-life balance, or believing you have to get all of your work done before you can relax. Whatever the challenge, it stems from your deeply held value system about yourself, your worth, and the world you live in, which may be more aligned to performance than to fulfillment or meaning in life more generally. I explore this further in Chapter 10.

>> **The people pleaser:** Having people-pleaser tendencies can get you into trouble because you are much less likely to speak up if you are feeling unchallenged, unsupported, or overloaded. Your desire for approval or appreciation by your manager or senior leaders (and friends or family for that matter), while well-meaning, may easily lead you astray and into that swamp. Like the workaholic, this pattern is deep-seated and complex, and profoundly

connected to your value system. When you understand how to discover your true value or even just rediscover your sense of value, you can create a new pattern for yourself. The first step is to want to do this for yourself first and foremost, and by picking up this book yourself, you have taken the first (and perhaps most important) step in the right direction.

>> **The perfectionist:** The perfectionist strives for flawlessness (which is particularly challenging if you are a human, given that we are all inherently imperfect to start with!). This striving for perfection is usually maintained by a harsh inner critic (also addressed in Chapter 10). The perfectionist seems to dwell somewhere between the people pleaser and the workaholic, so it is something of a double whammy. If the perfectionism is inward-directed, you may be prone to workaholism, and if it is addressed toward creating an impression of perfection for others, it can lead you to people-pleasing.

In Chapter 6, I delve a bit deeper into personality types and how you can find out if you are a good fit for your particular working environment and job description.

A few other notable features of individuals who are prone to burnout are health-related behaviors, age, and gender. People who don't exercise regularly, are over-weight, or who drink heavily are especially vulnerable to experiencing burnout (not to mention raising their risk of significant health problems). Women are more susceptible to burnout for reasons that are not entirely clear, although the multiple demands upon women involving both work and home caretaking respon-sibilities, and the stress of wage disparity and the "glass ceiling" are likely fac-tors. And finally, some age groups (younger workers in particular) are more prone to burnout, perhaps in some cases, due to the rise in technology and the tempta-tion to multi-task as a result. More on this topic in Chapter 5.

How Burnout Affects the Individual

There is such a thing as being too close to something. This includes your own experience of burnout, and actually one of the first steps toward shifting away from burnout is really to start to put the tiniest bit of distance between *you* and *it*. As I note in Chapter 1, you are not your burnout, and when you can see that bit of space between you and it, big things can happen. Burnout isn't just a problem to be solved; more importantly, it's a relationship to be addressed. Like it or not, you're in a relationship with your burnout. The good news is that this is like being fixed up on a blind date by your mom. You may have to put up with it for now to keep the peace, but you are not obligated to marry it. This blind date with burnout can end amicably with burnout in your rear-view mirror and joy and fulfillment on the horizon.

The following sections explore the various ways that burnout shows up, including not only how you experience it emotionally and psychologically, but also how it impacts your relationships and your work in both obvious and more subtle ways. This is all by way of helping you fully appreciate how intertwined you may have become with burnout and how it has perhaps "infected" all aspects of your life. Knowing this information helps you address burnout with a comprehensive "cure" of sorts, rather than a "Band-Aid" quick fix. As much as we would all like the quick fix (in pill form, if possible), you may already be realizing that something a bit more involved is required.

The physiology of burnout

In his book *1984*, George Orwell wrote about the challenges of physical pain: "On the battlefield, in the torture chamber, on a sinking ship, the issues that you are fighting for are always forgotten, because the body swells up until it fills the universe." The same could be said for the physical challenges that you may experience when you are feeling burned out. These problems can swell up to obscure your view of the larger picture. You may feel so physically exhausted or experience so much physical pain, that you have little bandwidth to focus on anything else. As such, your physical symptoms may very well require your attention first, so I give you some things to consider so you can tend to your human body if necessary, before looking at anything else.

As noted previously, stress plays a role in burnout, even though stress and burnout are two different things. One way to think about the relationship between the two is to think of burnout as a potential *result* of chronic (meaning persisting for a long time) stress that isn't managed. We all have stress from time to time, but having constant demands on us that never seem to let up can lead to stress overload and overtime, resulting in burnout. Looking to the physiology of chronic stress can give you some clues as to why you may experience certain physiological symptoms.

What happens when you experience acute stress

When you first experience a stressful situation (for example, you are given a new project with a tight deadline at work), your body tends to react as if it has been threatened (akin to an ancient ancestor of yours looking up from drinking from the stream to find a tiger licking its lips). It goes into "fight or flight" mode because the body has released epinephrine or norepinephrine (also known as adrenaline and noradrenaline).

In that stressful moment you may notice your heart racing, your face flushing, or any one of a number of symptoms of what is referred to as sympathetic arousal. This simply means that your alert system has been activated to help you protect yourself. But given that neither fighting (slapping your boss), fleeing (running screaming from the room), nor freezing (like a deer in headlights) is conducive to job security, you usually have to contain this reaction for the sake of a regular paycheck and a little dignity in the workplace.

When acute stressors become chronic stress

Suppressing the stress reaction now and then isn't particularly problematic in and of itself, but if the same thing happens repeatedly (you keep getting assigned more and more projects with crazy deadlines, or the original stressor persists for a while), the acute aspect of stress becomes chronic and a different part of your nervous system kicks in. A string of three structures called the hypothalamic-pituitary-adrenal (HPA) axis (stretching from your brain to your kidneys) becomes active when your stress persists, and a whole cascade of things unfold that are less important than the result. The end product of HPA activation is the release of hormones called glucocorticoids, the most famous of which is cortisol.

Cortisol has a number of effects that are intended to help you cope with a stressor by, for example, raising your blood pressure and cardiac output so that your muscles can help carry you to safety. Cortisol also increases glucose (sugar) in the bloodstream to provide nourishment for your muscles and organs, so you are equipped to put up a fight or run for your life. In addition to activating some systems, cortisol also inhibits others that are not needed to deal with a threat. For example, it suppresses reproductive activity because engaging in sexual activity when your life is in danger (however titillating that may be for a small segment of society) is usually not what you need in a dangerous situation.

It all ends up downstream as symptoms

All in all, it was a pretty impressive system for keeping us alive when our ancestor's lives were frequently in danger, but in modern society with modern stressors, it's a little less helpful. And as our non-life-threatening stressors pile up with the demands of work and personal responsibility, this process that was intended to keep us from getting eaten is now eating *us*.

Stimulation of the HPA axis too much or too often can lead to a suppressed immune system (more frequent colds and infections), a higher incidence of type 2 diabetes, obesity, and cardiovascular disease. As helpful as cortisol can be in some ways, it can be nasty when it continues to course through our veins on a regular basis, leaving us with impaired memory and reduced ability to pay attention and concentrate (not to mention vulnerability to depression, discussed in the later section "The psychological effects of burnout"). Other symptoms can include fatigue, muscle tension, disrupted sleep, headache, difficulty breathing, gastrointestinal symptoms, and sexual problems.

Not a pretty picture, to say the least, and when you factor in the various ways that we humans use to cope with a menu of problems like this (such as drinking, smoking, eating, using illegal substances, and so forth), the likelihood of multiple medical problems only intensifies.

The physiological signs of burnout

Repeated experiences of stress, especially high stress, lead to the activation of the stress response system and release of stress hormones from the adrenal glands like adrenalin and cortisol. Over time, some individuals can show signs of physiological burnout, whereby the adrenal glands can't mount the appropriate response to stress such that levels of one or both stress hormones are inadequate to match the needs of the body. In such cases a person who is normally a get-up-and-do kind of person becomes a get-up-and-go-back-to-sleep kind of person. Symptoms like chronic fatigue, chronic pain, or atypical types of depression, for instance, may show up.

TIP

Don't just gloss over the impact of burnout on your body. You may be aware of some symptoms, but other problems caused by burnout may not yet be obvious to you. It's important that, first and foremost, you make sure that you are taking care of your body and tending to your physical health. By listing potential problems here, I am not suggesting that they are simply interesting facts — if you are experiencing any of these symptoms, I strongly recommend that you have them checked out by a professional. Addressing the symptoms won't eliminate burnout, but if the underlying medical issues are not addressed, you could end up in serious trouble where burnout is *not* your biggest problem. Be wise and be prudent when it comes to your health.

REMEMBER

The beauty of the body is that it has an incredible capacity to heal. It can be rewired, so if you are experiencing any physical or psychological symptoms, it's not too late to address them. It takes time, and only you can take charge of this change. Are you in?

The psychological effects of burnout

Not surprisingly, burnout is often associated with depression and/or anxiety, but the nature of that association is multifaceted and worth exploring briefly. There is no question that people who are experiencing burnout have symptoms often associated with those of depression or anxiety, but there is also solid research suggesting that burnout is substantially separate from these two psychological afflictions. In other words, burnout and depression are not basically the same thing, and the same is true of burnout and anxiety.

What researchers do understand more clearly is that a history of problems with depression or anxiety probably sets you up to be more vulnerable to experiencing burnout under the right conditions. Unfortunately, it's also likely that if this is your history, you are also prone to a worsening of your symptoms when you are also going through burnout.

If you have no history of depression or anxiety, it's possible that you could develop some of these problems if you are also developing burnout symptoms. This isn't really surprising, since many of the typical symptoms of burnout tend to be those associated with anxiety and depression. For example, low mood, feeling anxious, difficulty concentrating, listlessness, and fatigue occur in the context of burnout as well as depression.

So how should you respond to these experiences if they arise? This book is particularly aimed at helping you contend with and transcend burnout specifically, which means if you suspect that you are struggling with anxiety or depression more broadly or chronically (because of a history of it or simply feeling as if it is something unfolding separate from your burnout) or you have increasing worrisome symptoms, such as thoughts of suicide or harming others, your best bet is to seek out a mental health professional to support and guide you in addressing these conditions as soon as possible. Likewise, if you are experiencing physical symptoms, do seek medical help as well.

In fact, sometimes depression can go undiagnosed far too long because people think, "I'm just burned out. I'll be better when my workload lightens up." By treating depression or anxiety (or some of the underlying processes that lead to these problems) that arises in the context of stressful or unworkable burnout-producing conditions at work, you give yourself a significantly better chance of leaving burnout behind you. Do yourself a favor and take good care of your mental and physical health in this way.

The social impact of burnout

I have worked with many patients who were faced with debilitating illnesses and the treatments associated with them. One heartbreaking phenomenon I observed over and over again was when a couple or a parent-child duo was facing the challenge of one person having cancer and the other being the primary caregiver. The patient would tell me (in confidence) that they so appreciated their partner or child/parent for their support and love, but they also felt so badly about all the care that partner had to provide them. They felt like a burden and tried to spare the caregiver by not conveying how much they were struggling with fear, sadness, or shame. I would then subsequently hear from their caregiver something like, "Nancy is going through so much already with her cancer and her treatment; I don't want to burden her even more with my own fears and worries about the future."

Out of concern for each other, each was retreating from the one source of strength and resilience that science has known about for years: each other! A vast field of research clearly shows that high-quality relationships with others are the key to flourishing and thriving in life, as well as having resilience and strength in times of difficulty and challenge.

This withdrawal from others is also often the case when people are experiencing burnout. As I note earlier in this chapter, a person's tendency when they are distressed or feeling burned out is to feel alone and perhaps uniquely flawed in some way, leading them to retreat from the connection with other people that, ironically, could help them feel much better (or at least less alone).

Burnout as an obstacle to making meaning

Making meaning out of your work or obligations may sound like a rather esoteric and theoretical exercise, especially if you are immersed in the throes of burnout and just trying to continue to put one foot in front of the other and hold it all together. But seeing the meaningfulness of the work that you do is really what gets you out of bed in the morning, sends you back into the operating room, or steels you for whatever unpleasant or demanding task is put in front of you. And therefore, it may be a lack of a sense of meaning that underlies burnout itself and becomes the most important barrier that we need to address.

You can think of meaning as the power source from which you draw to do what you do in the world, and the "lubrication" that keeps you moving when you are in danger of getting stuck. To quote Viktor Frankl again, "Those who have a 'why' to live can bear with almost any 'how.'" In fact, Frankl's words may point to how some people seem to be able to thrive in difficult, highly stressful situations while others can feel crushed by the same circumstances. The difference may be the meaning that one takes from the work itself.

What is your why?

In this discussion, I am not referring to the specific tasks of work (for example, answering emails, caring for patients, writing proposals, or attending meetings) but instead the larger context of *why* we do these things. For example, when I was working as a primary care doctor over 20 years ago, I felt overwhelmed by the demands that were being made on me by the new hospital policies to see more patients in less time to either get paid more or less, depending on my numbers. (It was the beginning of how medicine was to change to what it is today in the United States.) The work that used to give me pleasure was now eliciting anxiety and resentment. I was exhausted, unhappy, and disenchanted. I knew that I could not see people as "numbers." So instead, I asked myself, "What do you want?" I knew what I didn't want, but I did not know what I did want. I didn't know my "why."

On reflection (more on this later), I discovered that I wanted the opposite of what I was experiencing and that my "why" was to provide support to individuals so that they could heal themselves. I found the motivation to leave my job and change the trajectory of my life to bring me where I am today.

This is not to suggest that the meaning you get from your job or obligations must be lofty, humanitarian, selfless, or altruistic. If your job is simply a means of adequately supporting yourself, feeding your children, and building a better life for your family, then even the most mundane and unskilled labor can hold meaning and purpose that keeps you going.

Where do you find meaning?

One way of looking at our need for meaning is to think of this as a spiritual quest or purpose. Everyone gets a little nervous when people use the word "spiritual," as if the next thing I'm going to do is whip out some incense and begin chanting or teaching you a secret handshake. But spirituality need only point to our innate human desire for connection to something bigger than ourselves.

As mentioned earlier, humans are social beings who need the presence of others in their lives to truly survive and thrive, so being a part of a family, a spiritual or religious tradition, a club, or even a rock band can help you feel safe, supported, and fulfilled. When you experience burnout, you lose track of that connection (even if it is still there), feeling adrift and purposeless. From there, it's a short hop from purposelessness to the depersonalized, robotic, empty, vacant feelings that are a big part of the experience of burnout.

The Impact of Burnout on Organizations

Burnout is not a solitary phenomenon, even though the label typically refers to a set of symptoms or problems that arise for an individual. In fact, as burnout arises for individuals within a system (like an office, a company, or a family), the whole system begins to show the effects over time. Again, this is not to lay blame on a person experiencing burnout for why a whole system is impacted, but instead to highlight the interconnected nature of our lives as humans and how our inner state can impact those around us.

At a very basic, neurological level, there is a growing awareness among neuroscientists that people actually resonate with the emotional experiences of others. While there is much debate about the specifics of this phenomenon, the essence is that we seem to be able to sense and feel the emotional state of others we come into contact with. You know this experience if you have ever come home to a grumpy or angry partner, without any context for understanding why they may be feeling that way. You can simply feel their hard feelings and may even take them on and get grumpy and angry yourself. Imagine the fateful question that you might ask your significant other, "Why are you so grumpy?" The response is likely to be "Me? Grumpy? Why are *you* so grumpy?" And so begins a downward spiral of grumpiness, all because you could sense your partner's grumpiness and named it. Sound familiar? (The same can be true about positive emotional states. Can you think of a person or two who might have a more positive influence on your mood?)

Looking beyond the emotional and psychological impact of your experience of burnout on those around you, your low energy, impaired concentration, lack of motivation, and bad mood all likely contribute to reduced performance in various ways. The quality and quantity of your work are likely to decrease, sometimes in the face of increasing demands for *more* and *better* work from your supervisors. You start missing deadlines or quotas, and take longer and longer to produce what you used to do in a fraction of the time. Of course, this likely further lowers your own mood, raises your anxiety, and generally makes things more unpleasant for you. But it also impacts your working environment, your co-workers, your department or unit, and ultimately the performance of your company or organization. It's a domino effect.

The financial costs of burnout

The *Harvard Business Review* recently reported that burnout adds between $125 billion and $190 billion every year in healthcare costs, and stress alone accounts for about 8 percent of what people spend on healthcare overall. Those are big numbers, but if you break them down to individual employees, the Gallup Organization calculated that for every $10,000 in salary paid out, $3,400 of it is eaten up by employee disengagement (of which burnout is the biggest culprit). When you look a bit further into the numbers, there are also significant costs when it comes to low productivity, high turnover, and simply the loss of good talent and the cost to replace it.

These are among the reasons that companies and bosses do need to take burnout seriously and look at how they may be contributing to a workplace that leaves their employees vulnerable to burnout. They also need to make sure that employees who do experience burnout get the care and relief that they need.

But beyond these big sweeping numbers and costs is the very real economic impact of burnout on *you*. Naturally, you may lose income if you must miss work on an unpaid basis for whatever reason, but there are also financial implications to not performing your best (missed promotions, falling short of bonuses, being assigned to dead-end jobs). Furthermore, the fatigue and exhaustion of burnout may make you less likely to seek out and pursue new career opportunities, especially if you are doubting your own abilities or capacity to learn something new. All in all, the financial effects of burnout can be devastating up and down the organizational chart and beyond.

The insidious effects of a culture of burnout

There is a danger that as the incidence of burnout increases (as it seems to be doing over time), it can become normalized in really harmful ways. Some studies of burnout cite 75 percent of people reporting having experienced burnout at some point in their lives, and the number in some professions, such as physicians and law enforcement, is even higher than that. As long as this continues to be alarming, then people, supervisors, companies, and whole systems can respond to the alarm and do something to address it. But when the alarm continues to sound and nothing changes, over time we all stop hearing the alarm and start to treat the status quo as the "new normal."

In healing, there's a concept called *entrainment,* which is when one body falls into step with the rhythms and patterns of another body. It can be positive, like when a dysregulated body entrains to a settled nervous system and finds ease. But if entrainment orients toward a disharmonious (or dysfunctional) system, it can decrease ease and create inner turmoil and suffering.

This is why it's important to "call out" the way that burnout has wormed its way into our lives as an almost acceptable way of being in the world, so that you and the system in which you work don't fall into a pattern of accepting and even embracing burnout, or treating it like an individual failing that needs to be rooted out and corrected rather than as a symptom of a bigger problem or challenge in the workplace. (It is for this reason I chose to shift my work to creating cultures of care within companies.)

Burnout as commonplace in society

There is an old story about a village long ago, where the peaceful villagers went about living their lives on the banks of a beautiful river. One day, someone sounded the alarm that there was a person flailing about in the river, flowing downstream, and the villagers rushed to retrieve the poor soul and save him from drowning. Everyone was quite relieved with the rescue, but then the next day another person came floating down the river again. Pretty soon they set up sentries to watch for the increasing number of drowning people coming their way. They constructed elaborate structures to drop rescue ropes and a space to resuscitate the unfortunate victims as they continued to appear on a regular basis. They developed a quite elaborate system to pluck these hapless victims from the raging torrent.

And they never had the presence of mind to perhaps go upstream and see why so many people were falling in the river in the first place!

In many ways, our western society is like those villagers. A great effort is made to detect and even support individuals suffering from burnout, as well as to better select and hire people who are more likely to be impervious to it. But by doing this, we (as a culture) are starting to treat it as an inconvenient reality (like people drowning in the river) rather than a problem to be addressed.

Burnout as a badge of honor

The situation in our modern working culture is compounded by the fact that most organizations are likely to reward employees who put in longer hours and to replace those folks who aren't willing or able to take on a larger workload. In fact, quite often the overachievers are celebrated or rewarded with bonuses and other perks.

It isn't just the modern workplace where burnout is celebrated. Psychologist Sheryl Ziegler wrote a book entitled *Mommy Burnout* where she profiled women who had simply run themselves into the ground in a vain attempt to be seen (and celebrated) as a supermom.

Executive coach and teacher Kim-Elisha Proctor recently wrote of her experience working in Silicon Valley: "It was a badge of honor to say I worked 50–60 hours a week and commuted 3–4 hours a day. Anything else felt like I wasn't working hard enough. I was on top of my work and got a lot done. I was running on adrenaline, stress, and the joy of checking something off my to-do list. You don't realize how intoxicating adrenaline is until you run out of it. I was so focused on work that I didn't see the cost until it was too late."

Proctor really highlights the bind that you may find yourself in. The adrenaline is indeed addictive, but like an addiction, at some point you leave behind the madness of your reality (overworking or people-pleasing), and all you are doing is chasing the next "high." At some point you may find yourself bragging about how incredibly busy you are in a way that invites others to express some combination of pity and awe. There is something quite twisted and dangerous about glorifying busy-ness or burnout. Imagine if you were bragging to a friend, "You think *you're* depressed? That's nothing! I'm *so* depressed that sometimes I can't even get out of bed, and I consider suicide on a regular basis!" How crazy is that? Pretty crazy (I think you'd agree), but sometimes we take unreasonable pride in being burned out as though if we're going to be miserable, we would like to think that we are the *most miserable* person we know.

PTSD AND MORAL INJURY
IN THE WORKPLACE

Some psychologists have suggested that in addition to burnout, there are two other kinds of workplace stress reactions to consider, depending on the kind of impact that the stress has.

If the stress largely impacts your sense of engagement, efficacy, and purpose, it is likely to result in burnout. If you feel literally physically unsafe or in danger in the workplace, then *post-traumatic stress disorder* (PTSD) may be the result. And if the stress influences your sense of trust, self-respect, and values, it is termed *moral injury*.

If your workplace puts you in physical danger and at risk of PTSD, your way forward to addressing this is fairly clear in terms of reducing the risk and seeking mental health treatment for the disorder.

The fine line between burnout and moral injury is a bit trickier and worth looking into a bit more fully. Essentially, moral injury occurs when the system in which you work pushes you to do things that are not only difficult, but also against your deeply held values and principles. For example, if you are a classroom teacher who has a passion for educating the next generation, and your school district forces you to implement poorly researched or potentially harmful curriculum, testing, or disciplinary practices, you may suffer from moral injury.

Huge debates are ongoing in the medical field over whether the demands we make of physicians, the policing profession over the expectations we have for police officers, and the age-old challenges within the military community over the things we ask our soldiers to do. But even in a more routine way, moral injury may arise from a toxic workplace where people are either asked to do, or are witness to, things that violate their principles of honesty, fairness, equality, or human decency. Such experiences shake people to the core of their identity and self-concept and lead to crises of confidence and meaning. While painful and incredibly difficult to navigate, these kinds of experiences are not really burnout per se, although some of the felt sense of them is similar.

Remember: No amount of self-care, or even mindfulness and self-compassion is likely to have long-lasting positive effects for you if are stuck in a position of having to routinely violate your own sense of ethics, morals, or values.

TIP

As you become more educated and informed about what burnout is, how to recognize it, and where it comes from, you can do your part for the cause, so to speak, and be sure to use the term accurately. When you have a bad day and have worked especially hard, you're not burned out, you're simply tired. When you have a stressful job and you spend a day working like your hair is on fire, you may be frazzled, harried, or just plain overworked, but unless this goes on day after day without end and you feel unable to cope with it, you're not burned out. Do what you can not to "cry wolf" about burnout and cheapen the importance of that label. Those who are truly suffering from burnout will benefit from your careful choice of words.

The Wisdom of Paying Attention to Burnout

As you come to the end of this chapter, if you are still with me in this investigation into the various aspects of burnout and the territory of workplace stress, know that you are already laying the groundwork for a change and a move toward greater joy, fulfillment, and ease in your work and relief from the pain and suffering of burnout.

"How is all this information helpful to me in trying to get over my own burnout?" you may be asking. Well, the answer is simple, if a bit counter-intuitive. When we experience something we don't like or something that hurts, most of us have a tendency to (naturally) turn away from such painful things. You don't put your hand *back* on the hot pan after you burn it the first time. When it comes to thoughts and emotions, we want to do the same thing and avoid getting "burned" by them by trying not to think about them, trying not to feel them, or even trying to eliminate them. These are all forms of resistance, and as the evil Borg ship communicated in *Star Trek,* "Resistance is futile." In fact, one could easily say that "what you resist, persists," and so it goes with the signs and symptoms of burnout.

REMEMBER

The only way out of burnout is through it. You can't go around it; you can't run away from it; and you can't surgically remove it like an inflamed appendix. This is the hard truth of overcoming burnout: You have to be willing to encounter it face-to-face, look it in the eye, and say "I see you, but I am *not* you, and I am going to make myself stronger and more resilient so you cannot overtake me. I deserve better." This chapter is about bravely beginning to turn directly toward burnout and to acknowledge its presence. Much more on this ahead, but congratulations on taking this big first step, even if you didn't know you were taking it!

Chapter **3**

Getting Ready to Tackle Burnout

Recently, my client Andrew complained, "It seems like everyone on our team is stretched too thin and working extremely hard just to keep up with a huge demand and heavy workload. I'm exhausted but feel like I don't have a choice, being second in command. I have to set an example. People have to work hard, but they are passionate about our work so it's okay that they're stretched. It comes with the territory." I commented that though this is the nature of a new, small, and growing nonprofit organization, to what end does being stretched thin get you? What good is all the work you do if you end up sick and/or burned out? Who benefits then? Is it really okay? Isn't this a house being built on a shaky foundation?

I asked him, as I ask you, why is it okay for anyone to have to be pushed beyond their limits, to be expected to work long hours, or to function in an environment that almost assumes that stress and burnout are simply occupational hazards of the job? How has this become okay?

I'm putting this out there to challenge you to consider what sort of unspoken (or spoken, for that matter!) assumptions *you* are making about a culture of being overworked, under-appreciated, and pushing past your limits. Think about what the driving force is behind these assumptions and subsequent behaviors or actions. Is the driving force based in fear of not having enough or maybe not being enough?

The thing is, life will always be demanding and full of stress. Such is the nature of running a business, especially a start-up; working while trying to take care of others; and managing through the myriad of life's trials and tribulations. The ability to thrive in life requires a full gas tank, and if your gas tank is constantly being depleted because you are motivated by fear of the unknown or the what-ifs, you can't really make the drive, at least not without running out of gas.

My hope for this chapter (and the book overall) is to make the unconscious conscious and to shed light on some fundamental assumptions that you may be making that are dead wrong and leading you down a path of further burnout. I begin to map out a way forward to find your way through and out of burnout, and I encourage you to form some assumptions going forward that can help you keep your gas tank full so that you can enjoy the ride we call life.

Burnout Is Not the "New Normal"

It's a fundamental error to believe that because something is widespread, it must be the "new normal." At one point in human history, having other humans as personal property was commonplace and nobody batted an eye. At another time in U.S. history, women were not allowed to vote, which was "just the way it was." One can come up with a lot of examples of things or beliefs that were widely accepted as "conventional wisdom" when in fact society later realized that they were neither conventional nor wise.

True enough, burnout has been with us for quite a while, but that only makes it more recognizable and, in some ways, inexcusable that we continue to foster it (wittingly or unwittingly) in our organizations, companies, and culture. Monks in the fifth century suffered from burnout, and 16 centuries later, it has only become more commonplace and almost a badge of honor, as I note in Chapter 2. What if modern science had taken the same approach to smallpox or polio? Where would society be if we simply accepted what was widespread and just found a way to live with it?

Perhaps right now you're saying to yourself, "Damn right! This is wrong!" Or maybe you're quoting the 1976 classic movie *Network*, where a key character says, "I want you to get up right now. And go to the window. Open it and stick your head out and yell, 'I'm as mad as hell, and I'm not going to take it anymore!'" As good as that may feel in the moment, I'm not confident you'll notice much in the way of results from doing so, except perhaps waking the neighbors and scaring the dog. But maybe a little outrage over how you have come to this place would be a helpful energy to move you to make changes: in yourself, your job, and maybe even in the larger system in which all this unfolded.

When you have closed your window and settled down, take a closer look at how burnout weasels its way into your life without you even being fully aware that it's doing so. It's a sneaky adversary, burnout is, but I have confidence in your ability to detect it and begin to disentangle from it, with a little help from me and this book.

Recognizing the chronic and insidious nature of burnout

Say you've recently graduated from school with a shiny new degree and big plans to make your mark in your chosen profession. You go online to a few job posting sites, and you find a job description like this:

> *Attractive entry-level management position in the rewarding hospitality industry for just the right candidate with energy and ambition! This is your opportunity to get in on the ground floor of Hotshot Hotels as it prepares for explosive growth, by signing on to work ridiculous hours (including overnight shifts, weekends, and sometimes both!), work with untrained and incompetent junior colleagues, and be asked to engage in questionable accounting practices. All with great health benefits, unrealistic bonus plans, and other attractive fringe benefits. Apply today and be burned out in no time!*

Or maybe you're looking to climb the corporate ladder with this position:

> *Are you ready for the next step up in insurance claims management? If you've got a solid background in the insurance industry and would prefer to work harder and harder until you can barely drag yourself into the office every day to do the soul-crushing work that we will pile on you, then LMNO Insurance has just the place for you. Be another cog in the big insurance machine, stand tall in your ridiculously small cubicle, and push a mountain of paperwork for the good of the company. Apply today and earn an attractive salary that will seem less and less attractive the more you toil away for us at LMNO.*

Okay, I may be exaggerating a bit for effect here, but the point should be clear. Companies and organizations don't set out to burn out employees or even to treat them badly or disrespectfully. The vast majority of companies simply want to be successful, make money, serve their constituency, or achieve a goal of some kind. They do their best to make jobs sound attractive, interesting, challenging, and rewarding because they want good people to come to work for them to help them achieve those goals, and they believe they can do that if everyone works hard.

It typically starts small and fairly innocuously: A project needs to be finished up for a looming deadline, or a colleague calls in sick and your boss asks you to step up and help out in a pinch. Being a team player and perhaps wanting to please your boss (can you hear the echoes of the people pleaser from Chapter 1 here?), you say "Sure! I'm happy to help." You do your bit, the outcome is good, and everybody is happy (maybe even you), and you don't think much of it. Until it happens again. And again. Until at some point your boss or colleagues simply expect you to come through for them and go above and beyond the call of duty even though they don't seem to recognize that what you are doing is, in fact, above and beyond.

In other cases, it may not come as part of an inadvertent ramping up of expectations in an ambitious, high-growth work environment. Instead, it may simply be the nature of a job that is known to be stressful but may seem noble enough or important enough to cause you to overlook the potential threat of burnout. Healthcare and law enforcement are two great examples of professions that are well-known to be inherently challenging, but the romance of the profession may be the bright lights that obscure the shadow side of the role. The idea of saving a life, curing disease, or arresting a bad guy can seem worth some extra exertion or putting up with a demanding work schedule. This can be the case, but over time this sort of environment can take its toll, and the bloom comes off the rose when it all becomes routine or expected.

Observing your own pathway to burnout

Consider tracing your own pathway to burnout because, as in the preceding examples, it can really sneak up on you without you even realizing it's happening. In fact, this is the most common way burnout arises. So if this was your experience, you are not alone . . . by a long shot.

I challenge you to consider pausing and taking the time to see when the long, meandering, steady but persistent pathway to burnout began and then take note of a few milestones along the way.

Making a personal timeline is a wonderful way to see the big picture of your own life. You can write down some observations of key points that you remember when you found yourself a little farther from an easeful, rewarding job and a little closer to the painful and exhausting state of burnout. For now, put aside blaming anyone or anything for any of these steps on the road to burnout, which means you can also be truthful with yourself and admit that you may have made some of these steps on your own, without provocation and for the best possible motives. Just retrace your steps so you can begin to recognize how you got to where you are standing.

You may want to get a big sheet of paper and draw the following timelines for your life, including all the events that you deem significant that may have led you to where you are today — burned out or on the verge of it:

>> **Physical timeline:** Significant events affecting you physically like illness, childbearing, accidents, and so forth

>> **Mental timeline**: Key moments of feelings of confusion, loss of focus, or mental fatigue

>> **Emotional timeline**: Milestones of sorrow, worry, anger, or fear

>> **Spiritual timeline:** Experiences of loss of faith, disconnection, loss of hope, and so on

>> **Relationship timeline:** Impactful moments involving loss of a relationship, becoming a caretaker, and the like

>> **Global timeline:** Key events like the fall of the twin towers, an earthquake, the pandemic, or economic collapse

What did you feel as you recalled key points along the way? There are no invalid emotions, so whatever you felt was fine to feel; it just was what it was. See if you can remain present and aware of how it felt to feel what you felt and try to name the emotions that came up. Did you feel anger, frustration, guilt, shame, sadness, anxiety, fear, despair, irritation? All are okay, simply because you felt them. They don't have to mean anything; they're just markers of how moments or choices felt. And if you didn't feel anything at all, that's okay too. Much more on this topic and this practice in the coming chapters, but it's a great place to start, even if it's not entirely clear why you are doing it just now. Trust me; it will become apparent over time.

A disturbing (but telling) urban myth has been around for years that illustrates how this happens. (Frog-lovers note: If you happen to love frogs, I'd skip the rest of this paragraph.) Urban myth has it that if you put a frog in a pot of boiling water, it will instantly leap out. But if you put it in a pot filled with pleasantly tepid water and gradually heat it, the frog will remain in the water until it boils to death. Please do not try this at home, but see if you sometimes feel like that slowly simmering frog in your work environment. You don't necessarily have to hop out of the pot that is your job, but you can explore many ways to turn down the heat and make yourself boil-proof.

WHEN CARING IS WEARING

Angie had known she wanted to be a pediatrician for as long as she could remember. She was the girl who not only had dolls (like her friends) but would turn the corner of her bedroom into a makeshift clinic with an examination table, lots of colorful medicine bottles on the shelves, and a sparkly stethoscope around her neck. She sailed through medical school with a single-minded focus that ultimately landed her in a growing midwestern city in a group pediatric practice with several other colleagues with a similar passion for caring for kids.

The practice thrived, and its reputation as a welcoming space with talented and caring doctors grew quickly. More employees were hired, the office space was expanded, and the future looked bright. There were challenges, to be sure, especially as the environment for healthcare (and health insurance in particular) in the United States became more and more challenging over time, but somehow the practice continued to do well. Angie was riding high, working hard, and loving her work. Her lifelong dream was being fulfilled every day.

And then came the global pandemic, and the tide began to turn. The stress on the practice rose, especially as kids began to get sick with COVID-19. That would be bad enough, but Angie found her team dwindling as the demands on her doctor colleagues, her nursing staff, and even her office staff began to grow. Compounded by irate parents who believed that the disease was an elaborate hoax or that Angie was "inventing it to get insurance money," Angie did her best to engage in good self-care, find creative and fulfilling activities outside of work, and to generally remain resilient and strong.

But the challenges kept coming. Her colleagues were dropping like flies and choosing to retire early or take sabbaticals to try and find their own ways of coping. Angie scrambled to keep together a skeleton staff and decide whether she was going to renew her office lease or just "chuck the whole thing and take early retirement."

This is not an uncommon story, with different details of course, but I share it to show how a dream job can slowly but steadily become a nightmare scenario through no fault of your own, and how good work (helping sick kids) can get completely lost behind the clouds of real-life events or circumstances that can't be avoided.

Thankfully, there is a way through even challenging times like a global pandemic, and it has to do with paying close attention to your experience moment by moment, building further resiliency through identifying your needs and meeting them, and keeping a broader perspective on the situation. This is the message of this book, and you're already on the path to building a work life that is rewarding, joyful, and fulfilling, even while being challenging and stressful at times.

Responding to Burnout Rather Than Reacting to Suffering

When you picked up this book (or read about it online), you probably hoped you would find that it was really more of a booklet than a full-on book. You hoped that there was a simple solution for the predicament of burnout you are experiencing (or witnessing in someone close to you), and if you just discovered a few well-timed and wise tips or tricks, you could banish burnout from your life forever. Sadly, you've probably figured out that this process isn't like the *Tighter Buns in 30 Days* title that sounded so appealing (and efficient) a few years ago.

When it comes to dealing with burnout, I advocate for a wiser, long-term approach that focuses on *responding* in a thoughtful, strategic way rather than *reacting* reflexively to the pain of burnout to make it go away as quickly as possible. I'm not a sadist and I don't want you to suffer, but there is a better way if you are willing to be brave and try it.

Think about the last time you had a headache. You may have simply noticed the headache and popped a pain reliever to make it stop. A perfectly reasonable response, but think about it for a moment: Did you get a headache because your body was low on Advil or Tylenol? Probably not. Something else was going on: You were dehydrated, you were stressed out by a deadline, or maybe your hormones were out of whack. This is not to say that taking a pill was not a good idea at the moment, but if the underlying cause could be attended to in another, more effective way, you might want to prevent future headaches and future consumption of pills.

To be sure, there are some things you can do in the short term that will provide you some immediate relief and periods of ease while you build a repertoire of skills and capacities to truly transcend burnout for good. I lay out a few possibilities in the next section that should help you feel a bit better and give you the "gas in the tank" to explore the larger landscape of burnout prevention. But the real value in being willing to come with me on this journey of exploration, understanding, and self-reflection is that you will be able to truly transform your life (and your work) into something that feeds you as it was intended to do and will sustain you through the long haul of a happy, fulfilled life.

No quick fixes, but relief is possible

When the "Check Oil" light comes on in your car, you can certainly go to a convenience store and top off your oil with a quart, but if the light keeps coming on, you really need to look into the cause of the oil loss and address it. This book is the equivalent of pulling into a service station to have a mechanic lift your hood and tinker with the engine. The good news in this scenario is that you are a fully qualified "mechanic" who has everything you need to find and fix the things that need attention, so you can get back on the road to a flourishing and satisfying work life. Here are a few "quarts of oil" to get you where you need to go for now.

Creating little islands in your day

The biggest challenge that arises for people struggling with burnout is that all the best, most well-meaning advice revolves around getting away, taking time off, and removing yourself from your work and responsibilities. As nice as this may be (and I heartily endorse it when you can make it happen), what if you can't get away to get a massage or take a weekend at the beach? The answer is that you may want to redefine what "time away" means. In other words, what if your little "self-care holiday" involves pausing and simply looking around for what catches your eye (colors, light, beauty) while you wait for the microwave or taking the time to savor the cup of coffee that you usually slurp down while on the run to the next appointment?

Don't expect miracles while you're visiting your island (or afterwards), but drop in and simply notice these little openings and let your nervous system have a break. Humans have a natural tendency to compare things to "see if they worked," and this will happen if you open up some islands in your day. You will check in to see, "Do I feel better now after I simply took the time to notice the warm water and slippery feel of soap as I washed my hands just now?"

TIP

See if you can catch yourself trying to do a "before and after" comparison and simply be present for the moments in between for what they are: precious moments all by themselves. Those of us who are parents or grandparents often look back on periods when the kids or grandkids were small and making little discoveries or reaching milestones. Those special moments of joy and delight often get swept away in the rush of a growing human life, but they are the gold in that fast-rushing stream. Make your own golden moments and let them stand on their own.

Taking care of your body

The good news about taking good care of your body is that you don't need any special equipment; you don't even have to fully stop the flow of your busy day to tend to it, and it's always right where you left it: here! But given the ever-present nature of your body, you may often forget that you have one, and only really tune into it when it is sending signals like pain, hunger, or fatigue.

Human beings are sentient beings. This means that we "feel" or experience life through our senses. Your senses inform your brain so that you can exist in the world and adapt to challenges as they arise. When you take the time to look a bit closer, you will find a virtual cornucopia of sensations that span the gamut from unpleasant to neutral to quite pleasurable. For modern-day humans, gadgets and technology (like watches and light bulbs) have taken over to do the job, and for the most part, people have lost touch with these sensations in favor of getting things done or getting somewhere faster. This need to get things done leads many to push past exhaustion, persist with pain, or ignore hunger, effectively shutting down communication with this incredible machine that supports us 24/7/365. (Remember the earlier example about how your body signals you with a headache as a way of alerting you to a problem? That's just one minor example of the miracle of the human body.)

So here's your chance to reverse the trend of pushing past or ignoring the sensations of your body. Instead, pause to listen and hear what it's telling you. And if you're really interested in turning the tide on burnout, maybe take some small actions to give your body what it needs. Here are a few suggestions:

>> **Pause and release:** If you notice tension in your neck, back, face, or shoulders, see if you can simply pause long enough to let go of that tension for the moment. This isn't about any elaborate exercises, but simply noticing what you're holding that you could actually just let go of. For example, take a moment right now to notice your face, especially the areas around the mouth and nose, and the brow. Do you notice any furrowing, frowning, or tightness that you could simply release in a moment? Don't worry, that wrinkled brow isn't actually serving any useful purpose, and if you release it, I can guarantee that your face won't fall off.

>> **Take a stand:** If you sit a lot (as I do), see what happens if you take the time to simply stand up for its own sake, even if only for 10 seconds every half hour or so. I know that, for me, even though my lower back bothers me a lot as a result of spending too much sitting at my computer, when I'm actually sitting there, it feels fine, and I forget to move my body. And if you stand a lot in your work, what about taking the time to savor sitting? Actually notice the act of choosing to sit, the process of sitting, and how it feels in that moment of release when you finally let go into the support of the chair, and savor it all. And don't forget to get back up!

>> **Enjoy a food gift:** If you take a little time at home to consider your food choices, you may find that you can give yourself some relatively healthy "food gifts" as snacks or meals when you're working. Then when you connect to your body's hunger and don't have time to seek out the best choice for your body, the thing at hand can be the better choice for your ultimate well-being. You don't need to have a pocket full of carrot sticks and kale chips all the time, but if you know you have a favorite snack that outperforms stale chips from a vending machine or a sugary drink, why not make it handy? And while you're at it, consider noticing that inner voice that says, "I *deserve* this jelly doughnut

after the day I had" or "I *earned* this second beer by meeting that crazy deadline." If you want the doughnut or the beer, have it, celebrate it even, but life does not have to be all about transactions. You can choose to give yourself something you like or want simply because it's what you want. You deserve joy and happiness independent of what you do, whether you believe that or not just now. You will. Trust me. Check out Part 3 for more on that.

Taking a breath . . . or three

You may as well get used to it; I'm going to talk a lot about the breath as you take this journey with me. I go deeper into this in Chapter 8 when I explore the power of mindfulness, but for now, no need to make too much out of the breath, except to notice it and play around with it a little bit as a gift to ourselves in the midst of difficult circumstances.

Nothing is more immediate (and frankly, important) than each breath. If you doubt the importance of breathing, see what happens when you try to stop doing it for a couple of minutes. Somehow the importance of breathing becomes more apparent quite quickly. But more than keeping your body alive, breathing happens without you having to do anything; it has continued virtually unabated since your birth. (And you thought *you* were a faithful employee!)

TIP

Take a moment to reflect on the beauty of the breath. Inhale deeply and hold it for a second or two; then exhale completely. Really and fully let every ounce of breath out of your lungs until there is nothing left. Get it all out. Then what happens? That's right. You breathe in again. No matter how much you let go, a new breath will always come in. So imagine right now letting go of everything that you have been holding on to — tension, thoughts, to-do lists, and so on. Just for this moment in time, imagine all of it is in your breath. Exhale everything out, and without effort, a new breath will come in that is a little less filled with tension than the first one. Do this a few times as you clear out your thoughts (take a break if you feel dizzy) and then let your breath move into its own regular rhythm. How do you feel?

When it comes to finding time to breathe while you are working a busy shift at the fast-food restaurant, pounding out the work on the assembly line, or changing yet one more dirty diaper in the middle of the night, guess what? You're already doing it! The difference is that you can take a little time to simply pay attention to breathing while you're already doing it. Making the unconscious conscious is a simple shift in your attention to actually notice breathing happening in your body.

Give it a try. Stop reading right now and see if you can simply pay attention to one full breath from the beginning of the inbreath to the conclusion of the outbreath. Simple, right? Easy? Not so much.

For now, like finding the islands in your day that I mention earlier, from time to time, simply shift your attention away from whatever has captured your attention and see if you can follow three consecutive breaths. Your mind will wander, you will get lost in thought, and frustration may arise, but you're beginning to practice presence, which will ultimately be among the best gifts you can give yourself over time. And it all starts with a single breath and your ability to remain present to it.

Cultivating patience, curiosity, and vulnerability

My message has hopefully been clear to you from the beginning: The only way out of burnout is *through* burnout. There are no quick fixes that really work in the long term, and trying to resist or avoid burnout is destined to be a frustrating and unfulfilling approach. I say this not to discourage you at all, but to say that what I'm proposing is something much more profound and powerful than "simple" self-care or finding momentary escapes from the pain and fatigue of burnout. Burnout is a worthy adversary in the struggle to becoming more resilient and joyful, and this means we need to understand and appreciate that adversary. Just as football coaches study films of their upcoming opponents so that they are prepared to compete and hopefully win, I am suggesting that cultivating some presence and clear-sighted awareness of burnout itself will set you up for success. My recommendation as you continue on this journey is to consider cultivating patience, curiosity, and vulnerability.

Find patience

You may be noticing some impatience to "get started" in tackling burnout, and I can totally relate. To be honest with you, I know I have some wonderful tools and approaches to share with you that will make a difference, and I feel some of the same impatience to get to those resources that will help you. Having said that, the wiser part of me also knows that if those things are going to work for you, you also need to have the right relationship with burnout itself and the right approach that will set you up to truly transcend this difficult experience and thrive on the other side of it. Think of taking one breath at a time as you explore how you got to burnout. Stay focused on the now, rather than the past or in anticipation of the future.

Be curious

We humans don't think much about our relationships with things because our brains tend to think about the things themselves. If I asked you what your relationship with gravity is, you would look at me funny and question my sanity. But think about it: You do *have* a relationship with gravity. You just don't think about it very much. Your attitude is probably something like acceptance or resignation.

When you trip and fall and skin your knee, you probably don't shout, "Stupid gravity!" When you look carefully at yourself naked in the mirror and see that some things aren't where they used to be, you probably just sigh and shrug your shoulders. And when you wake up in the morning and put your feet on the floor, you probably don't exclaim, "Damn! I'm still stuck to the earth!" But as a human on this planet, you have your own relationship with gravity, and it's mainly not that conflicted. Isn't that so interesting and curious?

When you shift your mindset to one of curiosity and willingness to explore, you may begin to find that there is a more promising way to deal with burnout that is sustainable and powerful. Perhaps you can shift your perspective to see this relationship with burnout as an opportunity for growth and learning. This is why I invite you to find out more about the background and history of burnout and why I explore the different forms and sources of burnout in Part 2. It's all in the service of helping you cultivate a patient, thoughtful, responsive relationship with this experience that will serve you best in overcoming it in time.

Let yourself be vulnerable

And finally, a note on vulnerability. Perhaps when you saw that word in the preceding headline you hesitated or even stiffened just a little bit. Vulnerability sounds scary, and it may even seem like weakness to you, and if so, you're not alone. But vulnerability, as researcher and author Brené Brown makes quite clear in her work, is what is needed for courage. When you are willing to be open and admit your feelings of vulnerability (even just a little bit), only *then* can you take wise and brave action for change. To be honest, just by purchasing a book called *Burnout For Dummies*, you actually signaled your willingness to admit some degree of vulnerability. Congratulations on that move — I encourage you to keep it up.

What Taking Action May Look Like at First

For all my talk of patience and shifting your relationship with burnout, please don't get the idea that what you're doing here in these chapters is not actually action in the service of reducing burnout. It's just early action that may not look like what you expected. Think about an Olympic skier and how they get ready to compete in the premiere athletic event on the planet. Sure, they ski, but they also lift weights, run sprints, and engage in nearly endless other training activities. By inviting you to try a few self-care practices to find small moments of relief in your day, I'm not trying to stall you until you get to the good stuff. That *is* the good stuff for where you are in your journey. And there's much more that you can do to "train for the Olympics" of burnout reduction and prevention.

Preparing to take action and taking the first few steps isn't particularly sexy. It may not seem that bold, and nobody else may notice you doing these things. But trust me; you'll be glad you did. Comfort yourself in remembering the Chinese proverb that says, "A journey of a thousand miles begins with a single step." Your journey may not be a thousand miles, but every journey, no matter how long, still starts with those first few tentative steps.

Enjoying the lighter side of managing burnout

Don't get me wrong; I certainly appreciate the gravity and burden of burnout — on lives, on systems, and on society. In fact, it is a hugely growing problem that is taking on epidemic proportions, but at the individual human level, if you are to loosen the grip of burnout on your life, you need to use every resource at your disposal to break free and move forward.

The *Cambridge Dictionary* (who would have thought that a conversation about humor would include reference to a dictionary!) defines humor as "the ability to be amused by something seen, heard, or thought about, sometimes causing you to smile or laugh, or the quality in something that causes such amusement." So, the question remains: Is there anything that you've seen, heard, or thought about regarding burnout (your burnout in particular) that has caused you to smile or laugh? Perhaps not.

Take a moment to see where you may find a smile or some humor in the situation you find yourself in and how you can cultivate good humor going forward as you navigate the territory of burnout.

The best source of endless entertainment (at least for me) is my own mind. Of course, my mind also serves up a fair amount of drama, angst, fear, and anxiety as well, but mostly I'm entertained and even amused at what my mind has to say. The key here is realizing that the mind is just part of you that has no more authority than your left kidney or your earlobes. In fact, the comedian Emo Philips once remarked: "I used to think that the human brain was the most fascinating part of the body. Then I realized, 'Whoa, look what's telling me that.'"

So I guess I'm saying, "Consider the source." See if you can look at your mind as simply the equivalent of a radio playing constantly in the next cubicle over — you can choose to listen to it, let it fall into the background, or believe everything that comes out of it without question. You get to choose.

TIP

I sometimes observe myself and my actions or those of others as if the observer (me) is from another planet. I shake my head with a smile on my face and think, "Humans. They are so interesting." This imaginary exercise enables me to be both curious and more lighthearted, which then allows me to learn more about myself or the situation. Give it a try. Imagine you are an alien observing yourself or any given situation, tickled at how humans do things!

One last note on humor for now (and hopefully you have detected a fair amount of it already in what you have read so far in this book), is to recognize the profound truth of the statement "If I didn't laugh, I'd cry." This "counts" as finding humor because it captures a beautiful (and poignant) moment of surrender and letting go when someone realizes the gravity of a situation and the futility of fighting it even more. These moments are when we have the deep realization that truly resisting further will only cause more suffering, which is my point in bringing up humor in the first place.

And by the way, crying is okay too. It's the body's way of releasing pain and fear and can also help you loosen the grip of burnout. Think of the child who gets separated from their parents in a crowd at Disneyland. They wander around looking terrified and wide-eyed, gazing into the eyes of strangers, silently or frantically searching for the safety of their parent. And when the moment of reconnection occurs and the child finally feels safe again, it is usually only *then* that the tears come, as a release of the pain and suffering of separation takes place. So whether you laugh or you cry, you begin to find some space between you and your experience of burnout.

Discovering a place for warmth, kindness, and compassion

Speaking of humor (see the preceding section), one of my favorite twisted management slogans is "The beatings will continue until morale improves." One of the many myths about being harder on yourself and feeding your inner critic is that somehow if you were *more* critical and demanding and perfectionistic with yourself, you would get better results. (Humans!) This is different from having high standards for yourself and expecting good performance; this is beating yourself up to achieve more. And not only does this not work, it also actually makes things worse in many ways.

Remember that old saying "You can catch more flies with honey than you can with vinegar"? (Putting aside the question of why on earth you want to catch flies or share your honey with insects.) Like any cliché, there is truth to it, and it applies to your inner experience (sans flies) just as well. I share more about self-compassion in Chapter 9 and delve more deeply into this topic, but for now my suggestion is that you simply consider being as kind with yourself (internally and externally) as you would be with a good friend going through the same experience.

You may be a highly ambitious person who has motivated yourself to achieve great things over the years by being relentless in your pursuit of perfection, achievement, approval, or whatever. You may feel that if you hadn't constantly beaten yourself up, you would never have achieved what you have in your life.

However, the research backs me up when I say that actually, people who are more self-compassionate actually try harder and persist longer in the pursuit of what's important to them than people who are self-critical. You can think of self-compassion as a form of fuel that goes into your proverbial gas tank, while self-criticism creates a leak. The core message here is that you can cope better and achieve more when you cultivate a safe and supportive "inner space" to acknowledge when things are hard and when things hurt, the way you would do for a friend. I talk more about how to do this in Chapter 9.

Perhaps you can try balancing your inner critic with some kindness. Try saying to yourself (or perhaps imagine yourself saying this to your friend): "Of course this is painful. You're in a period of burnout. You've tried so hard for so long, and you feel discouraged and hopeless. It's okay to feel this just now. I'm here for you and I care about you. What do you need right now?" You know how to do this for others. Can you do even just a little bit for yourself at this moment? And anytime you remember to do it?

Recognizing your power

The heading of this section may seem a bit lofty and unreachable to you right now, struggling as you may be with feelings of fatigue and exhaustion, but its message is true. I am reminded of a quote from *A Return to Love* by Marianne Williamson that is often shared. Here is one portion of it that I think is relevant:

> Our deepest fear is not that we are inadequate. Our deepest fear is that we are powerful beyond measure. It is our light, not our darkness that most frightens us. We ask ourselves, 'Who am I to be brilliant, gorgeous, talented, fabulous?' Actually, who are you not to be? You are a child of God. Your playing small does not serve the world.

If I had to guess, I would say that you would take issue with that first sentence of Williamson's quote. You are very likely feeling highly inadequate right now, in the throes of burnout and all that comes with it. You're not feeling anything like powerful in this moment, and frankly you'd settle for being of average IQ, not repulsive-looking, and generally seen as a nice person over being brilliant, gorgeous, talented, and fabulous. But bear with me for a moment.

There's no doubt that you may feel (or fear that you are) inadequate. But I would suggest that this feeling of inadequacy bothers you. In fact, it really rankles and unsettles you to feel inadequate, and that discomfort with how things feel right now is part of why you sought out this book. To quote *Star Wars*, you feel a "disturbance in the force." Am I right? Okay then, ask yourself, "Why does it bother me to feel burned out?" It may sound like a silly question, but you've come this far, so stick with me.

Why does it bother you? I would suggest that it bothers you because there is another part of you that isn't burned out and believes you deserve better. This part of you is not okay with the status quo, and this part goes very deep into your very being. This is the part of you that gets you up in the morning, envisioning a future for yourself, and the part that sees hope and possibility in things. *This* is the part of you that is "powerful beyond measure" but is kind of in hiding, and its voice is very quiet just now.

Your process in this book is to slowly amplify and listen to the voice of this part of you that wants more and better for you. I know it's there, because it is the only reason that you aren't simply accepting the current reality of your burnout as permanent and just surrendering. You are not giving up because you have a deep sense that there is room for something better for you. You're right.

Keeping your eye on the prize

In Chapter 2, I talk about the physiology of burnout and chronic stress in general. One of the symptoms can be tunnel vision. Evolutionarily, it served humans to become hyper-focused on a threat because it frequently meant the difference between life and death. When the source of the stress is more widespread, pervasive, and complex (as it is with burnout), then having tunnel vision can severely limit your awareness of options available to you and cause you to become preoccupied with one detail (like pain in the body or the memory of a certain incident) such that you lose sight of the larger picture of your situation. It's natural to find yourself in this narrow preoccupation with one part of your experience, because your neurobiology governs this tendency. It's not your fault because it's in your neurobiology. In the short term, the task for you is to disentangle your attention from just one thing and purposely encourage your attentional system to broaden and to allow you to formulate different responses to the situation because you have the larger perspective.

American psychologist and researcher Barbara Fredrickson's broaden-and-build theory in positive psychology suggests that positive emotions (such as happiness, interest, and anticipation) broaden one's awareness and encourage novel, exploratory thoughts and actions. Over time, this broadened perspective helps you build useful skills, psychological resources, and responses to challenges. In the short term, making room for humor, warmth, awareness, and your deeper motivations for joy and satisfaction (all the topics of this chapter) helps you "broaden and build" your perspective and your sense of mastery over burnout.

Ultimately, the goal of this process (and this book) is to not only help you emerge from burnout and go back to baseline, but to actually fix your attention on the many ways you can find to flourish and thrive in your work and in your life. Begin now to formulate at least the seed of an idea for what a flourishing and satisfying life might look like for you.

REMEMBER

Don't worry about other people's ideas of what's right for you, because you know what brings you joy, even if you aren't feeling much of it just now.

As you set your course for flourishing and burning brightly rather than burning out, this vision will guide you like a North Star in your journey of overcoming burnout.

2

Sorting Out the Sources of Burnout

IN THIS PART . . .

Explore what may have led to your burnout.

Dive deeper into examining your own situation of burnout.

Examine your job as a source of burnout and see whether it's the right fit for you.

Find out if you have compassion fatigue, if caring is your job.

Chapter **4**

What Caused Your Burnout?

I magine this scenario: It's a freezing winter morning with at least a foot of new snow having fallen overnight, and you're late for work. You race to the garage to get into your car to make your morning commute, coffee in hand, but you find the garage empty! "Oh man!" you say to yourself, "I had to park on the street last night because the kids' toys were in the driveway, and I forgot to bring the car in later." You get one look at your car in a minor snowbank and think something that we won't print here. After clearing the snow off your car, scraping ice off the windshield, and settling into your seat, you turn the key. Nothing. Well, the engine does turn over, but it doesn't start, and it sounds terribly sluggish. You slump back in your seat and think more unprintable things, about yourself, the car, the weather, and so on. "Now what?" you ask to nobody in particular. "I'm such an idiot for not moving the car last night!" You berate yourself as your head drops on the steering wheel.

Eventually, you consider the possibility that this may not be all your fault, and you go back inside and decide to Google, "What do I do if my car won't start?" Google serves up a link to your local mechanic shop and basically all you can find is the "advice" to call them up and have them come and fix it for you. You check another search result, this time for a gas station down the street, and it says you should check to make sure you're not out of gas, and if you are, to call them and they will bring you gas. Another site tells you that it's probably just too cold and you should really consider moving to Arizona where they will gladly show you some houses there that you might like. And so it goes. All (including your own failings) are possible causes, each with a very simplistic explanation, and none appreciates the complexity of the actual problem.

This is the situation with burnout, and you have probably already gathered that while it is pretty easy to identify much of the time, the causes and various factors that contribute to burnout are complex and varied. This means that the solution is not likely to be simple. In fact, if the solution *were* simple, you probably wouldn't be suffering from burnout right now and you wouldn't be reading this book.

If you were feeling burned out and someone told you to just take a nice long vacation and you'd feel better, they would be right. But if you went right back into the same work situation with the same attitude and approach, those good feelings would eventually fade (if nothing else had changed), and you'd find yourself right back where you were when they gave you the advice in the first place. You could go on vacation again, but that's not really a practical (or affordable) solution, and you'd end up with the same situation again.

This chapter is dedicated to untangling the various threads or contributors to burnout so that you know how to approach your burned-out state with a sense of what needs attention, what will help you, and what may be a total waste of time.

The Multiple Sources of Burnout

There's no quick fix to burnout, and it arises from a confluence of a number of different factors. If you have a fever, you can take medicine to lower your fever, but if the cause of the fever is an infection in a wound you have, eventually the fever will be back when the medicine wears off. Better to treat the wound infection itself first and *then* take the medicine to keep the fever down. The same is true with burnout.

I hope this exploration helps you sort out where and how to move forward to address your burnout, not just for the immediate future but the long term as well.

Taking responsibility without shame or blame

If you're like most people, and frankly, you are (we humans share 99.99 percent of our DNA with each other), I would be willing to guess that when you try to identify the cause of your burnout, you are focused outwardly: on your boss, your co-workers, your working conditions, a pandemic, or any one of a hundred different things outside yourself.

At the same time, I'd be willing to bet money that a little voice in your head is quietly eating at you. That little (or perhaps not so little) self-critical voice might be saying: "You brought this on yourself," or "You just aren't strong enough; you aren't cutting it as a (doctor, daughter, chef, air traffic controller, whatever the case may be)," or maybe "If you were smarter, this wouldn't have happened to you."

Do these (or similar self-critical words) sound familiar? (I go deeper into working with this inner critic in Chapter 10.) I am here to tell you that, while you may have played some role in getting to where you are, there is absolutely no useful purpose for self-blame or self-flagellation to deal with burnout, and that little voice is not as smart as you may give it credit for being (see the previous chapter on that). Burnout is not your fault. Period. It can be, however , your responsibility to heal.

In fact, while seeking out blame is a natural tendency (as if once you know who or what is to blame, you can fix the problem), it's a fruitless endeavor. As the Vietnamese Buddhist teacher Thich Nhat Hanh once said: "Blaming has no positive effect at all, nor does trying to persuade using reason and argument. That is my experience. No blame, no reasoning, no argument, just understanding. If you understand, and you show that you understand, you can love, and the situation will change." So, in this and the subsequent sections, I hope to help you to understand, so that you can let go of any shame and instead focus on change.

Changing your relationship with yourself and your burnout leads to a change in the burnout itself.

Your history sets the stage

I saw a bumper sticker recently that said, "If at first you don't succeed, blame your parents." When I say that your history plays a role in your current situation (whatever your current situation may be), it should be clear that I'm not trying to help you find someone or something to blame. But there's no denying that the particular details of your life journey definitely influence the choices you make, the ways you cope with challenges and opportunities, and how self-confident or self-compassionate you are likely to be.

My client Alice grew up with a highly critical mother who judged her daughters more on how they physically appeared than what they accomplished. No matter how well Alice did at school, she never received accolades. She recalled asking her mother one time why she did not show up at an academic awards ceremony for which Alice was receiving an honor, to which her mother replied, "Your weight embarrasses me." The memory had stayed with Alice for over thirty years, being the basis for her negative self-image and lack of confidence.

Your history may or may not be scattered with memories such as this, but given it is rare to grow up in a perfect home as we do not exist in a perfect world, chances are, there are some key moments in your life, both positive and negative, that have influenced how you see yourself and your world, be it with self-doubting or self-confidence.

Think back to the key moments — the high along with the low points — the events that really stand out for you as being memorable, impactful, or influential in some positive way. Don't worry about making sense of these events or formulating an explanation, interpretation, or excuse for any of them — just make a list.

This is not your "greatest hits," but it may be a "highlight reel" as long as you are willing to list the pleasant along with the unpleasant highlights of your life. Imagine you were making an autobiographical documentary about you that only you would watch. Can you make a simple accounting of noteworthy things that you did or things that happened to you in the course of living your life?

TIP

You may want to go back to the timeline you created, review it, and see how those events may have shaped your way of thinking or the actions you decided to take. You may also want to add some positive highlights to the timeline.

How do you feel when you recount these experiences? Allow yourself to let go of shame or blame as you become the observer of your life.

Acknowledging your history can be fruitful

Your life events do not define you, but they can provide insight into how you do things in your life. For example, the middle child of three, I was far more responsible and reliable and steady than most people my age (I also didn't know any better). I identified with being "the responsible one." I remember being 17 years old and my father saying to me the night before he was scheduled to have heart bypass surgery, "Eva, you are the responsible and strong one. If something happens to me, promise me to take care of the family." I kid you not; this statement was not taken from a movie, but from my life. (When I told my mother about it 30 years later, she was shocked and said, "What am I? Chopped liver?")

I took my role very seriously, and it served me in many ways in that it propelled me to excel academically, take care of people in need, become a beacon of strength and support for others to lean on, and go into and survive the profession of medicine. At the same time, my attachment to being responsible and strong (and people-please) prevented me from accepting help from others and from allowing myself to be vulnerable and let my guard down. I became uncomfortable and anxious if I was late or things weren't well-organized (which is still challenging for me). It led to my own eventual experience of burnout, pushing me to look honestly at myself and my history and what got me to that point.

Tracing the path of your life for clues

Your experiences can have upsides and downsides. Neither is good nor bad, but rather part of your history. The point is that you come by your tendencies honestly, and sometimes your history can set you up to be vulnerable to things like burnout. For example, if you had a demanding parent who (out of a desire to see you succeed in life) always pushed you to do more and better and never seemed to be satisfied with who you were, you're likely to have internalized that influence and dialogue such that you find yourself like a rat on a wheel, trying desperately to achieve more and become perfect (good luck with that one!) but feeling as if you're never quite enough. Put you in a situation where there is a lot of work and even a subtle expectation that you will produce big-time, and it's a recipe for burnout.

Every story is more complex than and different from this example, but see if you can identify some key milestone moments in your life that have contributed to who you are today. Consider how those experiences play out in your work or your other life obligations. You may already have some ideas, but doing this little reflection can be quite eye-opening and begin to give you greater perspective on how you have been overcome by burnout.

REMEMBER

Keep in mind that critical life events have shaped the way you approach life, your work, and yourself. Consider how you have responded to and dealt with any life events that could have had an influence on your burnout, such as a sudden illness of a loved one, being a primary caretaker for your family, having to work two or more jobs to make ends meet, or balancing work with major life changes like a big move, going back to school, or going through a divorce.

Please do not forget to forgive yourself for all of it, for whatever role you played for the experiences to happen the way they did. As the old saying goes, "Forgiveness is giving up all hope of a better past." Don't let this reflection become a "pity party" or an opportunity for further self-flagellation. Remember that you only know what you know when you know it. Whatever it was, it happened in the past, and now you are in this moment. As the turtle dude in *Kung Fu Panda* once wisely said, "Tomorrow is a mystery, yesterday is history, and today is a gift. That is why they call it the present." What will you do with your gift?

Personality is the spice of life

Humans are interesting bundles of experience, genetics, skills, and talents. *Personality* is the term used to describe the combination of characteristics or qualities that form a person's distinctive character. In general, that distinctive character is relatively stable and consistent, and is like the through-line of a human life. We can easily get caught up in the age-old debate of nature versus nurture to try and sort out *why* we have the qualities, tendencies, skills, and talents we have. But instead, I think it's most helpful to look at how the personality you happen to possess may be contributing to your burnout (or supporting you in dealing with it).

Know that your personality is not your identity. It is a reflection of a conglomerate of tendencies and characteristics. It is not entirely separate from your personal history (which I explore earlier in this chapter), but it is definitely just as interesting and just as big of a predictor of how you cope with chronic workplace stress and how (or if) you develop burnout symptoms and the syndrome of burnout itself.

Where you stand on "The Big Five"

The topic of personality fills many volumes, and as you may imagine, tons of different theories about personality are out there. Many of these have proved to be quite useful to psychologists and others in helping sort out what makes us humans tick, how we get into difficulty, how we solve problems, and how we relate to others. Taking a personality test can be quite enlightening, and I highly recommend it if you are interested in finding out more about yourself. Of course, there are a variety of personality traits that are more closely linked to burnout. These include (but are not limited to) the following tendencies:

>> Striving for perfection

>> Comparing yourself to others and/or being competitive

>> Having difficulty asking for support or help

>> Fearing failure or rejection

>> Being unable to prioritize and organize tasks effectively

>> Having a hard time saying "no" as a result of wanting to please

>> Overidentifying with your job or passion so that it is all consuming

Know that these traits reflect the parts of the personality that are out of balance — I examine these further in the next chapter. For now, I look at one major theory of personality to see why these traits may be showing up and why you may have developed burnout in your work.

Many contemporary personality psychologists believe that there are essentially five basic dimensions of personality and that each of us falls somewhere on a continuum along each of these dimensions. The Big Five factors are sometimes remembered with the acronym OCEAN. Keep in mind that every trait can be a gift to growth and resilience, but when out of balance, can be a tendency that may lead you closer to burnout:

- **Openness:** This personality trait reflects the person who is open to new cultures and experiences, and can be inventive and curious versus cautious and consistent. On one hand, openness can lead to professional productivity and efficacy, and on the other, according to experts, it can also be negatively associated with emotional exhaustion and depersonalization.

- **Conscientiousness:** This personality trait is associated with people who are organized, efficient, responsible, achievement-oriented, and self-disciplined. Conscientiousness can also lead to professional productivity and efficacy, but according to research it's also associated with emotional exhaustion and depersonalization.

- **Extraversion:** People with this trait tend to be outgoing and energetic versus solitary and reserved. Again, you may be able to see why such a trait supports a person to be successful professionally. Too much extraversion can also be associated with burnout, including emotional exhaustion and depersonalization.

- **Agreeableness:** People with this trait are sensitive, altruistic, trusting, and cooperative. They tend to be less critical and sometimes less rational and more sympathetic. The same is true with this trait as with the others when it comes to emotional exhaustion and depersonalization.

- **Neuroticism:** With this trait, people tend to be very sensitive and nervous. The flip side of this trait is emotional stability (some authors deem emotional stability to be the fifth trait), where the person has a tendency to be free of guilt, anxiety, frustration, and other negative emotions. Perhaps you can see how the latter is associated with professional efficacy and success, while neuroticism is more associated with exhaustion and depersonalization.

A number of online, self-administered tests purport to assess the so-called "Big Five," and you can go to a psychologist to take the most widely utilized and empirically valid measure of these traits, the NEO Personality Inventory–Revised (NEO-PI-R).

TIP

Before taking a test, it can be an interesting exercise to simply go through each of these factors and see whether you can determine where you happen to fall relative to the two ends of the spectrum. This is what virtually all tests of the Big Five do for you, but reflecting on your perceptions of yourself can be particularly helpful in eventually uncovering any blind spots you may have regarding your personality. Be ready to potentially be surprised if you then take one of the tests and find something else! Remember, this isn't about any one trait being good or bad, positive or negative. It's about uncovering tendencies that bring you out of balance and can lead you down the path to burnout.

For example, you can take The Big Five Personality Test at truity.com. My client Beth found that she was high on Openness, Conscientiousness, and Agreeableness. She thought she was an introvert but found herself to be right in the middle between the two poles of Extraversion, and she was strongly on the side of resiliency and confidence, meaning that she could brush off misfortune and move on more easily than most. Check it out yourself. Did you discover something about yourself?

Connecting your profile to burnout

After you take some time to swim in the OCEAN of the Big Five and have emerged with a sense of what your particular profile looks like, take some time to reflect on how your burnout predicament may have arisen partially out of your personality tendencies. In Chapter 5 and ensuing chapters, I go a bit deeper into how it is not so much *how we are* that determines whether we burn out or not, but how those predispositions match up with the demands of our job or the system in which we work.

For example, if you scored high on Openness to Experience, being inventive and curious may sound good, but if your particular work situation is one in which those qualities are discouraged and you are feeling "boxed in" to doing things "by the book," then your inventive side is constrained. This may make you less patient and forgiving, paving the road to burnout. I had this experience myself, which is why I eventually left to start my own consulting practice.

Imagine being a customer service representative, where you are fulfilled by working with different people every day, facing a wide array of challenges, and helping people solve their problems. The work can be very fulfilling, but if you're really good at it, you may get a big promotion with a fatter paycheck and more responsibility. That may be okay, but if the title of customer service manager now means that your primary tasks are setting schedules, meeting quotas, and reviewing budgets, you may find yourself itching to get back on the phones or "into the trenches" where you can interact with the customers again. This can be a recipe for burnout as a result.

On the flip side, getting to know your own personality profile can help you begin to map a course toward a more fulfilling work situation or even to simply find different ways of doing your job that match your style. In Chapter 13, I explore just this practice, which is referred to as *job crafting.* Often, people find that they can't quite put their finger on why a job doesn't feel like it fits even if, on the surface, it's "a good job." Sometimes the mismatch is obvious, but sometimes it takes an appreciation for your own personality style and how it matches with your actual job.

Vision, meaning, and purpose: Is there a mismatch?

When your day involves emptying bedpans or poring over spreadsheets or driving a truck, you may scoff at the suggestion that your work is a spiritual practice or a step in finding the meaning of life. (Many of us who know the inside joke know that the answer to that question is 42. Thank you, Douglas Adams, for that.) But before you dismiss such lofty notions, give it a chance to sink in. Whoever you are, however modest or unassuming you may be, you are putting one foot in front of the other in pursuit of *something*. You may not have thought of this, but that something that gets you up in the morning may be more than just because you have to, because you have a job or a responsibility.

For example, perhaps you aspire to perform as a guitar player and entertain people with your talents. But for now, you're working in the local city planning department shuffling paper. Where's the meaning among all that paper? If the job provides you with food, clothing, and shelter, it may not, at first glance, feel meaningful, but if it also allows you to continue to practice or to afford that new guitar or next amp, then the meaning and purpose begin to emerge. Every moment is a step on a journey, and the question to ask yourself is this: "Does this step lead me in the direction of my vision?"

REMEMBER

It may be obvious when your sense of purpose or meaning in life is leading you down the slippery slope of burnout. If you don't have a sense that what you are doing has *any* connection to a larger vision for yourself, then you are likely to feel lost and without purpose or focus. This is a recipe for disappointment and, eventually, burnout.

There are two possibilities in this scenario, both of which can begin to lead you on a path out of burnout:

>> **You just haven't quite made that connection** (like in the preceding guitar example). Once you do, your whole attitude may shift such that the same tasks may now seem more important because they align with where you are headed. I live in a big fishing town, and I am constantly impressed by the tight family connections that form the backbone of the fishing community. Families fish together and support each other, because the simple act of pulling a ling cod or Dungeness crab from the ocean is more than a task (albeit with a delicious product!); it's a way of meaningfully contributing to the thriving of a close-knit family.

>> **The connection isn't there.** When you carefully reflect on both your vision for yourself and what you are doing now, you find no realistic connections or ways in which your work is supporting your sense of meaning. In this case, you have a terrific opportunity to explore making a change that aligns better with your dreams and your values. Chapter 10 delves into this challenging, but potentially rewarding, process of making change in alignment with your values.

Why the job is pushing you over the edge

Certainly, some jobs are inherently more stressful than others, but the exact job factors that may promote burnout are more extensive than simply a stressful job. So an underpaid police officer in a high-crime area of a big city may be quite resilient and burnout-free, while a highly paid accountant in a fancy office building may struggle constantly with staying on the right side of the same affliction.

At least six potential sources of burnout are inherent in any job:

>> **Lack of control:** An inability to have a say in the key decisions that affect your job (like your schedule, the specific assignments, or your overall workload) can lead to job burnout. Similarly, if you aren't able to assure that you have the resources you need, this feeling of helplessness and lack of control can also contribute.

>> **Unclear job expectations:** The best of job descriptions may create an impression of clarity that may not actually be present in your real job. In other words, if you're unclear about the degree of authority you have or what your supervisor or others expect from you, you're likely to struggle with your work and feel on edge or demoralized at times.

>> **Dysfunctional workplace dynamics:** While the environment in which you work isn't spelled out in a job description, it is certainly a factor in predicting whether you may have trouble with burnout. Perhaps you work with an office bully, you feel undermined by colleagues, or your boss micromanages your work. These are just some of the workplace dynamics that may impact your well-being.

>> **Extremes of activity:** Your mind probably goes to a fast-paced work environment as one that is most likely to lead to burnout, but you may be surprised to find that the opposite is almost as likely to be true as well. Whether a job is monotonous or chaotic, you need constant energy to remain focused, and this chronic effort is taxing on your system and can easily lead to chronic tension, headaches, fatigue, and eventually, job burnout.

>> **Lack of social support:** If you feel isolated at work and in your personal life, you may feel more stressed. Your working conditions and the nature of your job itself can lead you to be (or simply feel) isolated or separate from others. In Chapter 15 I go into greater depth on the truly transformational power of positive relationships as a protective factor as well as a facilitator of true thriving and flourishing at work.

>> **Work-life imbalance:** If your work takes up so much of your time and effort that you don't have the energy to spend time with your family and friends, you may burn out quickly. The topic of so-called "work-life balance" is a complicated one that I discuss more in the next chapter, but some jobs tend to pull you toward the work side of that equation and can lead to burnout.

It bears mentioning that a change in life circumstances, such as becoming a full-time caregiver for an elderly parent or spouse, or going through a trying divorce and becoming a single parent, can turn a semi-stressful job into the factor that pushes you over the edge into burnout. What may have been inconveniences to you — the dysfunction, lack of support, or unclear supervision — become burning issues that add to your disgruntlement, loss of motivation, and fatigue.

TIP

You may want to consider taking some time to look at your job through the lens of the factors that may contribute to burnout, but definitely don't forget to also consider what aspects of your job may actually help you thrive and be resistant to burnout. Every job or role has positives and negatives, and you know this going in or hiring on, but the key is how you manage it all.

For example, if you work for a monthly magazine, you may notice that going from a laid-back, creative environment mid-month to a crazy, deadline-driven, mad dash to finish each issue at the end of the month is a process that sets you up to burn out. But on the other hand, you may find that being in this cyclical process alongside co-workers you genuinely like and admire who are good-humored even in the most pressured moments tends to help you let off steam and navigate through those monthly deadlines in a way that leaves you feeling a sense of joyous accomplishment when you really stop to think about it. One balances out the other, leaving your sanity intact. How does your work both nourish *and* deplete you? The best jobs do a little of both, but the balance tends to lean toward the nourishing part.

Perhaps you can make a list made up of two columns, "fill up" and "deplete," with regard to whether the task or role fills up your gas tank or causes a leak, whether it supports you to thrive or dive, or whether you actually like doing that particular task or can't stand it. As with all the exercises, notice how you feel as you are creating the lists. I do a deeper dive into really dissecting whether your job is the right fit in Chapter 6.

Context Is King: Systems Can Create Burnout

You may very well be a highly resilient and capable individual with an adaptable personality and clear sense of meaning and direction in your work. You may also have your "dream job" that is a perfect match for your personality and temperament and pushes you just the right amount to keep you interested, challenged, and on your toes. Maybe you're a police officer or an X-ray technician or a senior postal worker. You may think you're immune to the ravages of burnout. But you're equally likely to be prone to burnout because you work within systems that don't function at their best, and in some cases, are downright dysfunctional, unrealistic, and fail in many ways to do what they are intended to do.

This is not intended as an indictment of policing, healthcare, or the postal service (these are just the most obvious current examples of systems with serious problems), but instead to help you consider the third contributing factor when it comes to burnout. You are an individual, inside of a job, which also exists inside a larger system, and any one of these elements (or all of them) may be a contributor to your burned-out state.

Keeping a wide view of your situation

As I have noted previously, when you are experiencing burnout, you are neurobiologically oriented toward tunnel vision to allow you to focus on your adversary and respond with fight, flight, or freeze. Among the hardest things to do in this state is to force your field of awareness wider to take in your immediate surroundings.

And now I am suggesting that you stretch that field even more broadly to encompass the whole system in which you toil and consider how it plays a role in whatever you are facing. I admit that this is hard enough under normal circumstances and may seem impossible if you are carrying the heavy burden of burnout. But be patient with yourself and try to look a bit farther out on the horizon for a bit to see what may be going on that may be relevant to your situation.

Take my client Jessica, for example. In her mid 30s, Jessica had already achieved a high level of success, functioning as the medical director of a nonprofit organization, aimed at helping patients access alternative healthcare while also doing cutting-edge research in the field. She was attracted to the mission and vision of the organization and was determined to put in the hard work to help the organization be successful, even though she was aware that money and cash flow were tight. Along with the other employees, Jessica worked long hours, sat in countless meetings, and accepted a paycheck that was much lower than her colleagues in similar positions. To her, it was "Okay, because we are doing good in the world." The problem was that the leadership team (her bosses) became so concerned with the bottom dollar that they pushed harder, imposed more meetings, acted punitively (blaming employees for failures), rarely rewarded anyone for their hard work, and imposed salary cuts (without taking cuts themselves). Can you see how this was a perfect setup for moral injury and subsequent burnout for Jessica, especially when you take into account her tendency to be a perfectionist, a workaholic, and a people pleaser?

REMEMBER

The point here, as I have made before, is that nothing happens in isolation, especially burnout. There are factors involved that you can be accountable for and others that involve assumptions and actions that are pervasive in the system. The next section looks at what some of these assumptions or actions may be so that you can reflect on your own situation.

Exploring and naming systemic assumptions and actions

As in Jessica's situation, there are certain pervasive systemic assumptions and actions that negatively influence you as an individual. In Chapter 1, I mention the different flavors of burnout — overload, underload, undersupported, and overpleasing — which are not just a reflection of the person experiencing burnout but of the system or job they are part of. Burnout by neglect, for instance, involves having an employer who is not supporting or guiding you, which over time, leads you to feel incompetent and helpless. Becoming aware of the assumptions and actions of the larger system can help you see the big picture so that you can make choices that are best for you. For leaders, understanding these pitfalls gives you the foundation upon which to create change in your organization to help your employees thrive (which means your company thrives).

Assumption: "Suffering is okay because we are doing good"

Many nonprofits live by this very common assumption that doing good justifies suffering. Funds are often tight while the goals to help are high. The culture of such an organization usually attracts personalities who care (a lot) about the issue or the people the issue protects or helps, so much so that they are willing to sacrifice pay, flexibility, and other factors that might support them to thrive.

Assumption: "We need to collaborate, discuss, and meet on everything first"

A major factor that I have witnessed in companies (as have other researchers) is the need to have countless meetings and conversations about pretty much any decision. Whether it entails face-to-face meetings, emails, or phone calls, it can get to the point where there simply isn't enough time in the day for people to do their actual jobs.

Assumption: "Everything needs to happen now (or yesterday)"

The notion that every email or text or question needs to be answered immediately is also a common assumption that can lead to eventual burnout. Do you remember when we didn't have the internet? We waited for phone calls or actual snail mail. Technology and the digital world have certainly enabled more productivity and the ability to multi-task, but the subsequent expectations have become counter-productive, as the need to be constantly "on" and responsive can eventually become a stress overload, triggering that fight, flight, and/or freeze response.

Assumption: We don't care how you manage your time; just get it done.

Even though meetings and emails pile up, the actual work that has to get done does not go away, nor does the expectation that it gets done on time. Oftentimes, leadership doesn't care how it gets done, only that it does. I have found in my coaching practice that one of the biggest sources of stress for even the top-level executive is time management and how to be better organized.

Assumption: Figure out your work-life balance on your own time

More and more companies, especially in the wake of the COVID-19 pandemic, are now realizing that if they want to keep their employees, they need to become more creative about supporting them in having some semblance of balance and flexibility, whether by providing childcare resources, letting people work from home on occasion, or carving out time in the day for employees to take breaks. Historically, the job and getting it done have superseded how well-functioning a given employee is, and the expectation is for the individual to figure out their work-life balance on their own time.

Assumption: Recognize the best and give them more . . . to do

Often, organizations verbally recognize the employees who have been the most productive and then give them more work to do. If anyone else chooses to be recognized, they, too, have to do more work. The result is work overload that doesn't match the purpose of recognition.

Connecting the dots

Perhaps after reading through the assumptions, you may be thinking, "Yup, that's me," or perhaps they don't seem relevant. Know, however, that burnout happens when there is a disparity between the stress that you are exposed to and your ability to handle it over time, which is predicated on the strength of your own internal resources and the environment that supports you (or doesn't). You may or may not be able to change the system within which you work right now, but you can find ways to work with it without shame or blame. You can start by breaking down how you got to burnout into a Four Factor Model.

Explaining Burnout with the Four Factor Model

Paula Davis, founder of the Stress and Resilience Institute (www.stressandre silience.com), notes that in her research she has discovered that there are three causes of burnout in organizations: a high workload, lack of recognition, and lack of support. As noted in the earlier section "Personality is the spice of life," personality tendencies also play a role, so I've added a fourth factor to this model, which is based on you, or rather, your belief system, habits, and tendencies.

High workload

The most common problem, Davis noted, was the high workload, whereby responsibilities did not match the resources needed to get the work done. I have had many a client complain that they are doing the work of three or four people. This situation is exacerbated when team collaboration and cohesiveness is missing. Having balance between workload and your personal capacity is the recipe for success. More often than not, this is not the case.

Lack of recognition

How people want to be recognized may vary, but the desire to be recognized is universal. In both my personal and professional experience, I have found that recognition can be fuel in the proverbial gas tank, giving people the energy, purpose, and passion to work hard. Words of praise, however, can only go so far, so uncovering what kind of recognition best serves people is also an issue, as different individuals perceive reward differently. Whether it is regular positive feedback, a promotion, or being given comp time, being recognized can come in a variety of forms.

Lack of support

Support comes in many flavors as well — financial, physical, or psychological. When people feel cared for and safe, they are more likely to voice their ideas or concerns. Support shows up as fair and equal treatment, a sense of community, and an ability to share values and have a voice. I coached several executives in one company who offloaded their problems in our sessions but refused to share their concerns with leadership for fear of being punished — rightfully so, because the president of the company led in a style that was highly punitive, was known to yell frequently, and regularly fired people if they disagreed with his direction.

Personality tendencies and habits

Most of us have a pattern of behavior whereby we find ourselves in situations that seem to be repeating themselves. One pattern that may show up is the tendency not to make yourself a priority. Lack of self-care or self-value can often be what drives individuals to take on too much work, unable to say "no" or be able to find their voice and stand up for themselves and their needs. Sometimes, it is not exactly a pattern in your behavior, but one that results from life events, like being a caregiver and having a full-time job, or going to school and working at the same time, whereby it's difficult to find time for that balance. I use the term "care" not only to reflect ways in which you can take care of yourself, such as exercise, good sleep, and healthy eating, but also in ways that prioritize you. Self-care, which often reflects self-value, highly influences how in or out of balance your Big Five personality trait is and can therefore positively or negatively affect if or how you get to burnout. (I review some of these tendencies in Chapter 5.)

Connecting the dots with your life experiences exercise

Hopefully, you are starting to see that burnout involves a bigger picture and is quite complex. It may seem overwhelming at first, but there is no rush to figure it all out at once. *Slowly*, you can begin connecting the dots.

I encourage you to try to do the following exercise in Table 4-1 that involves establishing how each of the four factors may be showing up in your workplace or life, how they may be pervasive in your environment, and how they personally affect you. You can create a chart where the three factors associated with the larger system or organization along with other external influences, such as critical life events, are listed in one column, and a list of your personality traits, personal beliefs, or tendencies are noted in the column next to it. For instance, you may write down the different ways your job is demanding, while also noting ways in which you have a hard time prioritizing tasks or perhaps your own belief around having to work hard and not take breaks.

TABLE 4-1 The Four Factor Model and You

Systemic Factors	Systemic Issues (The problem is pervasive)	How It Affects Me	Personality Traits, Beliefs, and Tendencies
Workload (For example, high demand, not enough time, deadlines, extremes of activity)			
Recognition (For example, no feedback, no raises, lacking rewards, lacking clear expectations)			
Support (For example, no sense of community, dysfunctional dynamics, punitive environment, no flexibility)			
Personality tendencies (For example, can't say "no," make little time for health)			
Critical life events (For example, being a primary caretaker, working a job and going to school, dealing with illness of yourself or loved ones)			

You want to ask yourself questions like these:

>> What is my workload?

>> What are the things that I am responsible for?

>> How many people's jobs am I really doing?

>> In what way do people get recognized?

>> How often am I recognized?

>> Do I feel safe to voice my ideas or concerns?

>> Am I offered flexibility to take care of myself?

>> Would I voice my ideas or concerns even if I could? Is my tendency to take on a lot and not be able to say "no?"

>> How does the system benefit by me not speaking up?

When you are working on uncovering your personal beliefs and tendencies, regularly ask yourself, "Why?" and look for patterns. You may ask

>> Why is it okay for me to take on a bigger workload?

>> Why do I keep on despite not feeling recognized?

>> Is this a pattern for me?

>> Why do I not get the support I need?

>> Do I consider it "bad" to ask for help?

>> Is it the culture or is it also me?

Don't feel the need to fill out this chart in one sitting. Keep a journal and take notes as you observe yourself and your environment. Add to your chart as you read along in this book, and the big picture will become increasingly clear.

Appreciating the complexity and taking your time

By now you've gathered that the myriad of factors that lead to burnout are intertwined and complex, some of which you do not have control over, and several of which you do. You have the ability, for instance, to examine yourself, your tendencies, your beliefs, and what drives you and figure out what you need and want. You can appreciate what is lacking in your work life and take measures that can alleviate some of the stress, enhance support in your life, and improve the ways you get recognized, including ways you can recognize yourself. It's just the start, but it's a good one to get you on the road through and out of burnout.

REMEMBER

Avoid shame or blame along this journey. As you are assessing burnout in your life through the Four Factor Model, take care not to lay blame or shame on others or yourself. You are working to unravel the puzzle one piece at a time, being accountable for what you can be accountable for, forgiving a lot, and establishing pathways of support and care that will serve you to thrive going forward.

Take your time. Do not be in a rush to fill out the preceding chart. Observe, learn, be curious, and take notes. Stay open, acknowledge, and appreciate. The next chapter dives more deeply into the makings of your relationship with burnout. What you discover will help you fill in the blanks in the chart, so hang in there and stay tuned.

Chapter **5**

Examining Your Relationship with Burnout

A s I mention elsewhere, burnout doesn't happen all of a sudden and it doesn't happen in isolation from everything else. Stressful life events, high workloads, lack of support, and personality tendencies are just some of the contributing factors. I must stress again that burnout is not your fault. You can be accountable for your role without incurring shame or blame. The goal for you is to discover ways to heal, grow, and ultimately reveal your own resilience. The path begins with you taking responsibility for *you*.

In this chapter, we dig more deeply into *you*. You have the opportunity to examine your tendencies — tendencies that may be unique not only to you but also to the larger culture that you are part of — and how they interplay with the other factors that create the perfect storm that results in burnout. You get the chance to implement tools for self-assessment and find out how to start taking action on your healing journey.

Shifting Away from Shame to Opportunity

I knew from a very young age that I wanted to be a "medicine woman." Whether it was a result of being surrounded by academics in medicine and science or because I loved watching *M*A*S*H*, *Marcus Welby MD*, *Wonder Woman* or *The Bionic Woman* (or Man), I wanted to save lives, be of service, and I cannot lie, be a super-hero. After years of studying and training, I was excited to finally be able to be a full-fledged doctor and fulfill my believed-to-be purpose.

The problem was that the actual practice of medicine was not what I thought it would be. The administration pushed us to be more money driven, to see more patients in less time, prescribe only certain drugs, and refer to only specific specialists. I watched good colleagues getting sued, often for reasons that were not valid. What I thought would be a loving and caring field to work in turned out to be punitive and fear based.

I was dedicated to my patients, but as my distress and anxiety increased, I became increasingly more resentful, which led me to be riddled with guilt. So I worked harder, but the harder I worked, the more helpless I felt to change anything. I felt angry at the system that I worked for and at the patients themselves for not doing as they were told and blaming us for their problems. This latter thought then led to feelings of shame and guilt for being angry with the very people I wanted to help, and for my inability to do better, be happier, care more, and be altruistic. "I should," I thought, "be able to provide care without the need to be rewarded."

The more I played the shame/blame game, the worse I felt. I eventually found myself having anxiety attacks in between patients and becoming physically, emotionally, and mentally exhausted. I didn't like it. I was used to feeling like a powerful, strong person who was capable of fixing anything. I didn't like being angry. I was supposed to be a "caring and nice person." I wanted to get back to her.

Interestingly, the shame I was feeling for not being who I thought I should be propagated me to do some self-examination. I did not like feeling angry, but I also did not like feeling so badly about myself. I recognized that I was in a challenging situation and that I wasn't alone in my plight. So rather than beating myself up, I honored the way I was feeling and used my feelings to guide me to figure out what I really wanted for myself that would especially fuel my soul.

REMEMBER

I encourage you to shift your view as well and begin to look at your situation as a journey and an opportunity for growth, discovery, and change. Be kind and patient with yourself. Approach your burnout with care and love instead of blame and shame as you begin to dig deeper into how you got there.

Digging In to How You Got to Burnout

Ultimately, only you can know what is right for you. The glitch is that you only know what you know when you know it. You may not know what you need or what is right for you — not yet anyway. So take some time to explore your tendencies and see if you can uncover where the mismatch lies between you and the system within which you exist and especially work for. Keep in mind that your tendencies may be unique to you, but they also have characteristics that are influenced by many other factors, including culture, socioeconomic status, spiritual belief, and gender, for instance.

As you read through the following examples, keep your journal and chart handy (see Chapter 4) so that you can jot down notes.

Fear of missing out (FOMO)

Fear of missing out, dubbed FOMO, has been described as a type of anxiety disorder that individuals may experience when they pervasively worry that they are missing out on having meaningful and rewarding experiences that other people are having. Researchers have found a connection between FOMO and rumination, depression, distracted learning, impaired ability to make decisions and make commitments, lower job performance, less life satisfaction, and burnout. If you have a fear of missing out, you may feel the need to sign up for every meeting or event, want to be copied on every email or group text, and have a hard time being present and concentrating on the task at hand because you are worrying about being somewhere else or contemplating what you could be doing instead. Burnout may result from too much socialization and feeling overwhelmed from the high workload or work hours, from the anxiety itself, and so on.

Passion outweighing all else

I recently became involved with a wonderful project aimed to raise funds and provide resources to displaced Ukrainians. The founder and head of the project, Fred, is so passionate about the work we are setting off, he is often brought to tears. His passion is infectious in many ways. The problem for Fred, as he will admit, is sometimes the passion is so strong that it becomes all-consuming as well as overwhelming. Often, he finds that activities that would normally fill up his gas tank, if you will, like regular exercise and sleep, go by the wayside.

Of course, it is wonderful when you get to do what you love. The pitfall is that when you love something so much, you tend to want to do more of it. The passion can then lead to an obsession and is often associated with feelings of perfectionism, anxiety, and fear of failing. When the passion also involves other people, meaning other people rely on you to do your job, your ability to create healthy boundaries for yourself can falter, paving the path to burnout. Mission-focused executives, teachers/principals, nonprofit employees, social workers, nurses, and physicians fall into this category, reflecting a group of people who are more at risk for burnout. As important as having passion to inspire and motivate you is, it can also be unhealthy if clear boundaries are not delineated.

Depending on technology and staying "connected"

As wonderful as technology is in helping us be more efficient, connect quickly, always be up-to-date, and be more productive, there is such a thing as being overly connected when these very same qualities are lost. The inability to shut off and be mentally present in the here and now rather than attached to the screen can lead to mental and physical fatigue; less motivation; and ultimately, burnout. In the workplace, a culture of being connected constantly can lead you to believe you have to be "on" all the time, even when you are technically "off" at home. It feels like there is no "off" switch; you can't take a breather, and if you do, more work will just pile up.

Putting off care of your own well-being

Most of us are so busy doing that we forget that our body and especially brain actually need high octane fuel to "do" or function well. As such, lack of exercise, poor nutrition or sleep, scant time for relaxation, cigarette smoking, and overconsumption of alcohol are examples of ways you may be putting off taking good care of your health and well-being that can add or lead to burnout. There just may not seem to be enough time.

Right now, I am writing this book, working with clients, and taking care of both my parents. My father was just in the hospital with chest pain and discharged just three days ago, and my mom had a total knee replacement six weeks ago, so she needs quite a bit of assistance as well. As a result, I am on the go and on the run often, doing for others. There are many days when I think I am too tired to exercise, or I can't be bothered to cook. The problem is that if I don't make healthy food choices and get sleep or exercise, I feel more tired and have a smaller bandwidth to handle my to-do list. So I am that much more diligent about making sure I do what I can to ensure my own well-being.

Without proper care, you are more likely to succumb to physical and mental health problems, exacerbating burnout as you may find yourself more fatigued, in pain, having reactions to medications, and so forth.

Seeking meaning when there seems to be none

Just as too much passion can pave the way to burnout, so too can lack of passion. Researchers have found that lack of perceived meaningfulness at work is associated with a higher risk of emotional exhaustion, as well as cynicism and lower work engagement. Some people are more affected by lack of meaning than others, of course. You may see your work as just a job and find meaning and spiritual connection in other areas of your life. On the flip side, you may think that your work is just a job, but you find it meaningless, the system does not share your values, and you do not feel like you're part of a community or whole, and you really crave those things.

Misappropriating work time

Whether you believe more is better, you have a hard time saying "no," you agonize over your work being perfect, or your tendency is to be more open and spontaneous versus conscientious and organized, the result can be that you misappropriate your work time. The result is a high workload, working long hours, feeling overwhelmed or rushed, or feeling inadequate because you keep missing deadlines or being late, putting you at a higher risk of burnout. Researchers have found, in fact, that people who work more than 40 hours per week have a higher rate of burnout than those who work fewer than 35 hours. It doesn't take a genius to figure that out, of course, yet employers don't compensate as much for fewer hours worked and often demand you work 60+ hours a week. The question to contemplate here is what role you play in working long hours or taking on too much.

Stepping Back to Self-Assess

As I stress in the earlier section "Shifting Away from Shame to Opportunity," understanding your tendencies is not a cause for blame or shame. The pathway to burnout is complex and involves the intertwining of many factors, including those that are systemic (see more about those in Chapter 4). You may want to take care of your well-being, for instance, but the culture of your work environment expects you to put in long hours and be constantly connected through technology. Perhaps you also have FOMO, or your tendency is that you are not detail oriented or organized, or perhaps you are so impassioned by your work that it takes over your life. The combination of these factors creates the perfect storm to bring about burnout.

The key now is to continue to look for patterns. You can examine yourself more deeply by asking yourself a variety of questions that take into account the personalities that are at higher risk for burnout, the flavors of burnout, and behavioral tendencies. What you uncover can hopefully serve as a guide for what you may want to work on in the future or focus on as you read through this book.

The questions are broken down into two categories:

» **Personalities:** Workaholic, perfectionist, and people pleaser

» **Tendencies:** FOMO, too much passion, over-connected, lack of well-being, missing meaning, and misappropriating time

Know that these categories are not separate entities in and of themselves, but rather each one is intertwined with the other. You may find that some questions seem redundant. That's okay. Simply take note and look for patterns, especially as you take into account the flavors of burnout:

» **Overload:** The demand of your work outweighs life balance.

» **Underload:** You are underchallenged, bored, and find your work to be mindless.

» **Too little support/neglect:** You feel unsupported and don't receive feedback, clear expectations, or guidance.

» **Over-socialization:** Your satisfaction is driven by receiving approval from others.

Self-assessment questions

As you read and answer the following questions, you may also want to refer back to the chart discussed in Chapter 4 as you discover more about yourself. Each question gives you the opportunity to answer "yes," "no," or even "sort of." If your response is the latter, try to break down what aspects of the question may pertain to you and which do not.

Personalities

The following list of questions provides you with the opportunity to help you better understand if your actions or beliefs influence your personality tendencies to be a workaholic, perfectionist, or people pleaser.

WORKAHOLIC

Do you . . .

>> Get more excited about your work than anything else out of your life?

>> Take work with you everywhere you go, including to bed, when on vacation, while eating, and so forth?

>> Work more than 40 hours a week?

>> Turn your hobbies into work or ways to succeed professionally?

>> Work such long hours it is at the expense of your relationships with your family or loved ones?

>> Get annoyed or irritated when people tell you to take a break from working?

>> Ruminate, think, or worry about work or that a job has not been done well when you are supposed to be "off" relaxing, talking to someone else, sleeping, or doing something else?

>> Feel the long hours you put in are justified because you love what you do?

>> Feel complete responsibility for projects even though other people may be involved?

>> Believe your value is predicated on how successful you are at what you do?

>> Take on more work concerned that it will otherwise not get done?

>> Skip meals to work or eat on the rush so that you can work?

PERFECTIONIST

Do you . . .

>> Keep working diligently to make sure your work meets your high standards even though time is running out (versus hand it in imperfect)?

>> Procrastinate because you want your work to be so perfect you have a hard time starting?

>> Stop doing things or trying things you believe you are bad at or at least not good at?

>> Look back at your work and focus on the mistakes and the faults?

>> Tend to look at yourself and focus on the things that need improving or change?

>> Predicate your value on the result of your efforts, not the journey?

>> Have a fear of failure or rejection?

>> Feel attacked when someone gives you constructive criticism?

PEOPLE PLEASER

Do you . . .

>> Not like conflict and avoid it by being more agreeable?

>> Soften your position on a subject if you see the other person will disagree with you?

>> Tell your boss, co-workers, or friends you can be reached anytime and actually answer texts, emails, or phone calls right away?

>> Worry a lot about what other people think?

>> Ask for approval before you move ahead with an idea, project, or endeavor because of your self-doubt and lack of confidence?

>> Have a hard time saying "no"?

>> Feel like you sometimes walk on eggshells to keep everyone happy?

>> Often feel overpowered by other people, as if you are being walked over?

>> Believe you are really good at anything?

>> Think of what you should have said to someone after the fact and never follow up on it?

>> Often partake in activities that please other people but not you?

>> Feel embarrassed that if you speak up or ask a question, you will sound stupid?

>> Get anxious when having to take on anything new?

>> Get anxious or nervous when you have to make a decision on your own?

Tendencies

The following list of questions can help you assess whether you tend to fear missing out (FOMO), have so much passion that it prevents you from finding balance in life, have a hard time disconnecting from the digital world, are able to take care of your well-being, can find meaning or purpose, and can manage your time.

FOMO

Do you . . .

- » Overschedule yourself, including meetings and outings, to avoid missing out on experiences or opportunities?

- » Revisit decisions after making them?

- » Compare your successes or failures to those of others?

- » Constantly or at least frequently check social media updates, emails, or texts?

- » Feel compelled to be everywhere or at least someplace where an opportunity for something exists ("something" being recognition, job success, fun times, and so on)?

- » Have difficulty committing to one event because of the concern that there may be something else you could be missing?

- » Feel the need to always be "in the know" and therefore sign up for every event and every meeting?

- » Think repeatedly about events you may have missed and why you may have missed out on them?

- » Have difficulty making decisions, worried that other options could be better?

- » Often experience doubt and regret after making a decision?

- » Find it challenging to disconnect digitally (from texts, emails, social media, and so on) even on vacation when you are "supposed" to be relaxing and "off"?

TOO MUCH PASSION

Do you . . .

- » Have a hard time delineating boundaries between work and personal life, often because you are so inspired by what you do?

- » Believe that what you do comes before your own needs?

- » Believe your value and/or identity is wrapped up in what you do?

- » Feel your job dictates what sort of care you take for yourself?

- » Believe that people depend on you and it's too important to rest?

- » Feel your work is largely or greatly purpose driven?

- » Sometimes feel exhausted to the core, but compelled to keep going?

- » Feel that keeping your passion or purpose alive and burning 24/7 (or at least most of the time) is absolutely necessary to hold onto in order to succeed?

OVER-CONNECTED

Do you . . .

>> Have a hard time disconnecting from your computer or phone?

>> Feel overwhelmed when a text or email comes in?

>> Get anxious when you see all the emails that have piled up?

>> Feel like you can't turn off your phone or computer?

>> Find yourself "on" at home even though you're technically off?

>> Feel obligated to respond immediately to email or texts?

>> Work remotely and feel the need to compensate for not being physically there by increasing your online presence and accessibility?

>> Work from home and spend the entire day on the computer without many human interaction breaks?

>> Need to stay connected to prove your value?

LACK OF WELL-BEING

Do you . . .

>> Take care of everyone else but yourself?

>> Find it hard to make time to exercise?

>> Know how to truly relax (without a phone or a computer)?

>> Tend to spend most or all of your day indoors without getting out in nature?

>> Still feel exhausted even though you slept?

>> Believe you don't need sleep when there is so much to do?

>> Consider yourself physically healthy?

>> Give yourself time to rest and recover from the difficult workweek?

>> Have a tendency to eat comfort food or foods high in sugar, chemicals, or fat when you're stressed?

>> Have a tendency to eat on the run or skip meals?

>> Smoke cigarettes, drink more than one to two drinks daily, or use drugs or food to help with your nerves?

>> Believe meditating or having a spiritual practice takes time which you don't have?

>> Find you have no time to spend with people you love who can support you?

>> Feel so tired that you don't have the energy to exercise, spend time with friends, eat healthy foods, meditate, or do much for yourself?

MISSING MEANING

Do you . . .

>> Feel like you would rather be doing something else, but don't know what it is?

>> Feel comfortable at work, but not challenged or motivated?

>> Feel unhappy doing what you're doing, but don't know what else to do?

>> Feel that you are working in a job you didn't choose, but it's too late to change?

>> Feel your job helps no one and that it is just mindless and pays the bills — sometimes barely?

>> Wish to somehow leave a legacy for others but have no way of doing so in your current position?

>> Find your job (and even life) monotonous and/or boring?

>> Find it hard to stay focused and concentrate?

>> Drag yourself to work everyday, just counting the hours until you can be done?

>> Get easily frustrated and irritated with your colleagues or clients?

>> Use alcohol, caffeine, food, drugs, or cigarettes to numb yourself and not feel?

>> Feel cynical or disillusioned at work?

MISAPPROPRIATING TIME

Do you . . .

>> Find that you are easily distracted even when you are trying to focus?

>> Have a hard time getting things done on time or even being on time?

>> Feel like you are always rushing and there never seems to be enough time in the day to do everything?

>> Have difficulty setting priorities?

>> Tend to procrastinate until the last minute?

- » Have a hard time setting clear goals?

- » Tend to avoid creating a plan or outline and prefer to "wing it"?

- » Seem to regularly underestimate how much time something takes?

- » Believe being busy and productive are the same thing?

- » Have a hard time carving out time to take breaks or time off of work?

- » Feel increasingly overwhelmed when more work is thrown your way?

- » Have a hard time turning down work requests or other obligations?

These self-assessment questions are intended to serve as a foundation for guiding you to understand yourself better and to recognize your tendencies, so as to give you a bigger picture of how you got to burnout. It may even seem overwhelming right now, but remember, this is just the starting point. You aren't going to fix burnout overnight. You are doing your detective work right now.

REMEMBER

You may also be wondering, "How am I going to change my tendencies? It's who I am." Know that your tendencies are not who you are. Rather they are traits and behaviors you have assumed because in some way and at some point in your life, they have served you to cope with challenges. They are just not entirely serving you right now, and as you learn to heal yourself, you will hopefully find that you are able to develop healthier tendencies and healthier boundaries for yourself that help you thrive versus dive.

Taking the Next Steps

Recall the Three R's in the process of moving through and out of burnout: recognize, restabilize, and resilience. You are establishing the "recognize" part of this process, which means you are pinpointing what needs restabilizing first. If you feel overwhelmed and are not sure where to start, that's okay. This is not about finding a quick fix. It takes patience, time, and a lot of care. Imagine you are a triage nurse or doctor, and your job is to calmly assess the situation without judgment and prioritize what needs attention first.

Establishing calm

When you are stressed and overwhelmed, it's hard to think clearly, let alone prioritize. For this reason, I encourage you to establish a state of calm prior to moving forward and taking further action. In fact, I recommend doing so any time you feel overwhelmed or stressed, or you need to make an important decision. One way to establish calm is through practicing the mindful breath, which can effectively slow down the fight or flight response, allowing your body to better relax, your mind to clear, and your emotions to be less charged. Doing so allows you to have better mental clarity and a more open and positive approach to whatever you may be facing.

It's key to understand that breathing changes with stress. When stress levels run high, the sympathetic nervous system is active, which stimulates your breathing rate to become more rapid and your breaths shallow. The physiological changes are meant to provide your muscles and brain more oxygen so that you can "fight or fly." Your breathing also changes when you are relaxed, when the parasympathetic nervous system is active, allowing you to "rest and digest." Stress hormones drop, and neurotransmitters that help you feel happy and calm, such as serotonin, dopamine, and gamma-aminobutyric acid (GABA), increase.

Researchers have discovered that emotions like anger, sadness, joy, or fear can elicit particular respiratory patterns. They've also found that by engaging in each specific respiratory pattern, the associated emotion can be provoked. In other words, you have the ability to affect your emotions with your breathing pattern. You can initiate a shift from the sympathetic nervous system (SNS) to the parasympathetic nervous system (PNS) by slowing down and deepening your breath, which can, in turn, improve your emotions and how you feel.

The practice of being mindful also lowers stress response reactivity, as you are not ruminating on the past or anticipating the future, but rather are in the here and now, in moment-to-moment awareness. When you practice mindful breathing, you witness the present moment of the breath experience without judgment. You don't attempt to understand, interpret, or conclude. You don't project your views or judgments. You instead allow yourself to witness the breath as it unfolds.

Taking the Mindful Breath

PLAY THIS

You may want to sit, or you may want to lie down. Whatever position you choose, ensure that you are comfortable and that you can stay alert, yet relaxed.

Consider the following as you practice mindful breathing:

>> Begin by breathing slowly, in and out.

>> Count 1-2-3 as you breathe in and then count 1-2-3-4-5-6 as you breathe out.

>> Breathe in through your nose and breathe out through your mouth.

>> Let the breath simply flow without trying.

>> Observe your experience of breathing, perhaps noticing the temperature of your breath as it moves in and out, the rising and falling of your chest, the

expansion and contraction of your belly, the way your lungs fill and the way they let go.

>> Allow your thoughts to rise and fall with your breath.

>> Allow yourself to be aware of how the breath fills your body with life.

>> Notice your connection with the breath of life.

>> Notice how you are not holding on to anything, letting go with your breath.

>> Simply observe your experience. Witness the breath of life filling your body and then being shared with the world.

The mindful breath is a wonderful tool that can be used anytime and anywhere to help you establish more calm. Practicing it frequently or for extended periods of time will eventually have the effect of lowering your stress response reactivity in general, and therefore it will help support you to feel more positive and a bit more rested.

Practicing self-forgiveness

Any action you engage in that minimizes unnecessary uses of your mental and emotional energy will ultimately help you heal and move through and out of burnout. Self-forgiveness is one way to do this.

Similar to mindfulness and meditation practices that involve breath work, self-forgiveness has been linked to lower levels of anxiety, depression, stress, and burnout. In the workplace, researchers have found forgiveness to be very effective in reducing burnout, partly because it helps individuals improve their ability to accept uncontrollable circumstances. In one study, forgiveness mitigated the effects of bullying (Ross & Fincham, 2021), and in another study, it helped health-care providers struggling with burnout (Firulesco, 2020). It is also suggested that forgiving yourself may be just as important or even more so when it comes to combatting burnout.

If you think about it, it makes sense. Think of how much energy you can waste being mad or beating yourself up. The more you beat yourself up, the worse you feel about yourself, the less you think of yourself, the more overwhelmed and stressed you get, and the more your negative habits and tendencies kick in. How often do you blame yourself for doing something wrong and generalize by using phrases that start with, "I never . . .," "I always . . .," "I am so . . .," "I should know . . .," and so on? These types of general statements only serve to exacerbate feelings of hopelessness and helplessness, and thus subsequent burnout.

Staying curious and open

In light of being more forgiving, you can also benefit from staying open and curious as you approach the process ahead. These characteristics help you be more lighthearted and perhaps sometimes see the humor, or as my dear friend and stress humorist Loretta Laroche likes to say, "See the bless in the mess."

I remember one time when I was sitting in a restaurant having a very serious conversation with a colleague, both of us commiserating over work. During the conversation I became distracted when I saw a boy, who was probably 3 years old, making funny faces — not at me, or anyone in particular for that matter — and mashing a paper cup against his face. It seemed he was trying to see what each facial movement felt like, especially with a paper cup mashed on his face. He then proceeded to jump off his chair and lie down on the floor, to get a feel for the cold floor against his face. Every time his face touched the ceramic floor, he would giggle. Before long, the mom picked the boy up, placed him back in his seat, and asked him to behave and eat his food. She was very sweet about it, so he didn't cry, but he definitely appeared disappointed. His pancakes were not as interesting as the floor, but the ice in his drink was! How quickly he forgot about the past and got right back into being curious about the present moment!

It made me think, "When did I stop being so curious? When did I start taking myself so seriously? When did worrying about the future or ruminating about the past become more interesting than what was happening in the now? I made a promise to myself in that moment to remember this 3-year-old boy and remind myself to lighten up and enliven my sense of curiosity, for even in challenging situations, there are opportunities for discovery and growth.

Yes, life can be difficult and challenging, especially right now, but curiosity and joy can help you manage it better. It can turn off your stress response long enough for you to get your head clear when you are feeling overwhelmed or down. You have a choice, even right now: You can worry that you don't have all the answers to fix your burnout just yet, or you can let the discomfort you are feeling propel you forward to be more curious.

TIP

To cultivate your curiosity, you may want to keep a notebook with you so that you can write down questions, observations, ideas, and insights as you go through your day. Stay open and curious, and look for road signs in unlikely places. A desk clerk might make a comment that reminds you of something or gives you an "Aha!" moment. You might read a book that explains something, giving you more clarity on a given subject. Use now as an opportunity to continually ask questions, explore, learn, and gather new information.

Compiling the Data and Prioritizing

At this point you are ready to review your self-assessment and perhaps the chart you fill out in Chapter 4. Do you notice a pattern or where a mismatch may lie between your needs or desires, your personality tendencies, and the atmosphere or environment at work?

I had my client Hellen do a similar exercise in the office with me. She came to me complaining of perpetual fatigue, depression, anxiety, chronic pain, and being "too fat." She said, "No matter what I do, I can't lose weight," and added that the reason she was being overlooked, ignored, and given menial jobs at work was because "I am fat. I would leave, but I don't have the energy to look for another job nor the time." On further questioning, I was able to gather that several co-workers had already left, and the company refused to hire more help. Hellen was left to do the job of three people and was unable to speak up for herself. She admitted that she didn't even like her job and that she wanted to go back to school to become a social worker, but she doubted her worth and capabilities and believed her only worth resided in making people happy. She also came to realize through the questioning that she felt guilty about succeeding or getting to follow her dreams because her disabled sister could not.

Through this line of questioning, we were able to establish that Heather was not only overworked and underappreciated at her job, but that she also did not like the line of work she was in. She wanted to do something entirely different but was wracked with self-doubt and guilt, which she stifled by eating a variety of junk food, her one source of comfort.

As such, our first priority was to find better ways for Hellen to love and forgive herself. We worked on cultivating self-compassion, becoming more mindful, learning to meditate, improving her self-care habits, and slowly building up her capacity to exercise. As she grew more confident, she was better able to address the mismatches at work, discover her voice, and act upon her true desires. She ultimately got herself a raise and went back to school to become a social worker, and today, she is a wonderful one at that!

The point of this story is that you want to prioritize *you* high on your list, and that means offering yourself compassion and acceptance first. Everything else will follow suit over time.

REMEMBER

The more love and acceptance you have for yourself, the better you will be able to take the necessary steps to effect change in other aspects of your life.

For now, take notes, gather information, and be curious. You are finding out more about yourself, what you want, and what you need.

Taking Baby Steps with Self-Care

As you prioritize yourself, start thinking about ways you can improve your self-care. It's difficult to think clearly, work effectively, or fully enjoy life when your body is sick, tired, inflamed, and not functioning at its best. Often the problem is that when you're overworked and overburdened, it's challenging to find the time or the energy to exercise, cook healthy meals, get enough sleep, or get any downtime for that matter. If *you* are not a high priority on your list, self-care will easily go by the wayside, which for many, is another source of shame.

You are not alone if self-care has been difficult for you. If it were easy, I wouldn't have a job! Seriously though, when you choose to treat yourself with compassion and care, you are more likely to incorporate healthy self-care habits.

So perhaps you may want to first look at the "well-being" portion of your self-assessment and ask yourself whether there are small steps you can take to nurture and care for yourself. Remember, there is no place here for shame or blame. There is nothing you "should" have done or "should" be doing. You have the opportunity now to reflect and do things a little differently. Can you go to bed a littler earlier? Eat less junk food? Add more plant-based foods into your diet or get out in nature? I review some healthy actions you can take in Chapter 11.

REMEMBER

Keep in mind that your body (and brain) is a vessel that enables you to do things. Fuel this vessel and you will have the capacity to do more without falling apart. Though burnout is not considered to be a medical problem, medical or health issues are often paramount in this condition. Seek professional help if you do have any health issues. Self-care includes making sure you are getting the support you need from others who can help you. If this is all you can do at first, that's okay. Baby steps.

Identifying what you want to feel to lead the way

You may be looking at your self-assessment results right now and feeling unsure of what to do, where to start, and what it all means. Maybe you have compiled that data and you're not feeling overwhelmed. Fear not and shame not. The goal for you right now is not to project into the future or feel badly about the past, but rather to focus on the right now. What you can know right now is how you feel and, perhaps, how you may *want* to feel. The key here is to pay attention to what you are feeling right now, accepting those feelings without judgment, and then to uncover what you would rather be feeling or *want* to feel. This information thus helps you discover more about yourself and your tendencies, while also providing you with more clarity of what you want to achieve.

In Chapter 1, I mention that part of you that isn't burned out. That part of you that believes in you and your ability and worthiness to thrive. That's the part of you that *wants* to feel at peace, enriched, energized, happy, and so forth. That's the part of you that believes getting out of burnout is possible and that you can feel differently. It is also the part of you that drives a lot of your other behaviors.

For instance, perhaps you note that you are feeling exhausted, and your *want* is to feel more energized. Now you have a goal. What supports you to feel more energized? Does working long hours support that feeling or zap it dry? Or maybe you *want* to feel at peace. Does ruminating over whether you did something wrong support the feeling of peace or annihilate it? In that same light, you realize that you avoid conflict because you want peace.

There you have it. You may not know how to go about changing your tendencies just yet, but you do know that you want peace. What other healthier actions can help bring about the feelings of peace? Meditation, mindful walks, listening to music, and so on. Get the picture?

In a recent coaching session, my client Jacky complained about how upset she was for not being recognized at a recent leadership meeting at work, while her colleagues were. She was upset and exasperated, stating, "They do this *all* the time. They recognize other employees, but *no one ever* recognizes me. I used to be okay being behind the scenes, but I still should be recognized." After making sure Jacky felt validated for the way she felt, I asked her if it was true that she was *never* recognized or valued by *anyone*. I asked her if she could recall ever being appreciated or recognized, at all.

Upon reflection, she admitted that there were times that she was valued and recognized by most people she knew, and she was regularly thanked by these same people. She realized that she was really upset because two people whom she deemed important did not publicly praise her achievements. She went on to say that both these individuals were her "best friends" and that she regularly bent over backwards to help them and make sure they were happy. "I know they love me, but they never recognize me in public," she said.

"Ah," I said, "So you do get recognized sometimes, but not by the people you work so hard to please in public? Have you spoken to them about it?" I asked.

Jacky responded that she didn't like confrontation and didn't want to see them upset. "I'm a people pleaser," she added. I asked why they would be upset if they truly cared for her. I added that when people are spoken to with love and compassion, they tend to be able to listen, especially when needs are voiced clearly. If you can voice what you want, you can usually get it. "What does this situation help you realize that you don't want?" I asked.

"I don't want to be taken for granted, and I don't want them to be upset with me," she answered.

"How would you feel if these two people did recognize you?" I asked.

"I'd be happy," she said.

"Why?" I asked.

"Because I'd feel valued," she answered.

"So you don't feel valued without their recognition?" I asked.

Jacky then understood the reasoning behind my line of questioning and answered, "No, I know I'm valued. It would just be nice if they were to credit my accomplishments in public," she answered. She understood now that she had been scared to speak up about her wants because, for one, she wasn't clear on what that want truly was, and second, she subconsciously was giving the power of who determines her value away to two other people and letting two people determine her value. Asserting her value within herself gave her the confidence to speak to her colleagues.

So try to create that feeling of peace and of being valued and seen within yourself. Then you can speak your truth calmly and compassionately, which Jacky eventually did. She found herself being publicly commended to the whole company and getting a promotion!

Connecting with your want and setting intention

Here's how you can go about the process of uncovering what you want to feel:

1. **Start.**

   Choose a tendency or flavor from your assessment.

2. **Acknowledge.**

   Acknowledge to yourself that you are feeling whatever you are feeling. There is no right or wrong, and no good or bad. Allow yourself to feel the emotion. Intentionally try not to suppress or repress your feelings or your thoughts. Recognize that they have been a factor in leading you to burnout.

   Ask yourself, "How am I feeling right now?"

Are you tired, frustrated, sad, angry, achy, or anxious? There is no shame in how you are feeling right now. It is important to make note of where you are right now, at this starting point. Write down as many adjectives as you can think of without questioning or judging yourself.

3. **Redirect.**

Redirect your focus for a moment to your breath:

Breathe. Focus on the breath as it moves in and then out. In and then out. In and then out.

Then, count 1-2-3 on the inbreath and 1-2-3-4-5-6 on the outbreath. Do this for five or more cycles of breath.

Allow thoughts to come and go with your breath.

Continue this breath focus for another ten cycles of breath.

4. **Ask.**

When you are ready, ask yourself, "What do I *want* to feel?" If you have trouble coming up with the feeling, ask yourself, "What is the opposite of the feeling I am experiencing?" Write down as many positive adjectives that you can think of.

5. **Sit with the feeling.**

Redirect your focus back to the breath. Count to 3 as you breathe in and 6 as you breathe out, and imagine the feeling you want to have. Imagine what being peaceful, excited, or joyful feels like. Allow memories to float through your mind and notice how your body feels.

6. **Set intentions.**

Once you have established one or more *wants,* set the intention to engage in actions to support them. You are just setting intention right now. That is all. With positive intention, especially one filled with self-compassion (which I explain in more detail in Chapter 9), you will find you are better able to effect the changes you need to get through and out of burnout.

Chapter **6**

Deciding Whether You and Your Job Are a Good Fit

A record number of burned-out or simply unhappy employees quit their jobs as a result of the pandemic, or rather, as a result of what the pandemic brought to light: The job was no longer a good fit, if it ever was. According to the U.S. Department of Labor, a record 4 million people quit in April 2021 alone. Named the "Big Quit" or the "Great Resignation," workers demanded better wages, more flexibility and mobility, opportunities for advancement, respect and recognition, and better working conditions. A Pew Research Center survey found that those individuals who quit and became employed elsewhere were more likely than not to say they were now getting paid better, had more opportunities for advancement, and had improved work-life balance.

Are you one of the people who quit or are you wondering why you didn't? Perhaps you love what you do, or maybe you used to and aren't sure what changed. Did you change? Your circumstances? Your boss? The nature of the work? Did the COVID-19 pandemic change your job, or at least how you view your job? This chapter helps you explore whether the job you are currently in is a good fit for you, whether it aligns with your core values and expectations, the implications all of this has on how you arrived at burnout, and guidelines for charting a course to freedom and fulfillment.

Do You and Your Job Have Good Chemistry?

When single and looking to find a romantic partner, most people have a set of criteria with regard to what they are looking for — tall or short, a sense of humor, rich, kind, fit, intelligent, and so forth. You meet one another, and if the chemistry is there, a second date may ensue. As you find commonalities, shared values or goals, and more good chemistry, the relationship usually takes off. But then, as so often happens in life, things change. You change, the other person changes, conflicts and miscommunication arise, life events throw you curveballs, and one day you find that good chemistry is now mostly bad chemistry. Do you stay together and work it out, go your separate ways, or change nothing and remain miserable and frustrated?

Like any relationship, jobs are rarely predictable. What you wanted ten years ago may not be what you desire today. Between changes in your own financial needs, the global economy, other critical life events, your personal need for growth, market fluctuations, and a myriad of other factors, you can rest assured that the relationship with your job — and for that matter, your career — is unlikely to stay the same. Indeed, researchers say that at any given time, 40 percent of professionals are interested in changing or pivoting their career, so you are not alone if you're feeling like you are ready for a job change.

Whether you are someone who wants to make this pivot or you want to find a way to be happy with your "relationship" or your job, exploring whether you and your job are a good fit can provide you with the information you need to chart a course to either find the job that is right for you or see whether you can fix the one you have.

What did you expect?

Jamal stared at his computer screen. He felt numb. "I can't take another Zoom call or look at another spreadsheet" he thought. "I used to love this job and working with my clients. I thought I wanted this promotion. But all I do now is sit in meeting after meeting, fill out reports, and wade through the quagmire of administrative duties. I thought this new role would be a good upward move and help hone my skills. I thought that being a direct report to Jeff would give me more opportunity to learn, but he's moved up the ladder now and the new guy is too busy and thinks I'm doing fine on my own. I need more direction. I have no idea if what I am doing is right. This isn't what I thought it would be."

You're not alone if you find yourself in a job that isn't what you thought it would be. In 2017, pre–COVID pandemic, 40 percent of people left their jobs because they did not like what they were doing. Maybe their expectations didn't match the reality of what the job was offering, the responsibilities of the job changed, or perhaps the core values of the company no longer matched theirs. Similarly, what may have started out as the perfect job for you may by now have become a nightmare.

The question is this: What were your expectations when you took this job? At that time, what was most important to you? Perhaps you were looking for a job that provided the best salary and were willing to sacrifice building your skills. Only now maybe you find yourself bored and underchallenged. Maybe you were so resolute to follow your passion that you were willing to accept lower pay. Only now you find yourself overworked, with a new mortgage and two new mouths to feed.

In order to understand how you arrived at burnout, you want to go back to where the path started and explore your early expectations and priorities. Your expectations and priorities serve as clues, guiding you to better understand your deeper needs, your goals and core values, and your behavior. Your priorities, of course, reflect what you deem most important.

REMEMBER

Your early expectations reflect what you thought would happen versus the reality that transpired. Disparity between your expectations and reality can result in discontent and disappointment, which fuel the fire toward burnout.

Why did you choose this job?

Like expectations, your priorities influence your decisions and subsequent actions. Asking yourself why you chose your job can help you further analyze whether your job is a good fit for you. The inquiry can guide you to uncover your motivations and goals, and find out more about what was and maybe still is so important and appealing to you that you chose that particular role. It may also uncover whether what was important to you then has changed. For example, say a high salary was at the top of your priorities list. As a result, you chose a job that paid well, even though you found the mission or culture (or both) of the company to be a little circumspect. The salary also trumped the daily two-hour commute. Years later, you find yourself making an exceptional salary but feeling rather empty inside because you're not fulfilling your desire to do good in the world and you spend much of your day in your car. Trying to fit in time to exercise, cook healthy meals, or spend time with your family just creates more stress. Factors that influence whether or not you choose a given job include the following:

>> **Salary or compensation:** Your priority was to get well compensated. You may have also needed to get a job with good benefits, especially health insurance.

>> **Tasks and skills:** You were intrigued by the opportunity to hone and engage your abilities. You believed that the tasks you would get to do would utilize your skill set and energize you to work hard and succeed.

>> **Location:** At that time, the location of the job was really important to you. You wanted to find a job close to home, near good schools, or near family. Or perhaps you wanted a job close to town so that you could be near entertainment, museums, or shopping. Or maybe you chose a job near nature so you could hike or do other recreational activities.

>> **Mission of the organization:** When joining, you felt impressed and motivated by the mission of the organization. You were excited about the goals, services, or products the company offered.

>> **Opportunity for advancement:** You may have wanted to move up in your field and felt this job was the starting point for you to either gain skills or be placed in a position to be promoted.

>> **Security:** You were under the impression that the company was growing strong. Layoffs weren't even a remote possibility. At the time, there was a high market demand for the product the company offered.

>> **Culture of the organization:** You do well when you feel socially connected to your peers and colleagues and felt the culture of this organization would be perfect for you.

>> **Management:** You were impressed by leadership and management, believing they would provide you with the right balance of mentorship, independence, and/or supervision.

>> **Prestige:** You were attracted to the name or brand and wanted to be able to tell people you worked for this prestigious company.

What, exactly, did you sign up for?

When you chose your job, the description served, if you will, as a map, providing you with the guidelines and road signs you would need to follow as you forged your path. It laid out the roles, tasks, and parameters of what would be expected of you (that's if the job description itself was accurate), so you could adequately or successfully perform your job.

Do you remember what your job description was when you took the job? Is it still the same now? Knowing what your job is or what your responsibilities are is an important part of figuring out whether the job is the right fit for you. Of course, it doesn't give you the whole story by any means. The job description, like a map, doesn't explain *how* you will do your job, *what* you will learn, *who* you will meet along the way, *if* there will be detours, *when* you will arrive at a given destination, and *whether* or not you will truly feel fulfilled. Nonetheless, it's a good idea to reestablish the baseline of expectations, both yours and those of the people who hired you.

REMEMBER

One of the reasons reviewing your job description is beneficial is that it helps you examine whether what you are actually doing on a daily basis matches the description. Many job descriptions are written up by the human resources department, especially in larger companies. This means that the person in charge of hiring or writing the description is not the person who is going to be your boss. The result is a that a job description is written that doesn't exactly match what the actual role entails. You may find, for instance, that you took on a job with certain expectations only to find yourself in an entirely different role, especially when it comes to day-to-day tasks.

Taking on multiple roles and wearing a variety of hats is not uncommon, especially in a small company that is growing. What started out as one job morphs into multiple jobs, so there really is no clear job description anymore. It may be that much of what you do isn't even in writing. Why is this important? It matters because without a clear map, you have no clear guidelines or road signs to navigate your way and to gauge whether your expectations or the expectations of your employer are being met. If much of what you do isn't in writing, how do you get compensated for it? If you don't feel that you're doing the work you were hired to do, how do you speak up for yourself?

Understanding what the job demands of you beyond the job description

Every job is a transaction of sorts. In return for some payment (in most cases), your employer is asking for you to provide something of at least equal value in return, and that something goes beyond just the job description.

Does your position call for an attitude of collaboration, creative thinking, self-sacrifice, determination, flexibility, persistence, good humor, or attention to detail? This set of qualities is not usually reflected in a formal job description and may not even be obvious right away when you take a new position. Quite often, it is these implied but not stated "asks" by your employer that can become a bit tricky to navigate without falling into a hole of burnout. Deirdre Maloney, in her book *The Mission Myth* (Business Solutions Press), writes about one of the pitfalls of working in the nonprofit organization world.

Maloney notes that many of these organizations attract passionate, committed, but sometimes completely unrealistic people into their ranks. This passion (which is valuable on the one hand) needs to be balanced out by a commitment to solid business principles and sound financial practices. If you are hired as an accountant by an organization dominated by passionate idealists, both of you will be frustrated and you will find yourself feeling that lack of control I describe earlier as a key predictor of job burnout. Interestingly in this scenario, you may also be inadvertently contributing to the burnout of your zealous supervisor who sees you as a "stick in the mud" and a "Debbie Downer" when you insist on being conservative with the finances of the organization.

Considering the value exchange

The flip side of what your organization asks of you is what you bring to the organization. Of course, the most obvious contribution that you make is the actual job that you do, the tasks you accomplish, the projects you complete, or the specific results that you produce. This is the most basic aspect of the value exchange between you and your employer, and it's worth evaluating all by itself, especially to see whether there's a fair exchange of value between what you provide and how much you are compensated.

Recall the six organization risk factors that can lead to burnout according to researcher Dr. Christina Maslach:

>> **Workload:** The work you are expected to do outweighs the support you need to get it done (including pay).

>> **Control:** You don't feel supported to handle your workload and are constantly trying to keep up with a moving target. You are unable to set up effective boundaries.

>> **Reward:** The company rarely presents bonuses and financial rewards, as well as opportunities for advancement, learning, growth, visibility, or positive feedback.

>> **Community:** Leaders do not ensure that staff feel supported and connected. You feel unsafe to voice concerns.

>> **Fairness:** Leaders play favorites, fail to set clear expectations across the board, and reward/punish employees inconsistently.

>> **Values:** The work or the values of the organization do not match yours.

Not surprisingly, if you feel underpaid, that means you feel undervalued, which can lead to feelings of resentment and, over the long haul, burnout. Be sure to consider your paycheck as only one aspect of what your employer or your job "gives" you. Although it's the easiest thing to quantify (and compare with others), it overlooks not only things like fringe benefits, but also the intangibles of flexibility, meaningful work, opportunities for growth and learning, and colleagues you enjoy. Factor it all in together and see where you stand. This may be another inflection point when it becomes clear that you need to bring about a change, either by asking for further compensation (in some form that may not be money) or by looking for another position or company in which to work. Regardless of the outcome of this careful reflection on the value exchange between you and your employer, you'll gain a broader perspective on your situation and the factors involved.

REMEMBER

Even beyond all of this, don't overlook your very particular unique contribution to your work and your organization. Often people are quick to overlook their own unique attributes, talents, and abilities, feeling as if they would be considered conceited or narcissistic if they were to embrace them and even share them.

Remember the Marianne Williamson quote from the previous chapter: "We ask ourselves, 'Who am I to be brilliant, gorgeous, talented, fabulous?' Actually, who are you not to be?" She's right; who are you not to be? What do you bring to the table that is worth celebrating? What do your colleagues and supervisors say about you when someone asks them to tell them about you? It may be your sense of humor, your creative way of problem-solving or your unique capacity to enjoy tasks that others just can't stand. Take the time to savor your unique contributions to your work.

Balancing your passion with the reality of the job

Some career experts may tell you that your passion for what you do is the most important factor. Other experts disagree. Cal Newport, the author of *So Good They Can't Ignore You* (published by Piatkus), is one of the proponents who think you should have a passion, but not follow it. He believes you are more likely to achieve career satisfaction, financial success, and a sense of control when you develop rare and valuable skills and put them to task. He advises figuring out how you want to live and then building your career around your vision.

REMEMBER

Don't get me wrong: It is wonderful to love what you do, but it's just better when what you do loves you too. You can love what you do but hate your commute, or the incessant paperwork or meetings that are involved, or the lack of independence or feeling of safety, or the lack of life balance. What good is passion when you are burned out?

CONNECTING WITH MY HEART'S DESIRE

When I was struggling with whether or not to stay in my job working as a primary care physician, I met with a colleague who told me, "Follow your passion; the rest will be gifted and given." I thought, "I can do this job. My passion is to help people heal. This job lets me do just that. I will figure out how to make it work." My feel-good feelings lasted about an hour, at which point I realized that my passion was not balanced by my work reality. I felt undervalued and overworked, and I was losing my compassion as a result. The reality of practicing medicine entailed looking at a computer more than my patients and seemed to have very little to do with following my passion. So I decided to approach the passion perspective differently. I asked myself, "Given your current passion (knowing it is fluid and may change) is to guide people to heal themselves, does your current place of work support you to do so, not only in the kind of contributions you can make but also in supporting you as an individual so that you can be at your best?"

Of course, the answer was "No" to all of the above, which led me to contemplate more specifically what I wanted. I wanted to help people, but I also wanted a life! I had lost much of it working so hard through medical school, residency, and now as a primary care physician. I wanted to travel, exercise, learn, and really live life. Within a month I quit my job, started moonlighting at an urgent care center to pay my bills, and began studying different forms of alternative medicine to gain the knowledge I believe I needed to be able to guide people through the healing journey. My goal was to be able to create a job for myself with flexible work hours and plenty of time to work with patients, while also having time to take care of myself, and travel and lecture throughout the world. A year later, I hung up my shingle, and the rest was history.

Figuring out what changed

Nothing in life is static, and nothing stays the same, including you. You and your job have been influenced by a variety of factors, including critical life events, both personal and global. Maybe you became a constant caregiver, went back to school, or perhaps got a new boss. Maybe your company went through a merger or the industry that you are in has become less or more relevant. It would be rare if your job and life were not somehow affected by the COVID-19 pandemic. Indeed, Brian Kropp and Emily Rose McRae projected huge changes in the workplace for 2022 in the article they wrote in 2021 in the *Harvard Business Review*:

> The level of volatility will only increase in 2022. New variants will continue to emerge and may cause workplaces to temporarily go remote again. Hybrid work will create more unevenness around where, when, and how much different employees are working. Many employees will be greeted with real wage cuts as annual compensation increases fall behind inflation. These realities will be layered on top of longer-term technological transformation, continued DE&I

[diversity, equity, and inclusion] journeys, and ongoing political disruption and uncertainty.

I don't mean to cause you more stress by referring to this statement, but the fluctuations in the global economy and political climate are very real and affect all of us, both our personal and professional lives. There is little point in ruminating about the past or worrying about a possible negative future because the past is gone, and the future is always going to be an unknown. There is benefit in being aware of the reality, as it is, and using the past to understand yourself better so that you can project a vision and chart a course that will serve you in the future, no matter what happens.

How was your job or life affected by the COVID-19 pandemic? What other events have transpired over the course of the time you have been at this job? In what ways have you changed personally? Has your passion, purpose, or outlook shifted? What were some key events that influenced you, your job, and your life? Perhaps you can review the timelines you create in Chapter 3 and journal your thoughts or add to your timeline.

Assessing Your Career

Hopefully, you've been able to paint a clearer picture of your work situation, your passion for what you do (or lack thereof), the factors that brought you to choose your job, and some of the reasons you are feeling burned out. When it comes to your job — or really any relationship — you have two options: Accept the situation and stay, or accept the situation and leave. Either option requires you to accept what is and then figure out a way to effect change in the ways that you can. Know that accepting your situation and your role does not mean self-blame or shame. Rather, it involves accepting reality as it is, mindfully and with compassion for yourself, so that you are better able to establish whether the role you are in is suitable for you, and if not, what role could be.

Are you in the right career but the wrong job, right job but wrong career, or are both wrong? Juanita worked as an executive in the construction industry. Upon reflection, she was able to recognize a misalignment between the nature of the industry (unpredictability, high tempers, high stress, and often foul language) and her personality or demeanor (rational, even tempered, conscientious, polite, and so forth). Understanding and accepting the nature of working in construction, she then had to decide if construction was the right industry for her to work in. Should she stay and shift her expectations or leave and find the right culture for her? There was no right or wrong answer for Juanita, nor is there a right or wrong answer for you. What is important is that you come to understand yourself better so that ultimately you can craft a job that supports you to thrive, not dive.

Performing a career assessment can further your understanding of yourself — your interests, values, skills, and aptitudes — and help you figure out what job market you do fit into. There are different types of career assessments that can involve personality tests, skills assessments, interest inventories, or values assessments, as well as a variety of tests to choose from. One test won't give you all the information you seek, so you may benefit from taking a bit of time to take more easy free quizzes on www.thebalancecareers.com/free-career-aptitude-tests-2059813. Doing so can help you figure out what career path is well-suited to matching your skills, values, interests, lifestyle, and especially, your current job.

Here are some examples of questions you can contemplate that may provide you with some guidance to figure out whether you are in the right career and wrong job or the wrong career altogether.

Right career, wrong job

Do you feel . . .

>> You need more support, feedback, or supervision?

>> The pervasive values of this particular organization do not match your own?

>> You are not being paid adequately?

>> Your particular position is not utilizing your strengths?

>> You are being undermined by colleagues or your boss?

>> Overlooked and lack the authority you need to get jobs done?

>> You love what you do, but not who you have to work alongside?

>> The financial stability of the organization you work is questionable?

>> Your commute to work takes up too much time?

>> There seems to be little upward mobility or advancement in this organization?

>> You cannot respect the current leadership who seem inconsistent, ineffective, or punitive?

Wrong career

Do you feel or believe that . . .

>> There is nothing about your job you enjoy doing?

>> The nature of the industry is one that is unpredictable or toxic and is not aligned with how you like to be or function?

>> If you have to do this kind of work for the rest of your life you may as well shoot yourself in the foot now?

>> No money in the world would convince you to take on your boss's job?

>> You are doing this job because it pays the bills, not because it satisfies any passion or matches your skill sets?

>> You desire more purpose in your career and there is none here?

>> You wish you had chosen a different path when you were younger?

Establishing Core Values as a Guiding Compass

Your core values serve as a compass that can help you navigate which direction to take when it comes to your job, especially when the path ahead is not clear. They represent your own fundamental beliefs that guide the decisions and support the actions that can lead to more fulfillment and inspiration. When a misalignment exists between your core values and your career, unhappiness, disgruntlement, depression, loss of motivation, disengagement, and fractured communication and relationships with your colleagues or clients can ensue, and of course, burnout is more likely. Ignoring your values usually only adds to your struggle to experience success and fulfillment.

Ask yourself what it is that you value most in your life. Is it integrity, passion, achievement, or honesty? Your values are shaped by what is important to you, and these values then influence how you function in your workplace. When your personal values align with the values of your workplace, you usually find yourself in a happy match. When people share the same values, they work better together as a team, communicate more openly and honestly, feel more committed to one another, are inspired and motivated, and see disagreements or conflicting opinions (versus conflict) as opportunities for learning and growth. In other words, there is synergy. In contrast, when workplace values are misaligned with your own, the consequences can be damaging to you and to the success of the organization. This mismatch can result in moral injury, unhealthy competition, unsolvable conflict, ineffective communication, loss of motivation and commitment, and loss of stability.

When you take time to reflect on what is important to you and what you want from your workplace, you gain a better understanding of yourself and your values and can better analyze current and future situations.

REMEMBER

Keep in mind that your values often change over the course of your life. What doesn't change is that your values are just that, yours. As such, they will always serve as a compass that guides you to choose the path that best suits you.

When establishing your core values, consider these three different categories:

>> **Intrinsic values** are values that are inherently rewarding to you, that motivate you to feel better fulfilled. Examples may be integrity, connection, or creativity.

>> **Extrinsic values** relate to external rewards that are important to you, such as wealth or financial security, social status, or influence.

>> **Lifestyle values** relate to how you want to live your life. For instance, you may value living near nature or in the city, living in a well-to-do neighborhood, or traveling across the globe.

The Job Doesn't Fit, So What Now?

Perhaps you've had a niggling feeling for quite some time that your job or role isn't suited to you, and you don't need to do a deep analysis to know that your job isn't the right fit. Nonetheless, here it is right in front of your eyes. The job doesn't fit. It explains why you've been experiencing increasing self-doubt, stress, anxiety, or irritability and have been pushing yourself to work harder or numbing yourself with excessive eating, drinking, or other self-destructive habits. You are in the wrong job or you are working with the wrong people, and whatever the case, it is bringing out the worst in you. What now? You can't just up and quit your job this very second, can you?

Even if leaving your job right now is an option, you may still want to chart your course. You want to evaluate your options, make sure you set reachable goals, and if appropriate, see whether you can create a more supportive work environment where you are.

Short term: Fake it 'til you make it

Misery begets more misery. Before I resigned, I spent much of my time hating my job and complaining about everything that was wrong, and feeling trapped because I was already in an incredible amount of debt due to medical school loans. Leaving my job was simply not an option. Though my concerns were valid and there was little I could do about the changing medical system, the decision to be angry and resentful was mine and in my control to change. My own negative mental outlook and lack of self-care were adding to my problems, not solving them. I either had to change my attitude for a while, or at least fake it while I examined my options. As long as I focused on the negative, my view of what was possible for me would remain limited and narrow. So I put a smile on my face, practiced self-compassion and gratitude, and took better care of my physical health. Even though my inner critic had something to say about all of it, my attitude did change, which enabled me to open my view of what was possible and chart a course to freedom and fulfillment.

REMEMBER

The point here is that often you can't just quit, but you can fake it until you make it while taking care of what you can until such time that it is possible to leave. Taking care involves taking care of the things that are within your control to change. It involves caring for your physical health and mental health, making sure you have the support you need (like money in your bank), finding ways to be mindful and grateful, and most importantly, giving yourself plenty of self-compassion, taking mini appreciation breath breaks if you need to.

Exercise: Mini appreciation breath break

Begin by sitting quietly and closing your eyes.

1. **Take a deep breath in, breathing in through your nose, and then exhale completely, breathing out through your mouth.**

2. **Bring your focus to the breath, observing the sensations you experience as you breathe in and out.**

    Notice what you feel and sense with each breath. If thoughts arise in your mind, allow the thoughts to be absorbed with your breath and watch them come and go with your breath.

3. **Begin to count 1-2-3 as you breathe in and 1-2-3-4-5-6 as you breathe out.**

    Count to three on the inbreath and six on the outbreath for the next ten cycles of breath, allowing all tension in the body and thoughts in the mind to be cleared with the breath, released out into the wind or air.

4. **Observe your body, noticing any sensations you may be experiencing.**

    Appreciate the silence. Appreciate your breath. Appreciate the opportunity you have right now to be silent.

5. **Breathe in appreciation and then exhale, letting go of everything else for another ten cycles of breath.**

6. **Sound a bell or chimes to gently bring yourself back into the present moment while keeping your eyes closed.**

Long term: Keeping your eye on the prize

What is the prize (or prizes) you have your eye on? Can you step back and try to view the bigger picture?

What would your life look like if you stayed at your job and what might it look like if you quit? What is most important to you? Do you want there to be an alignment of values? More professional advancement? A better location? To like your boss? To be able to have a healthier lifestyle? Do you want to change careers? What will it take to do so? Do you have to go back to school?

When you are burned out, exhausted, and overwhelmed, it can be extremely challenging to envision a different and better future. It is possible, though, to start holding a vision for yourself and begin setting small goals that are in your reach to achieve. For instance, you may decide you need a certain amount of financial security to leave your job. How long do you need to work to save up for this kind of cushion? Do you have the ability or bandwidth to take on a temporary job? Maybe you envision yourself someday being in a different profession. Are there people you know professionally with whom you can network?

Exercise: Creating your vision

PLAY THIS

You may want to set a timer for 5 to 15 minutes.

1. **Begin by sitting quietly and closing your eyes.**

2. **Take a deep breath in, breathing in through your nose, and then exhale completely, breathing out through your mouth.**

3. **Bring your focus to the breath, observing the sensations you experience as you breathe in and out.**

   Notice what you feel and sense with each breath. If thoughts arise in your mind, allow the thoughts to be absorbed with your breath and watch them come and go with your breath.

4. **Begin to count 1-2-3 as you breathe in and 1-2-3-4-5-6 as you breathe out.**

   Count to three on the inbreath and six on the outbreath for the next ten cycles of breath, allowing all tension in the body and thoughts in the mind to be cleared with the breath, released out into the wind or air.

5. **Observe your body, noticing any sensations you may be experiencing.**

   Appreciate the silence. Appreciate your breath. Appreciate the opportunity you have right now to be silent.

6. **Now let your mind wander into the future.**

See yourself full of energy, thriving, and successful. You are being interviewed on the *Today Show* or another talk show. The hosts are asking you about your work and giving the audience an in-depth report on your successes and how you've managed to overcome so much adversity. Let the scene play out as if you were watching a film.

7. **When you are ready, open your eyes and write down as much as you can remember.**

Focus on writing a full story from beginning to end, as if you were writing a newspaper article, starting with a headline. Good questions to guide you are

- Where did I come from?
- Where did I go? What did it look like? Did I want to be there?
- Where did I end up? What was the outcome?
- What did I accomplish?
- What did I feel? How did I feel?
- What did I need to do to get there?
- Who was with me?
- How did I measure success?
- What were my targets?

Think of this as a fun exercise to help you expand your vision beyond usual limiting beliefs or attitudes. The intention is for you to experience the notion that positive change is possible and to connect with how you want to feel.

TIP

Review your lists, assessments, or charts and note again what you don't want and don't like in one column, and what you do want or like in the next column. In the third column, write down what you wish for. Don't allow the feeling that getting what you wish for is impossible.

Charting a course to freedom and fulfillment

You know your destination; now you want to figure out how you are going to get there. When you create a broad vision with specific goals, you are better able to draw out a strategic plan that will help chart the course to freedom and fulfillment.

Keep in mind that you want to set goals that are in reach, especially early on. Your goals will continue to change as your situation changes. But initially, if your site is on a prize that feels like it will involve climbing a mountain and you only have enough energy for a little hill, the overwhelm may prevent you from moving forward. Your aim is to focus on the smaller goals that will help you get there. For instance, you can set goals for action steps that will help you develop the skills you need, connect with the right people, improve your health or your bank balance, and support your feelings of purpose or passion. You can set such goals as these:

>> **Networking:** Whether you want to continue forward in your current profession or in another one, it pays off to connect with others in the field, ask questions, and make connections.

>> **Doing research:** Find out as much as you can about the given field or job you are interested in. Be curious and consider finding a mentor.

>> **Getting a notebook:** Document your process, your plans, your budget, and whatever else will be going on in this process. Having an official place where you are recording the journey helps remind you that this is not just a pipe dream.

>> **Getting educated:** Maybe your goal involves learning a new trade or skill. Look into how you can learn, perhaps by enrolling in an online course or a class that is provided at a local college or community center.

>> **Ensuring an income:** The added stress of being unable to pay your bills is a surefire way to continue on a path to burnout. Make sure you create a plan to ensure your finances are stable.

>> **Improving self-care:** This really is a number-one priority goal. You can't get through and out of burnout and into your dream job or career if you are sick or broken. Set goals for the variety of ways you can take better care of yourself and improve your life satisfaction outside of work.

>> **Practicing the skill:** Your aim is to develop the skill you seek or get better at it. Practice makes perfect. Look for opportunities to build and use the skill. Volunteer for a project if you need to.

>> **Following a passion:** This passion doesn't necessarily need to be work related. You could have a passion for music or learning a new language. This passion can function as a means to help you feel fulfilled.

REMEMBER

Always remember to take care of yourself. Focus on how you want to feel and work backwards by improving your lifestyle, your knowledge, your skills, your relationships, and your feelings of purpose or passion. Create a plan for each objective with action steps that are realistic. Just knowing you have a plan is a big step toward getting yourself through and out of burnout, toward freedom and fulfillment.

Chapter **7**

When Caring Is Your Job: Dealing with Compassion Fatigue

s it possible to care too much? It certainly is, especially if your caring is tiring you out and causing you to get burned out. The syndrome is known as *compassion fatigue* and is more common in people who "care" for a living — healthcare workers, teachers, firefighters and full-time caretakers for elderly or sickly family members.

Indeed, if your job is to care, you are likely driven more by compassion than financial or material rewards. You are driven by your desire to alleviate suffering and to see another person be happy or get better. For many of you, your work often requires that you act selflessly, putting the needs of others over your own. If you don't receive material, emotional, and structural support to do your job, the chance of getting tired and burned out is quite high. Throw in a pandemic and a higher workload, less external support, less positive feedback, higher personal risks, and more fear, and it's no wonder you got pushed over the edge into burnout.

This chapter explores how burnout can happen when caring is your job. It primarily focuses on healthcare workers, but keep in mind that the information set forth is relevant to anyone who cares for a living and in life, and who doesn't receive the care and support they need to stay vital and purposeful.

The Unique Challenge of Burnout in Healthcare

Recent studies report that one out of every three physicians is experiencing burnout. A survey of more than 500 healthcare workers and first responders published recently in the *Journal of General Internal Medicine* found that 74 percent experienced depression, 75 percent experienced anxiety, and 38 percent had post-traumatic stress disorder as a result of the COVID-19 pandemic. Half those surveyed reported a low likelihood of staying in their field. Half! Burnout is indeed a crisis in healthcare!

Even before the COVID-19 pandemic, burnout was a common occurrence for healthcare workers, the highest prevalence being in the surgical fields, emergency medicine or those who deal directly with life-threatening situations, and those who regularly experience shift overloads. High stress scores and prevalence of burnout were also noted in nursing and medical assistants, social workers, and individuals with entry-level positions who had direct exposure to patients, especially those who felt there was little possibility for advancement. The consequences of burnout in healthcare have been far spread, as burned-out workers are more likely to provide less quality patient care, communicate less effectively, and are more likely to leave, decreasing patient access to care.

As such, the COVID-19 pandemic added further insult to injury. Labor shortages, larger workloads, a higher volume of critically ill patients, lack of equipment and supplies, rising anxiety about getting sick or putting their own families at risk, being isolated, and feeling demoralized due to the lack of support received from the administration or from the press created the perfect storm for burnout.

Paying the cost of care and . . . caring

Interestingly, burnout levels in physicians appear to decrease with age, theoretically because older physicians tend to have found more balance and have a less "idealistic" approach than younger physicians have. Does this mean older physicians care less? Personally, being an older physician myself, I don't actually believe that I care less. I think I am a bit wiser and have learned that I also need to take care of myself in a system that can't take care of me well.

The notion that you need to care less in order to avoid burnout as a healthcare worker is somewhat disconcerting in a field that requires you to always be compassionate. It's not like you can take a break or have a day off from caring. There is always another person who needs help. At the same time, selfless compassion or compassion without support or balance has a cost. How do you stay compassionate and attuned to patient needs when you are trying to manage unsustainable workloads; solve problems that are not easily managed with the medical knowledge and interventions that are available; and feeling sidelined by hospital infrastructure changes, availability of supplies, local and national politics, villainization by the media, and high administrative demands? It's no wonder healthcare workers feel battered and run down.

Healthcare workers are not alone in this plight either. Teachers, police officers, firefighters, counselors, therapists, and the like are also at risk.

REMEMBER

Whatever your job, if it involves caring for others and you are not receiving the appropriate support to do so, you are at higher risk of suffering from compassion fatigue and ultimately, burnout.

The high expense of compassion fatigue

Even without pandemics, working in a job that requires that you care about other people can lead to burnout because you are often helping people who are suffering, and witnessing suffering or trauma over time can have a detrimental effect on your psyche. In addition, if you are like many other caregivers, you tend to act selflessly, putting other people's needs before your own. Though selflessness has been shown to improve well-being, acting selflessly without ensuring that your own needs are met in the process can further increase your risk of compassion fatigue.

Compassion fatigue is described as a "combination of physical, emotional, and spiritual depletion associated with caring for people in significant emotional pain and physical distress." It was first noted in the 1970s by researchers who identified psychological symptoms among healthcare workers, including social workers. It then became an official term in the 1990s as a means to describe the symptoms nurses in emergency rooms were experiencing. It is important to note that compassion fatigue and burnout are not the same thing. Compassion fatigue usually has a quick onset whereas burnout occurs over an extended period. However, when compassion fatigue is left untreated, it can lead to burnout.

Symptoms that are shared in both compassion fatigue and burnout are poor focus and concentration, withdrawing, feelings of isolation, fatigue, loss of purpose, denial of emotions, minimizing distress, and other physical or psychological complaints such as an inability to sleep, headaches, or anxiety. Individuals may feel helpless or powerless to effect change (like when a patient is suffering); experience loss of empathy; become increasingly less sensitive and more impatient; and feel overwhelmed, exhausted, numb, and detached. People with compassion fatigue may also feel pressured to keep working and develop unhealthy behaviors to cope, such as self-medicating or using other substances like alcohol.

Self-medicating to cope

I can tell you from my own experience that many of us in the healthcare field are our own worst enemies. Trust me, I know. We are just as vulnerable to distress, fatigue, and personal problems as other people, yet somehow, we convince ourselves it's okay, that we need to save the world first, and that we can't possibly burden other people with our problems because they need us. Not only did I not want to be a burden, but I also felt that asking for help could brandish my image as a beacon of strength and support. After all, I went into medicine to help *other* people. I approached my work with almost religious zeal, despite losing years of my life, countless hours of sleep, financial security, and the time to adequately practice self-care. "It's what we do," I thought to myself. "If there is a problem, work harder. Besides, I am in too much debt to do anything about it. I must go on." I struggled, I normalized my distress, I kept silent, and I turned to food for comfort.

Think about it: Can you imagine the emotional pain of a healthcare provider who has made a decision that has led to a bad outcome, or who has witnessed trauma after trauma, or who is feeling severe anxiety and fear about making a life-or-death decision? How can they cope day after day?

Many healthcare workers turn to substance use for relief, especially doctors and nurses who have access to medication. The sad reality is that given the increasing stress, substance abuse is highly prevalent among healthcare workers, posing a big problem, not just because it threatens the livelihood of the health professional, but also because it poses a threat to patient care and safety.

I personally turned to overeating, which had no consequences on my patients but did negatively affect my mood and my waist size. Others, however, turn to alcohol, cigarettes, prescription drugs (especially narcotics), and whatever it takes to stay awake or numb emotional or physical pain. According to *USA Today*, over 100,000 healthcare professionals, largely made up of doctors and nurses, struggle with addiction, mostly involving narcotics like oxycodone.

Aside from having easy access to the medication, many turn to comfort by self-medicating because they are reluctant to seek mental health treatment. Many believe that they can handle it on their own. Another reason they do not seek help is they worry they might lose their practice or their image if it were known that they were getting mental health therapy. Would you go to a doctor for help or trust their advice if you knew they were suffering from panic attacks, depression, or another mental health problem? According to the Mayo Clinic, 42 percent of physicians are reluctant to seek mental health treatment, and according to a Medscape journal report, 43 percent of medical professionals isolated themselves from others when dealing with burnout in 2021. Bottled-up feelings, high stress, fear of being selfish, fear of job loss, fear of not being trustworthy, and access to drugs are situations that lend themselves to self-medicating.

Is your Caregiver archetype setting you up for compassion fatigue?

Swiss psychiatrist Carl Jung discovered that there are 12 character archetypes, or character models, that are shared among humanity: the Innocent, Everyman, Hero, Outlaw or Rebel, Explorer, Creator or Artist, Ruler, Magician or Wizard, Lover, Caregiver, Jester, and Sage. These archetypes shape our personalities and what we strive to be like. Each character type has its strengths and weaknesses, and different people are stronger in a variety of character types than others. As you can likely guess, the healthcare worker, teacher, firefighter, or social worker tend to match closely with the Caregiver archetype, or one who is driven by the desire to help and protect others.

The Caregiver is motivated by compassion and strives to be generous and selfless in their actions, as they put the needs of others before their own. They are trustworthy and responsive, communicate well, and are there for you when you need a shoulder to lean on or help being picked up. The Caregiver fears selfishness and can find acts of self-care to be selfish, especially when another person exists who is suffering. Their greatest weakness can be martyrdom, and their selfless acts can be taken for granted and exploited.

Think about it: The Caregiver archetype wants to help others and do good. They have a tendency to be selfless and silent, working long hours in a system that advocates for harder work, high demands, often crazy hours, high risk, or high trauma. This doesn't even factor in that the Caregiver has personal and home responsibilities as well. If you are the Caregiver type working within a faulty system where you are overloaded with administrative or clinical work, trying to help people who are suffering, trying to manage despite the labor and supply shortage, and so forth, and you're putting your own needs on the back burner, what is bound to happen? That's right. Compassion fatigue and eventually, burnout.

In my close to 30 years in the field of medicine, I have witnessed many colleagues and clients reach compassion fatigue and get burned out or come very close because they cared so much at the expense of their own needs and self-care, and because they worked in a system that didn't support their needs. Some individuals opted to eventually take time off, and some left the profession altogether. Others found their way to get help, enhance their self-awareness, and develop healthier coping strategies. There is hope!

It's important to point out that though the tendency to be more of the Caretaker archetype can set you up to be at higher risk for compassion fatigue, it's not the only factor involved that gets you there, and it's certainly not the only reason you get to burnout. I, for example, used to lean more toward the Caregiver archetype, but I also had a lot of the Rebel and Advocate archetypes in me. The sense of not having autonomy and feeling the system needed changing but that I was powerless to do so pushed me over the edge. Nowadays, when I check my archetype quiz, I am 60 percent Rebel (I enjoy bucking the system and getting new ideas out in the world), 25 percent Advocate, and 15 percent caregiver.

It's Not You; It's a Flawed System

Whatever archetype characteristics you may possess, know that getting to burnout or even compassion fatigue is not your fault. You care in a system that doesn't necessarily care about you, at least not enough to support you in the way you need. Did you know that despite having the world's most expensive healthcare system, the United States has been given the worst ranking for over five years, among wealthier countries, with regard to measures of access, equity, quality, efficiency, and healthy lives? In addition, in 2006, the United States was number one in the world for spending per capita, yet 39th for infant mortality, 43rd for female mortality, 42nd for adult male mortality, and 36th for life expectancy. This isn't happening because healthcare workers don't care, but because the healthcare system is inherently flawed, as are many systems that involve the care of human beings, education being one as well. When these flaws prevent healthcare providers from providing high-quality care or teachers from being able to fully teach, it is a ripe setup for burnout.

These statistics are from 2006. Imagine what the numbers are like now, post pandemic, where healthcare workers are walking around like zombies, exhausted, and possibly using substances to keep it together. The National Academy of Medicine released a report that found that malpractice claims, worker absenteeism, and turnover have increased, and billions of dollars have been lost due to medical injury, largely a result of doctors and nurses being burned out.

The same is true for our educational system. Teachers are overworked as a result of staff shortages and are underpaid, undervalued, and not respected enough. Throw in challenging students, lack of support, loss of autonomy, and time pressure, and the people whom children need most (other than family) are becoming more despondent, less engaged, and saying goodbye to their beloved profession because they are burned out.

When caring people make mistakes

As I was writing this book, an article was released in Medscape that brings to light how very real the situation is. On March 25, 2022, a nurse named RaDonda Vaught was convicted of two felonies for a fatal medication mistake that occurred in 2017 and is facing eight years in prison. Days later, nurses across the United States decided to quit. In the article, a nurse who quit said she did so because she felt it could be her the next time as in the "pressure cooker of pandemic-era healthcare, another mistake is inevitable." Nursing organizations have condemned the verdict and have warned of this fallout in a profession that is already demoralized, depleted, and stretched to its limits because of the pandemic.

Do note that this particular verdict is quite controversial, and just as many people believe that she was tried justly and that her actions were negligent. The question that lies therein is this: Could it have been prevented? Even prior to the pandemic, nurses had found themselves in impossible situations due to shortages and mounting responsibilities. This situation and the reactions of healthcare workers bring to light how broken the system has been and emphasize that actions need to be taken to ensure that we have viable, engaged, well-rested, educated, and supported healthcare givers.

The point is that when you are exhausted and burned out, you make mistakes. The mistakes may be significant or insignificant, having dire consequences or minor ones on other people. Either way, when you make mistakes, especially when you care, you are likely to feel more guilt and shame, or some kind of emotional, physical, or psychological distress. So how do you cope?

The key is caring for the caregiver

In order to prevent burnout, the system at large would have to offer more support, guidance, resources, and opportunities for self-care and a greater sense of control.

Given the burnout crisis in healthcare, more measures are now being taken to address why it is happening, how to prevent it, and how to help the staff. Some hospitals are creating new initiatives to help workflow or increase access to mental health resources, while in other places physician and nursing groups are forming teams to facilitate better support and communication. Globally and in local hospitals, wellness programs are being offered. Other efforts are being made to improve physician autonomy and the collegial work environment, and to allow participation in organizational decisions, giving physicians more influence over their work and patient care. Other measures, like providing childcare resources or more flexible hours, have been taken. Examples include the following:

>> The Henry Ford Health System in Michigan has implemented a new process whereby prior authorization specialists obtain and justify insurers' approval for a given treatment so that clinicians are spared the burden. "Getting Rid of Stupid Stuff" is a program that was initiated at Hawaii Pacific Health, giving employees the opportunity to designate which aspect of the electronic health-record could be eliminated. One suggestion was to get rid of the need for nurses and nurse aides to document that they had conducted hourly rounds. Getting rid of this task saved 1,700 nursing hours per month. Imagine how many seemingly minor tasks can add up to thousands of hours of work, time, and effort that have little or nothing to do with actual patient care!

>> The American Medical Association has developed STEPS Forward, an open-access platform that features more than 50 modules offering strategies and resources that are designed to improve workflow, decrease operational inefficiencies, and improve the clinical team's engagement as well as patient care.

>> Providence healthcare system in Renton, Washington, instituted a "No One Cares Alone" program offering support and practical suggestions to members of high-stress units (ICU, emergency, pharmacy, respiratory therapy, and so forth) provided by teams of behavioral clinicians, social workers, and chaplains.

In short, these examples show that caring comes in the form of mental health support, improving workflow, providing material support, finding ways to create more efficiency and improve communication, and so forth. We have a long way to go, as these efforts are localized for the most part, but they're a start and cause to have some faith!

Cultivating a Vision of Care that Includes You

It's important to stress here that if you are a healthcare provider, an educator, a social worker, a people's advocate, or you work long hours for a nonprofit organization and are feeling burned out or on the verge of burnout, you are not alone. Neither are you alone if you are suffering from sleep deprivation, substance addiction, your own physical complaints, depression, anxiety, or even suicidal thoughts. It's not your fault. You are driven to care in a system that seemingly is not caring about you. There are bigger issues in the environment within which you work.

So, given what is, what are you to do? In the end, you are responsible for your own well-being and taking care of *you* as best you can. Though you may be feeling exhausted and depleted right now, know that there is a part of you that has the wherewithal to feel better. To fix a broken system, we often need to start with ourselves and fix what may be injured or broken within us. Perhaps, for now, rather than focusing on everything that is wrong, you can focus instead on what you need to thrive. What vision can you project forward that also involves taking care of you?

Challenging the way you think

You may not have control over how the system within which you work functions, but you can have control over your attitudes and reactions. Again, I am not proposing that you are not justified in feeling the way you do. I am instead encouraging you to challenge any thoughts, beliefs, or personality tendencies that may be contributing to your burnout. You can begin by challenging some of your thoughts.

The American Psychological Association defines thought or cognitive distortions as "faulty or inaccurate thinking, perception, or belief," with negativity often being the defining characteristic. Being distortions, these beliefs or thoughts are often not based in logic or truth and effectively cause you to experience more stress and distress.

The following section lists common distortions. Take a moment to read through the examples and think about how this type of thinking shows up in your daily life and how it may be contributing to your distress.

Challenging your beliefs in action

If you are like most, you may not be aware of how often your behavior or actions are swayed by faulty or inaccurate thinking or beliefs. What follows are examples of such thinking and ways you can challenge the thoughts or beliefs.

> **All-or-nothing thinking:** You perceive your life in absolute categories instead of as a continuum. For example, if you believe that your care of a patient or client is less than perfect, you see yourself or the system that hasn't supported you as a complete failure.

Challenge: You can challenge this thought by recognizing what *did* go well. You can also recall times when you were in a similar situation, and the outcome was successful. Is it true that you are a failure?

Overgeneralization: You view a negative event as part of a continued pattern of negativity while ignoring evidence to the contrary — that many things in your life are positive. You may use the words "never," "always," "all," "every," "none," "no one," "nobody," or "everyone" to support your belief that you don't and never will have (or aren't and never will be) enough. For example, you may be upset at not getting the support you need and state, "I never get the support I need. I am always left to do things on my own."

Challenge: Challenge yourself to see if this is indeed true. Are you *never* supported by anyone, ever? What is actually true?

Magnification or minimization (making the negative bigger and the positive smaller, for example): You exaggerate the importance of a problem, making it bigger than it necessarily is. For instance, you tell yourself you absolutely cannot handle a given situation when the reality is that it is inconvenient, or that you can, but simply are tired and don't want to. You might say, "I just can't take one more day of this," or "That was a complete waste of my time. My whole day is ruined. The patient kept focusing on what the internet says instead of listening to me, and now I am behind."

Challenge: Challenge this thought by focusing on what you *did* accomplish and consider solutions that can remedy the specific situation. Did you really accomplish nothing?

Using stress-provoking statements: You use words such as "should," "must," "need," or "have to" that add more pressure and provoke a stress reaction. For example, you might be angry at yourself for making a mistake or even for not exercising, berating yourself by saying, "I should have known better."

Challenge: Challenge this statement by using the word "could" or "want." These are words that avoid shaming or blaming yourself and instead create opportunities for growth and learning. Does it feel good to use "should" on yourself?

Personalization: You hold yourself personally and entirely responsible for situations that are not totally under your control, or you blame others without acknowledging the big picture. For example, you blame yourself believing it is entirely your fault that your patient ended up in the hospital.

Challenge: Challenge this thought by pausing to ask yourself what other factors are likely involved. Would you accuse your colleagues of the same?

Catastrophizing: As with maximizing, you focus on the worst-case scenario and view the situation as a catastrophe. For instance, you may have forgotten to explain all the side effects of a particular medication to a patient, and now you believe you are going to be sued.

Challenge: Challenge this thought and instead be accountable for the error and seek solutions to remedy the problem. Can you take stock of what you need?

These are just some examples of ways your thinking may be adding to your distress. Later chapters in this book (especially Chapters 9 and 10) explain where these types of distorted beliefs and thoughts originate from and provide you tools and ways to improve your mindset and intention.

TIP

For now, try to pay attention to your words or wording, your thoughts, your perceptions, and see how they may be adding more stress to your already stressful life.

Knowing you are worthy of receiving care too

I know from personal experience that when I am feeling negative, be it resentful, anxious, depressed, or sad, my vision narrows as I focus on the negative feeling or the situation that has led to me feeling that way. I focus on what I don't like, don't want, or how the situation is making me feel bad, and of course, distorted thoughts or statements may fill my head and even slip out of my mouth. As justified as I may be for feeling the way I do, focusing on the negative only gets me more negativity making me feel emotionally exhausted and unable to move forward to envision and create new opportunities for myself. Before I left my job as a primary care doctor, I was only able to start shifting into realizing a new reality when I calmed my emotions, put myself in a more relaxed state of mind, filled myself up with hope and love, and then imagined how I wanted to feel.

You have the ability to do the same. You don't have to change anything right now. You just may want to start forming a vision for yourself that includes you being supported and cared for. What might that feel like or look like?

Indeed, the first step is to know that you are worthy of receiving love, support, and care, from the environment and other people, and from yourself. What might that look like? Yes, the system needs healing, and right now, so do you. So begin to create a vision that involves receiving the love and care you deserve and so greatly need right now. This will then pave the way for you to get the help you need and to take the next action steps that will support you to move through and out of burnout.

TIP

You may want to take a moment and flip back to Chapter 5 and follow the exercise on identifying your wants, or you may simply sit back right now and close your eyes. Appreciate that you are indeed a healer and caregiver and that this is a beautiful thing. Allow yourself to imagine that you are being supported both at work and at home to do what you love. What does that feel like?

Being Willing to Accept Help

Given that most of the ecosystems that many of you work in are flawed and broken, you may be asking, "Is it even possible to find my way out of burnout?" It is possible. How you go about it will vary from the next person, and of course, just because you decide to meditate, do yoga, or eat healthier does not mean that all the problems you face will go away. Even self-care has its limits when you are in battle or continuously overloaded. Having said that, when you take the steps to care for yourself and allow others to also care for you, you may notice that you start feeling better and have a larger bandwidth to handle the challenges that you face.

There are strategies that you can incorporate both in your personal life and work environment that may alleviate some of your burnout symptoms and help you get back to doing the work you love. Are you ready and willing to accept help from others to do so?

Seeking good care for your mental health

Most people forget that suffering from mental health issues is a widespread issue for many individuals, including healthcare professionals, and a stigma still exists around it. This means many of you suffer in silence as you worry about your image or your patients or clients losing trust in you. Please remember that we are of little use to others, make more mistakes, and have a higher chance of burnout when we don't take care of our mental health. I say "we" because I was guilty of keeping silent. I used to plaster a smile on my face while falling apart on the inside. I was embarrassed that I was the person who was supposed to be helping other people, yet I was depressed. Although I wasn't suicidal, I was having feelings of not wanting to exist at times, of feeling helpless and hopeless.

Have compassion for yourself and seek help. Take advantage of any counseling or therapeutic programs offered within or outside of the institution where you work. You can speak with the human resources department to find employee assistance programs or individual or group therapy options. Because speaking to someone or groups within your institution may be anxiety provoking, there are options for support through a variety of medical societies or associations as well.

Know that actions are being taken to support you and reverse the mental health stigma, including that which is placed on healthcare professionals. For instance, the National Academy for Medicine (NAM) released a report on taking action against burnout and made recommendations for action steps that protect clinicians' health data; support them when they are seeking help; increase access to employee assistance programs, peer support programs, and mental health providers without the information being admissible for malpractice litigation; and create policies to prevent discouraging access to professional or personal support programs.

TIP

Consider researching what sort of mental health support your organization offers that you might be willing to access. Who would you be willing to talk to?

No matter your position or job, you will benefit from seeking advice and support. Whether it's from a therapist or counselor or someone more experienced who can mentor you, it's important that you have someone who can listen to you compassionately, help you explore your feelings, and support you to find solutions.

Fostering a team of support

The ability to manage adversity is a lot easier when you have the confidence that you are supported by someone. Better yet is having several people with a slew of resources that you can count on to help you. So too, being overwhelmed, exhausted, and unhappy is that much worse when you feel that you are on the journey alone.

You are not alone.

Whether or not you opt to go to counseling or join a support group, you do have the ability to foster meaningful relationships that serve to support you through this trial. You can also put some focus on strengthening your connections with your family, friends, or significant others, as well as your colleagues. When it comes to the latter, you can try to meet together regularly, debriefing on what is working and what isn't, coming up with shared goals, and making commitments to find solutions together. You may find this shared connection helps you feel more engaged, improves your workflow, and helps you remember why you love what you do.

In a 2006 study, researchers Robert Huckman and Gary Pisano from Harvard Business School analyzed more than 38,000 cardiac procedures and measured the success rates, reflected in patient survival rates, of more than 200 cardiac surgeons working in 43 different hospitals, comparing highly experienced freelancers to those surgeons who were part of surgical teams. They found that practice and experience improved performance of heart surgeons only at the hospitals where they did most of their procedures, and it decreased when they left to work at other locations. Their study led them to conclude that heart surgeons were able to shine because of the support they received from a bonded team of colleagues.

Stay tuned and read on, as in the coming chapters (especially Chapter 12), you find out more about strengthening your social connections and fostering a team of support for yourself.

Shifting your approach to work by helping yourself

When caring is your job and you find that you are starting not to care, you either need to leave your job or shift your approach to work and make your own care and needs priorities, *so that* you can do your work. I emphasize the words "so that" because shifting your approach is not about being selfish, but rather filling up your fuel tank so that you can continue serving others. It means checking in with yourself and noticing how you feel and what your needs may be, and filling yourself up, be it with experiences of joy, better self-care, or finding purpose and meaning. Shifting your approach thus involves shifting your mindset so that you feel less victimized by your circumstance and find ways to get built up rather than be destroyed. Here are just three ways in which shifting your approach to work can show up in your everyday life:

>> **Setting boundaries:** I know it's challenging to go home and not worry about your patients, clients, or students, but take a look at your schedule and delineate what happens at work and what can happen at home. Set up sacred time and space for you to have a personal life, sleep, be with family and friends, and do the activities you love.

>> **Looking for meaning and fulfillment:** How do you find meaning and fulfillment at work when everything seems to be going wrong? Search for the blessings in disguise and also look into programs you can be a part of or research you may be interested in doing. Think about ways work could be more fulfilling to you that are within your control. In this light, you may realize that you may need to change your schedule to be able to achieve the meaning and fulfillment you desire.

>> **Taking a break:** Perhaps you are better suited to working part-time if that is possible, or maybe you can switch to doing more research, or take more vacation time. Do you have to work in the same fashion you have up to this point? What can change? Sometimes you need a life overhaul to be able to shift your approach, and sometimes you just need a little break. I find that taking breaks to do a meditation or mindfulness practice where you regularly clear the mind and relax the body is extremely powerful in reducing stress reactivity, improving energy, and opening the mind to new ideas. I therefore encourage you to carve out breaks in your day where you can walk, meditate, play sudoku, and simply do something other than work. Take five minutes if that is all you have and breathe. Just this little break will help you shift your approach to your work and your day.

TIP

Consider setting your watch to send you an alert every hour to take a "breath break". When that alert goes off, start counting as you breathe in, 1-2-3, and then breathe out, 1-2-3-4-5-6.

Follow this breathing rhythm for ten cycles of breath or for one minute. Every hour do at least ten cycles of breath up to one minute. This will keep your stress levels down, stimulate the parasympathetic nervous system, and help you stay calm and focused.

Continuing to grow personally and professionally

Another way to change your approach to work and get help is to continuously seek opportunities for learning and growth, and ways to expand your knowledge and breadth of experience. Not only will such endeavors help you grow personally and professionally, but they will also help you find more meaning and fulfillment.

You may feel so overwhelmed at this point that you don't think you have it in you to learn anything new. You are reading this book, are you not? You already are showing evidence of wanting to learn and grow. Interestingly, staff development programs have been found to help reduce burnout while also imparting and improving staff skills. Gaining new skills and learning can improve your sense of accomplishment and serve as a way to energize you. Are there programs at work you might want to become part of? Is there a skill you have always wanted to improve or acquire?

Whatever you choose to learn or grow in doesn't need to be work-related. The key for you right now is to stay curious and ask yourself, "What is it that I want to learn? In what ways is this situation helping me grow?" Indeed, a 2010 study by Kashdan, Rose, and Fincham shows that curiosity, whether in the young or old, is associated with less anxiety, higher life satisfaction, positive emotions, and psychological well-being ("Curiosity and Exploration: Facilitating Positive Subjective Experiences and Personal Growth").

Nurturing a spiritual practice

Changing your approach to work is interconnected with your ability to enhance your sense of meaning, purpose, connection, and accomplishment, enabling you to feel cared for and refueled so that you can care for others. It is for this reason that nurturing your own spiritual practice can also help you. A growing body of evidence is showing that spirituality is vital to human health. It has been found that a spiritual outlook makes humans more resilient and that people who have a stronger sense of purpose and meaning in their life are more likely to have a higher quality of life, better health and functioning, and greater ability to cope with adversity. Indeed, studies show that a stronger sense of spirituality improves

» **Coping skills:** A recent analysis of over 454 studies found a strong correlation between coping with adversity and greater spirituality in people dealing with a variety of stressful situations, including medical illness. ("Religion, Spirituality, and Health: The Research and Clinical Implications," Harold G. Koenig, 2012)

» **Social support:** The analysis cited in the preceding bullet also found that greater spirituality encourages community and a positive association with social support.

» **Optimism and well-being:** The same author, Harold G. Koenig, found evidence in 256 studies of a positive association between spirituality and happiness and a sense of well-being.

» **Healthy behaviors:** Most religious doctrines encourage taking care of the body and discourage behaviors that may cause harm. A review of the literature shows a positive correlation between spirituality or religiosity with healthier habits, such as a reduced incidence of smoking, and a higher incidence of regular exercise.

» **Mental health:** With greater spirituality comes improved mental health and positive emotions regardless of religion.

» **Resilience:** Research examining the connection between spiritual fitness and resilience in army personnel showed that different forms of spiritual intervention were linked with greater resilience and well-being. ("Spiritual Fitness and Resilience," Yeung and Martin, 2014)

Enhancing or nurturing your spirituality can come in a myriad of forms, including through your religious practice. Perhaps you may choose to frequent your temple or church; spend time in prayer or reflection; seek counseling through a spiritual advisor such as a minister, rabbi, or shaman; or meditate in nature. You can also access spirituality by belonging to a spiritual community, communing with nature, being driven by a sense of purpose or responsibility, or just by breathing and knowing you are connecting with something greater, like the breath of life, or the greater good.

The key is that feeling more connected to something greater helps you better find meaning and fulfillment, and feel less alone and more supported.

Enhancing your coping strategies

Another way to care for yourself better is by improving your coping strategies. Think about what your current "go to" coping strategy is when you are trying to get through a difficult day. Do you drink a gallon of coffee, eat a tub of ice cream, have a glass or two of wine with dinner, or binge watch TV until all hours of the night? All of our behaviors and habits are learned ways of coping with stress. The problem is that feeling better doesn't necessarily translate into managing a given stress or taking good care of ourselves. We might be coping, but it is maladaptive.

Maladaptive coping usually has negative consequences and is often counter-productive, working in the short term but causing trouble in the long run. Examples of negative consequences include substance addiction, impulsive decisions, rumination, and self-harm, to name a few.

Improving coping strategies therefore involves finding healthier ways to manage your stress. It means getting help if you are using substances to self-medicate. It can involve employing stress management techniques like meditation or mindfulness, cognitive behavioral therapy, or other behavioral techniques. Studies show that with the practice of mindfulness, for example, you develop improved mental habits that promote resilience, productivity, and fulfillment, both at work and in life (which is one reason you find a lot about mindfulness in this book!).

TIP

There are countless resources on meditation, mindfulness, stress management, resilience, and so forth, including several *For Dummies* titles. Join a group, take on online course, work with a professional, and keep reading, as strategies are continually presented in this book. In the meantime, take note of your tendencies for coping. Does the behavior serve you to thrive or dive?

Focusing on self-care so that you can care

No one can take better care of you than you. Again, self-care alone won't solve the problems you are facing. It will, however, help you put gas in your gas tank so that you can endure the drive required to do the work you do. Self-care involves practices that support you personally and professionally, such as seeking professional counseling, developing a spiritual practice, creating a schedule that serves you to thrive, meditating, or finding ways to continually grow and learn. Other examples of self-care include the following:

>> Get better sleep.

>> Incorporate movement and exercise.

- » Spend time with people you love.

- » Explore learning something new.

- » Create healthy boundaries and set limits.

- » Seek meaning and fulfillment daily.

- » Learn ways to manage stress more effectively.

- » Begin a meditation or mindfulness practice.

- » Connect with your spirituality.

- » Seek help.

- » Find mentors and create your team.

- » Challenge your thought distortions.

- » Have a good laugh.

The list is plentiful, which means you have options. I explore self-care more in Chapter 9, but for now, understand that it is important for you to allow time for what matters, and what matters is you. If you don't take care of you, who will?

REMEMBER

Most importantly, treat yourself with the same compassion you might offer a patient, a loved family member, or a friend. Ask yourself, "What will support me to be at my best?"

3

Building Essential Resources for Navigating Burnout

Cultivate self-awareness through the practice of mindfulness.

Discover why being kind to yourself sets the stage to heal burnout.

Find courage and safety within yourself to effect the change you need.

Embrace your life force and take good care to enhance your vitality.

Chapter 8

Building a Foundation of Awareness with Mindfulness

Cultivating self-awareness, or making discoveries about yourself, your beliefs, your motivations, and how your body functions and signals you, empowers you to be able to maneuver through life more effectively and heal from burnout. You can better monitor your inside and outside world, observe experiences as they transpire, and respond to them, rather than react. Heightened self-awareness helps you engage your higher brain centers and perform complex cognitive processing and emotional reasoning, even during times of duress. It enables you to self-evaluate, be thoughtful in your communication, and find objective solutions to emotionally charged problems.

The practice of mindfulness, a meditation practice that involves focusing your awareness on thoughts, feelings, and observations of your inside and outside world as it unfolds in the present moment, offers you a pathway to cultivating self-awareness. With mindfulness, you awaken your senses to notice and witness how and what you feel with open interest, without trying to interpret anything, judge it, or analyze it. It helps reduce rumination, improve emotional regulation, enhance concentration and memory, and lower symptoms of stress. Indeed, mindfulness has been shown to improve self-control, objectivity, flexibility, concentration, mental clarity, and emotional intelligence. It affects tolerance, self-compassion and self-acceptance, and one's ability to relate to others (Hayes and Davis, 2011). This chapter shows you how to enhance your self-awareness through building a foundation of mindfulness.

Awakening Your Senses to the Reality of Burnout

Your senses inform your behaviors, motivations, and mindset. They enable you to process information, learn, be creative, and assimilate memories. Your senses — what you see, hear, smell, taste, and feel — also influence your perception. When you pay attention to your senses, you are better able to be in the present moment and make informed decisions. If you're like most people in modern-day society, however, you don't spend much time engaging with your senses. You are too busy, stressed, burdened, or numb. You may inhale your food, speed walk to your destination, think or talk more than listen, and spend a great deal of mental effort judging, analyzing, or blaming yourself or someone else for the way you feel. Your mind may be active, reviewing your to-do lists or ruminating over situations that have happened or might happen, giving little attention to subtle and not-so-subtle nuances that may be occurring around you, like the flowers in bloom or the flavors in your breakfast, which is especially detrimental when you are feeling stressed and overwhelmed.

Imagine being fully present, aware, and engaged in the moment-to-moment experience, witnessing each experience along with your own reactions, even when you are feeling stressed, as everything unfolds. You aren't thinking about yesterday or tomorrow, but rather engaging your senses and observing your inner and outer world from one moment to the next. You step back and take stock of your reality while experiencing emotional balance. This means you can view the entire big picture that brought you to burnout, without casting blame or shame, or getting caught up in your emotions or thoughts. Instead, you are able to think clearly, have patience, and make the sound decisions required to chart a path forward.

All roads begin at awareness

The mind is a superb instrument if used rightly. Used wrongly, however, it becomes very destructive. To put it more accurately, it is not so much that you use your mind wrongly — you usually don't use it at all. It uses you. — Eckhardt Tolle, *The Power of Now*

When you use the mind, instead of letting the mind use you, you let go of thoughts, assumptions, or preconceived ideas regarding how something should be. You become aware of what you feel, hear, touch, taste, and smell. You allow yourself to be curious about other people, situations, and yourself. You ask questions, listen, and gather information that helps you communicate, respond, have insight, regulate your emotions, strengthen your relationships, and make sound decisions.

Brenda walked into work and discovered that yet another colleague had quit. She now had to cover and had triple the amount of work on her plate. She was already feeling burned out, and this situation now left her feeling angrier, more exhausted, and overwhelmed. Rather than canceling her session with me that day, she decided to take a break and see if I could help. I guided her through a mindfulness breath exercise, which helped lower the emotional charge she was experiencing and find more equanimity within herself. Feeling calmer, she was better able to take stock of the situation, figuring out who she could delegate responsibilities to and how she could carve out time to take care of herself and still experience joy, even if briefly at first. She was then given instructions to continue her mindfulness practices and to keep examining her personal and professional life to uncover ways she could build support for herself, internally and externally.

Brenda gathered information, discovering which tasks, actions, or personal behaviors were adding to her burnout. She began carving out small pauses throughout her day to savor moments of appreciation and as a result, experienced more joy and respite, as well as more reward in her relationships. Brenda also started discovering aspects of her job that she loved and those that she did not, and which tasks she could delegate to others. Believe it or not, Brenda noticed a marked difference in her energy level and attitude within two weeks of upping the ante of her mindfulness practice. It didn't solve everything, but the path to healing burnout did become clearer.

REMEMBER

The same can be true for you. Your path to healing burnout can begin with becoming more self-aware — of how you feel, your thoughts, your behaviors, and your situation — providing you with a myriad of benefits, including more energy, patience, access to positive emotions, and the ability to better gauge which situations, beliefs, and feelings can support you to thrive, and which ones may leave you drained.

Knowing where you are before you chart a course

It's common to identify with feeling angry, frustrated, overwhelmed, or anxious as you think about how exhausted you might be, an event that just transpired or anticipate another hard day tomorrow. The problem is that when you do so for too long, your emotions and thoughts end up controlling you instead of the other way around, keeping you from gaining a full perspective of the situation and yourself. Without this information, it's difficult to effect the change within yourself that will serve as the foundation to build your better future.

The key is to put both feet in the present moment, instead of one foot in yesterday and the other in tomorrow. By learning to focus your mind on the present moment, you discover how to have a healthier relationship with your emotions and your thoughts. You understand how to observe your internal and external world, without identifying with anything in particular, enabling you to gather information about yourself and your current experience, including your tendencies, needs, and goals.

Wherever you are right now is . . . well, where you are right now. You are not going to solve your problems all in one go, and worrying about what will happen next won't help. The key is to be patient with yourself, let go of how you think your life should be, and take stock of where you are right now.

Being patient and persistent

For the most part, our behaviors and reactions are instigated by our desire to achieve relief or immediate gratification. But as you well know, there is no quick relief remedy for burnout, and the thought in itself can be daunting or depressing, which is of no help to you. You may feel as if your patience has already run out. Practicing mindfulness or being aware of the present moment can help you build up this patience. It also helps you gain clarity because you don't focus on a given arbitrary destination, but rather on the very real present moment.

What if I invite you not to think about getting out of burnout and to simply focus on the fact that you are experiencing feelings? Notice *that* you are feeling tension, or heaviness. Notice *that* you are breathing and the rhythm of your breath. Notice *that* you are thinking. Notice it all with openness and curiosity.

By becoming an observer of yourself and the world around you, you disengage the power your thoughts and emotions can have on your energy and your need to *do*, and instead create space for yourself to simply *be*. The more you can be in the state of *being* instead of *doing*, the more patient you will find yourself, able to observe life as it unfolds with openness and interest, while also conserving some energy.

Practicing mindfulness is both simple and challenging, as the practice itself is rather simple, yet the ability to do it is challenging when you get caught up in daily challenges, worries, pain, wandering thoughts, or feelings of discomfort. The very practice of mindfulness means that you are agreeing to sit with your discomfort and choosing not to do anything about it. You are, rather, allowing yourself to just *be*. That's the crux of what makes this practice simple and challenging: You are *not* doing anything. The practice helps you cultivate patience, and at the same time, it also asks you to have patience to do the practice. My recommendation is to be persistent and to practice *not* doing as often as possible. Can you practice *not* doing?

TIP

You can practice mindfulness, being patient, and *not* doing by listening to a sustained tone, using a guitar string, or a glass or metal bowl or cup. Create the sound and then focus on the tone until the sound stops. The louder the sound at the onset, the longer the tone will sustain itself. Repeat this several times, each time listening to the tone and sound until it is no longer there. Then notice how you feel.

Accepting what you can and can't change

Being comfortable being uncomfortable, accepting your circumstance, not doing, and letting go of "knowing" the future can be big asks, especially when you're faced with uncertainty and hardship, and you consider yourself a doer. Finding your way to embracing uncertainty and ambiguity, will, however, help you find your way to becoming more patient, resilient, flexible psychologically, creative, and adaptive to make change, and ultimately pave the path to healing from burnout.

Accepting pain, uncertainty, and hardship doesn't mean you have to like it. It just means that you accept that it is part of life, and you will do what you can when you can to effect change when possible. It means you can be open to a variety of thoughts and feelings without the need to avoid or self-soothe in destructive ways.

The good news is that you can improve your psychological flexibility by practicing mindfulness and working toward being open and accepting of your feelings of uncertainty, of what you can control and what you can't, like the Serenity Prayer guides us to do:

> ". . . grant me the serenity to accept the things I cannot change, the courage to change the things I can, and the wisdom to know the difference."

Minding Your Physical, Mental, and Emotional Self

Much of life is going to be uncertain. It's just the way it is. It will throw you curveballs and be unpredictable. You may not be able to understand why something has happened, what someone else is thinking, or what the future holds. You can know, however, how you feel in any given moment. The fact that your body signals you through physical sensations, thoughts, and emotions is a constant. The fact that your physical experiences affect your mind and that your thoughts influence your physical experiences is also a constant. The more frequently you listen and attune to this mind-body connection, the better able you are to read your body's signals, manage your emotions, and understand the hidden messages behind your feelings and emotions. You become better equipped to take better care of yourself and your needs.

As such, your first step when practicing mindfulness is to scan your body.

Your body: Your constant companion

You are a sentient human "being," meaning you exist through the experience of feeling. You are not a human "doing" or human "thinking." You act in response to how you feel. When your body does talk to you through your senses and you take a moment to listen, you can learn a great deal about yourself and your needs. Paying attention and attuning to your body can also save you from reacting automatically, making a poor decision, or heightening your level of stress and anxiety.

Practice: Scanning the body

You can begin to understand the language of your body by doing a foundational mindfulness practice that involves scanning your body and tuning in to your body's sensations and feelings. The intention of the body scan is to shift your mind away from thinking and toward the sensory experience of being present in the here and now. The beauty of the body scan is that you get to lie down, observe your experience, and otherwise *do nothing*.

There are a variety of ways to do a body scan, and there is no best or better way. It can take you one minute or thirty minutes. The practice you do is the one you benefit from. During the process, you may discover that your mind wanders. You may feel discomfort or irritation, a sense of peace, or even anxiety. You may notice tension, perhaps pain, or even areas of ease. The key is to simply notice *that* you are having the experience that you are having. There is no right or wrong, good or bad.

Here's how you perform a body scan:

1. **Find a comfortable position, preferably in a quiet place, and close your eyes.**

2. **Take a moment to bring your awareness to your body, as it is right now.**

   Notice any sensation you may be experiencing: where you may be holding tension or ease, whether you're feeling warmth or coldness, and how your body feels resting on the chair or lying on the floor. Notice if the sensations vary or change without judging anything.

3. **Let go of preconceived ideas of how you think this experience should be.**

   Allow yourself to be curious, directing your senses to awaken to how your body feels and what you feel. If you find your mind wandering and thoughts start creeping in, that's normal. You can say to yourself, "thinking, thinking, thinking" and bring your focus back to scanning your body.

4. **Bring your awareness to your breath.**

   Notice the rhythm of your breath. Notice how and what you feel.

5. **As you exhale, gently shift your focus down to your right big toe and notice any sensations.**

6. **Then notice the sensation in all the toes on your right foot, one by one.**

7. **Gently shift your awareness to the left big toe.**

   Notice any difference or notice nothing at all. Then move your focus to the other toes in your left foot. You are simply observing what you do or don't feel.

8. **When ready, gently shift your focus upward, through one leg and all the way up to your hip.**

   Notice what you feel, and allow yourself to be curious, observing nuances and changes as they occur.

9. **Continue to observe the rest of your body, one part at a time, until you get to the top of your head.**

10. **When you have scanned your whole body, stretch if you feel the need to.**

    Appreciate each body part you are stretching and notice the sensations that arise. Take your time.

11. **When you are ready, open your eyes and gently stand up.**

12. **Notice how you feel.**

Practice: Focusing on the breath

Mindfully focusing on the breath, especially the rhythm of the breath, can be quite relaxing. You can also learn quite a bit from the breath. It continues to do what it does without you having to think about it. It comes and it goes. You can't hold on to your breath even if you try. Every time you let go, another breath comes right back in, without any effort on your part. Your breath doesn't try to change itself or be something different. It isn't going anywhere in particular. It's just doing what it does. Though the breath doesn't take credit for anything itself, you can give it credit for being a constant for you and a wonderful teacher and guide on how to let in and let go, not try to go anywhere or do anything in particular, and to simply *be*.

Here are the steps for the Awareness of Breath meditation:

1. **Find a comfortable position, preferably in a quiet place, and close your eyes.**

2. **Take a moment to bring your awareness to your body, as it is right now.**

   Notice any sensation you may be experiencing: where you may be holding tension or ease, feeling warmth or coldness, or how your body feels resting on the chair or lying on the floor. Notice if the sensations vary or change without judging anything.

3. **Begin by inhaling and exhaling as deeply as you can for two or three breaths.**

4. **Notice the breath as it enters your nostrils.**

   Notice the feelings or sensations. Do you notice a particular temperature?

5. **Notice the breath as it enters into your lungs and causes the lungs to expand along with your abdomen.**

6. **Notice how the lungs and abdomen contract and fall as the air leaves and moves back out through your mouth as you exhale.**

7. **Observe your experience of breathing.**

   Notice the temperature of your breath as it moves in and out, the rising and falling of your chest, the expansion and contraction of your belly, the way your lungs fill and let go. Invite your full attention to the cycle of the breath.

   You are not aiming to change anything about the breath. You are observing without judgment. You aren't trying to control anything, including your breath.

8. **If thoughts arise, simply witness them arising and imagine them floating away with your breath. Then bring your focus back to observing the breath.**

9. **If thoughts, emotions, or unpleasant sensations arise, witness those as well.**

   Observe that you are having them, and then bring your focus back to observing the flow of your breath.

10. **When you are ready to bring your practice to an end, gently expand your focus to include your entire body.**

    Notice how you feel, how your body feels sitting or lying down wherever you are, and any other sensations you may be experiencing.

11. **Notice the room you are in, the sounds, and the temperature as you open your eyes and see what's around you.**

    Welcome back.

Minding the chatter of the mind

I believe the average person generates 70,000 thoughts a day. Seventy thousand thoughts stream through your mind every day, creating a lot of stories! It's important to remember that the stories are, well, stories, and your thoughts are just thoughts. They are not reflections of what is happening in the moment, right now, and they don't define who you are. You are not your thoughts, and your thoughts are not you. Rather, you have thoughts, and you create stories with them in order to better understand and make sense of your world.

When you practice mindfulness, you can better disentangle yourself from thoughts and stories. You approach the process with kindness, accepting what is transpiring and witnessing it with interest. It's as if you are standing back and watching the flow of a river with quiet curiosity and, if desired, gently guiding the river in a new direction.

In 1984, psychologists Lazarus and Folkman coined the Theory of Cognitive Appraisal, which describes the different ways individuals perceive and appraise threats. Primary appraisal involves how you initially perceive a given stressful situation, whether you appraise it as a threat or as an opportunity. With secondary appraisal, you gauge your ability or capacity to cope with the situation or take advantage of it, as you appraise the benefits of either acting on or avoiding the given threat. People who can positively appraise situations, viewing threats as opportunities, tend to adapt more successfully to adversity and be more resilient.

Practicing mindfulness can help you reappraise situations, or in other words, shift how you appraise life events to being more positive and adaptive. This is partially due to the role mindfulness plays in fostering more objectivity so that you can be more neutral when assessing a situation. It lets you step back and consciously reinterpret and reappraise a situation in a way that supports you to find meaning, change perspective, and reduce the emotional impact, even though the situation has not objectively changed.

Being aware of your emotions

Emotions are part of your human makeup. They serve a purpose. Like the sensory fibers in your hand that tell you that the stove is hot, your emotions act as sensory signals, letting you know when you are safe and when you are being threatened. They serve the purpose of motivating you into action to warn others to back off or urge them to come close. They inform your mind, letting it know whether it's okay to stop and smell the roses and see the big picture of life, or whether you need to focus and get the heck out.

As sensory messages, your emotions occur as automatic responses to stimuli, like the tingling in your left butt cheek that urges you to shift positions. You can't control *that* you are sensing tingling or numbness or *that* you are experiencing sadness or joy. You feel what you feel. You can, however, control how you react or respond. You can choose to get upset because your butt cheek is numb, or you can appreciate your body for letting you know it's time to move. The same is true with your emotions. You can choose to be upset that you are feeling troubled, or you can appreciate that your body is letting you know that you are feeling threatened and in need of care and compassion.

REMEMBER

You are *not* your emotions, just like you are *not* your thoughts. You have them. And when you practice moment-to-moment awareness of what is, you can find your way to witnessing your emotions as they transpire and get back in charge of them.

Reacting versus Responding: Mindfulness in Action

Emotions and thoughts are not meant to control you and your life, but rather to guide you in life. When your emotions and thoughts control you, the tendency is to be more reactive in stressful situations, which often makes the situation worse, and at least makes you feel worse. When you are in control of your emotions and thoughts, you are better able to respond to stressful stimuli rather than react.

For instance, say you really want to go for a long walk. You have been looking forward to it all week. But on the very day you want to walk, it's raining. You have a choice now:

> Do you get upset and mope around indoors all day, feeling miserable, eating yourself to a tizzy, feeling guilty about it, and then going to bed pissed that the day didn't go your way?
>
> Or . . .
>
> Do you acknowledge that it is raining and that it isn't your preferred weather? You honor the way you feel, mindfully appraise the situation, and decide that you still want to walk, put on your raincoat, and go for it.

Your decision or response changes the trajectory for the course of your day. The key is to first acknowledge that your emotions are signals, letting you know that you are feeling threatened, in need, running on empty, or feeling somehow inadequate. You have the choice then to let your emotions drive you to react or mindfully appraise how you feel, regulate your emotions, and respond calmly.

Mindfulness in action practice

PLAY THIS

The following exercise guides you to observe your body, emotions, and thoughts; label your experience; and use your breath to achieve a better sense of calm. The goal is to help you reappraise a given situation.

1. Set the stage.

Perhaps you can think about a situation that upsets you or causes you to feel anxiety, anger, or any other negative emotion. Let your mind go to the story.

Now take notice of how you feel. Notice the physical sensations that arise in your body, where the story goes in your mind, and how your body reacts to the story your mind is telling.

You may want to label your experience by saying, "Noticing the sensation of a pit in my stomach," or "Observing tension in my chest with this thought," or "Noting the experience of anxiousness and neck stiffness."

Notice with open curiosity.

2. Shift to the breath.

Redirect your attention and focus on the ins and outs of the breath for a few minutes and follow the breath as you inhale and then exhale. In and out, back and forth, as if you are watching the waves of the ocean.

Perhaps you can appreciate the breath or how it changes in relationship to your thoughts and emotions. Does it change when you feel angry, sad, nervous, and so forth? Observe changes to your breath as your thoughts or emotions change with interest and curiosity for another minute or two.

3. Reappraise.

Pause now to allow thoughts of the situation to come up in your mind. How do you feel about the situation now? How does your body respond? Take note with open interest.

Is it possible to see the situation differently? Is the situation triggering something in you, like feeling inadequate, undervalued, unsupported or unworthy, and so forth? Observe and take note of any thoughts or ideas that arise, without judgment and with compassion and kindness.

4. Breathe in kindness.

When you are ready, bring your focus back to the breath and imagine you are breathing in compassion and kindness, letting it flow into your lungs and the rest of your body with every cycle of breath.

Take note of how you feel, any sensations that arise, as you let thoughts and feelings come and go with your breath.

5. **Settle back out.**

Take a deep cleansing breath and then let your breath assume a natural rhythm, gently bringing yourself back and opening your eyes.

Reflect on how you may respond now.

Remembering to pause

To get better at responding instead of reacting, it may help if you remember to take a mindful pause for reflection before acting. When you pause, you aren't ignoring your emotions, feelings, or reactions, but instead you're identifying each part of your experience, distancing yourself from the experience as you watch the thoughts transpire in your mind or the emotions or sensations occur in your body.

You essentially insert a space in time where you can observe or be the observer of your experiences. It is the space in between your reaction and your next response, where you allow some time for your reaction to fade, the stress response to calm down, and your nervous system to rebalance. This then gives you better access to your more rational mind and positive emotions, and gives you the ability to make measured decisions.

Letting thoughts be mental objects that come and go

According to the Buddha, there exist four parts of life where mindful awareness can be employed — the body, feelings, the mind, and mental objects — and these parts make up the Four Foundations of Mindfulness.

>> **Body:** Mindfulness of the body involves bringing your awareness to the sensations you experience in your body, which you have hopefully experienced through the body scan and the breath focus.

>> **Feelings:** Mindfulness of feeling involves witnessing the effect a given sensation or thought creates (pleasure or displeasure).

>> **Mind:** Mindfulness of mind involves dispassionately observing yourself and labeling the experience. You notice if you are attached or unattached, focused or distracted, calm or agitated, wanting or not wanting, and so forth. It's not a process of analysis, but rather labeling, noting "there is wanting," or "noticing agitation," or "observing confusion."

>> **Mental Objects:** Mindfulness of mental objects or phenomena involves observing the comings and goings of circumstances or occurrences

happening around you (rather than within you). For instance, you observe the waves of the ocean rolling in and rolling out. You notice a wave that starts large and eventually becomes a tiny ripple on the sand. Everything you observe is a mental object that comes and goes.

TIP

You can apply these four foundations to your thoughts and everything else in your life, seeing it all as coming and going. Nothing is permanent, and everything is open to be observed.

Accepting obstacles that appear along the way

You may find yourself getting distracted or having doubts while trying to focus on your breath or a bodily sensation. Know that it is totally normal and not uncommon at all to feel that you are incurring a variety of obstacles when practicing mindfulness — or any meditation for that matter. The key is to accept what is happening and be open to observing and learning.

The following are common obstacles and what you can do should you encounter them along the way.

Feeling sleepy

As stress reactivity falls, so do your adrenalin levels, which means that you may notice as you take a mindful pause that you are, in reality, feeling sleepy. Sleepiness may also be a reaction to stress (fight, fly, or freeze/sleep). Often, a client will complain to me they can't meditate because they keep falling asleep, and I tell them how wonderful the body is in telling them that they are sleep deprived. Rather than letting sleepiness deter you, instead observe the feeling and delineate whether your sleepiness is from sleep deprivation or a result of feeling overwhelmed. Honor the experience.

Having doubting thoughts

It is also normal to doubt that taking a pause and being mindful actually works, especially when you are so used to thinking your way out of problems. You may doubt that your mind will ever quiet down and question your ability to "do it right." Feelings of self-doubt, insecurity, or unworthiness are common obstacles that many people incur during their practice. Observe the doubting thoughts, remembering that they are mental objects. Appreciate that these objects beckon you to ask questions and be curious, and observe them with open interest.

Getting irritated

I know when I first started my practice, I would become irritated at people making noise in the background or any noise for that matter, like the humming of the refrigerator, dogs barking, or passing trucks. I would also become irritated with myself for being irritated and not doing what I was "supposed" to be doing. Again, normal. Notice that you are feeling irritated. You might say, "observing irritation," or "noticing humming." Then, move on to the next mental object, thought, or sensation to notice. You may also investigate why you are irritated.

Feeling restless

Most people find it challenging to sit or be still, as our tendency is to *do*, not to *be*. Like other feelings, restlessness or even boredom happens. Observe the sensation for what it is, without judging it or yourself, and if you like, you can further investigate why you are feeling restless. Perhaps underneath it lies fear of failure or anxiety.

Having the pull to do something else

Just as my mind felt still, thoughts of food or something I wanted to buy or look up on the internet would pop up when I first started to meditate. "Why just now?" I would ask myself. But no matter how much I berated myself and brought myself back to my breath focus, that craving or want would creep back into my thoughts, which brought on my restlessness, irritation, and self-doubt. The key here is not to judge yourself. Accept the thoughts, feelings, or sensations. Perhaps label the fact that you are thinking by saying, "Thinking, thinking, thinking," and then gently bring your attention back.

REMEMBER

Whatever the obstacle, be kind and gentle with yourself. Notice and witness everything with open interest. There is no perfect practice. There is only the practice that you do.

Building Your Mindfulness Platform

Jon Kabat-Zinn, a leader in the field of researching mindfulness and the founder of the Mindfulness Based Stress Reduction program (MBSR), says that mindfulness ". . . is not a technique. It's a way of being in wise relationship to experience as you find it, and that means pleasant, unpleasant, and even the neutral stuff that you never bother to notice because it doesn't seem to have a big effect on you." He explains that the practice influences people to take responsibility for their own well-being and develop a new relationship with themselves, their discomfort, pain, or stress, that is kinder, more loving, and compassionate.

Having a mindfulness platform can support you in every aspect of your life. It can bring healing and balance to your interactions, perceptions, and relationships. It can help you assess situations more effectively, make wiser decisions, and be better able to access healthier behaviors. If being still, self-compassionate, self-forgiving, and patient are not your strong suits, it's okay. As you practice mindfulness, you may find those qualities improve. Accept what is and where you are right now. Be open to your experiences, whatever they may be, without striving for perfection. Enjoy the journey.

Do or don't do, but there is no "try"

If you remember the character Yoda from *Star Wars*, you may remember him saying, "Do or not do. There is no try." Essentially, this quote offers the lesson that if you are not doing some, you aren't doing it. You can't try to do it. You either are or you are not. You can either feel hungry or not feel hungry. Trying to feel hungry is just that, trying, but not actually being in the state of hunger. You are in the state of trying.

Decide to commit yourself to the process of being in the present. There is no point in getting upset with yourself. You are either in the now or you are not. If you are not, notice it and accept it as what you are experiencing right now. Do your practice or don't do your practice. Be present or don't be present.

Trying implies effort. Let go of effort. Observe, witness, and accept all that is happening. When you accept, you bring yourself into the present moment. Do or don't do. Be nice or don't be nice. Be angry or don't be angry. Be mindful or don't be mindful. There is no trying. Get the point?

Adapting seven essential attitudes

As you build your mindfulness platform, it may be helpful to uphold the seven key attitudes Kabat-Zinn noted in his book, *Full Catastrophe Living* (Delacorte Press), that support bringing mindfulness into a way of being. The attitudes are interconnected and support one another, and practicing one attitude helps you practice another. They guide you on how to be, accept and un-try.

» **Non-judging:** Having a nonjudgmental and unbiased attitude as you bear witness to your experiences is an essential attitude when practicing mindfulness. The key is to witness your experiences as they unfold, rather than judging them or yourself, even when it means witnessing your own judging.

» **Patience:** You can't force the seasons to change, nor can you speed up night turning into day. With the attitude of patience, you accept that things unfold in their own time. Your ability to be in the state of patience often requires you to be patient with yourself, loving, compassionate, and kind so as not to rush from one moment to the next.

- » **Beginner's mind:** Like a child seeing something for the first time, you want to stay open, curious, and receptive to what unfolds. You let go of "knowing everything" or being "the expert." You allow in new possibilities, seeing each experience as new. What if you were to imagine that you were seeing your thoughts as if for the first time, every single time, discovering new nuances or details?

- » **Trust:** Trust yourself and your feelings. Trust your body's signals. As you develop your practice and trust yourself and how or what you feel, you will be able to discern the difference between what is transpiring in your mind versus what is happening in reality.

- » **Non-striving:** The non-striving attitude is reflected in "not trying," as discussed previously. Keep in mind that you are not in a race and there is no absolute destination. If you feel that you are striving or trying to change things, notice it with compassion and without judging yourself.

- » **Acceptance:** Acceptance involves accepting everything as it is, with open interest, remembering that everything, including you, is perfectly imperfect. Accepting negative feelings doesn't mean you have to like them or that you are condoning the situation that has brought them about. It does mean that you are willing to accept and see things as they are.

- » **Letting go:** This seventh attitude refers to letting go of whatever you are clinging to, be it a thought, emotion, or feeling. It refers to being unattached to a particular outcome or result and instead accepting what is, letting it be, so that you can let it go and come back to the present moment.

Getting started with two simple practices

A myriad of exercises exist that you can partake in to develop your mindfulness practice, and countless resources are available to you in books, on the internet, on apps (like Insight Timer or Calm) and through courses. For now, here are two simple practices to get started with.

Where are my feet?

This is a wonderful grounding practice that guides you to bring your awareness to your feet. It is very effective in calming the stress response, engaging the parasympathetic nervous system, and affecting a state of calm, especially when you are upset, as you shift the focus away from your mind to the neutral grounding point of your feet. You can do this practice anywhere and anytime, sitting or standing. It is an especially effective meditation to do when your emotions are highly charged. There is no time frame for doing this and, of course, if you are feeling emotionally charged, you will know when it's time to stop because you'll likely be experiencing a greater sense of calm and peace.

Here is how to do it:

1. **Breathe naturally. Do nothing and then bring your awareness to the soles of your feet.**

   Notice how they feel resting flat on the ground. Scan the heel of the foot, then the arch, the ball of the foot, then each toe and then the top of the foot.

2. **Slowly move your toes. Notice the sensations.**

   Notice how the shoes or socks feel covering your feet. Notice the texture or temperature. Perhaps you are barefoot and notice the texture or temperature of the floor or carpet.

3. **Keep your focus on observing your feet as you breathe naturally.**

Here and now stone

I love this practice because it involves having something, in this case a stone, that I can hold onto, which serves as a reminder for me to stay present and grounded. It's called the "here and now stone." The practice invites you to let go of anything else you may be holding onto, be it your thoughts about the past or the future, and instead redirect your focus to being in the present moment. I keep a "here and now stone" on my desk and in my purse, so that I can intermittently, throughout the day, wherever I am, be reminded to pause and get grounded in the here and now.

Here's how to do it:

1. **Find a stone that you are drawn to.**

   It could be in your yard, on a beach, or on a mountain, or you might buy it in a store. I found one of my stones while hiking in Taos, New Mexico, when I stopped mid walk because I felt the urge to simply stand still, close my eyes, and experience my feet connecting to the earth. When I opened my eyes and looked down, right by my feet was a stone that was shaped like a heart.

2. **Really look at it. Notice the details, colors, texture, and subtle nuances of your stone.**

   What does it feel like in your hand? Does its temperature change the longer you hold it? Rub your fingers over the stone. How long has this stone been in existence? Where did it originate? Could it be millions of years old or is it brand new and human made? Still, the person who made the stone needed a stone to create it.

3. **Enjoy the site, touch, feel, and experience of holding the stone with all of your senses.**

IN THIS CHAPTER

» Exploring the practice of
self-compassion

» Approaching the humanness of
burnout with kindness

» Bringing self-compassion into your
life with pocket practices

Chapter **9**

Being Kind . . . to Yourself

A s burnout symptoms persist, it's not uncommon for people to experience more negative emotions, less emotional balance, less self-kindness, more isolation from everyone else, and a higher tendency to judge and berate themselves and others for failures and inadequacies. Burnout is a state of depletion. It's natural for the fight or flight response to be activated in response to keeping you safe. The problem is that this reactive state depletes you further at a time when you need more love and compassion for yourself, not less. To quote the Buddha, *"You yourself, as much as anybody in the entire universe, deserve your love and affection."*

Indeed, evidence suggests that self-compassion is associated with resilience to burnout and that interventions like mindful self-compassion programs can reduce symptoms of burnout. The pioneer researcher in self-compassion, Kristin Neff (along with Christopher Germer), says that self-compassion involves kindness toward oneself, recognizing that suffering is part of a shared human experience, and mindfulness or the practice of nonjudgment toward failures and inadequacies. This chapter guides you on cultivating self-compassion and self-kindness, the foundation for healing from burnout.

Treating Yourself as You Treat a Good Friend

"That was so stupid!"

"I can't believe I did that! What an idiot!"

"I should have known better!"

"I'm such a loser!"

"I am so pathetic!"

The preceding statements may seem innocuous. You may not realize how often you say such things, and perhaps you even think berating yourself motivates you to do better and push harder. But can you imagine speaking this way to a dear friend who is struggling? Would you berate them and put them down? Highly unlikely. Indeed, it is more likely that you would speak to a dear friend with tremendous care and encouragement, understanding, and support. Imagine if you treated yourself with the same kind of care! Treating yourself with self-kindness, as you would care for a loved one, is what Neff says is the first component of self-compassion.

Such a simple concept, and yet, so difficult to do! Why is that? Being self-kind is challenging because most of us tend to give more credence to our harsh inner critic. Your inner critic berates and vilifies you and reminds you of your inadequacies. You may believe that your inner critic motivates you to do better or push harder toward achieving a goal, and to a certain extent, it might.

REMEMBER

Ultimately, however, your inner critic mostly succeeds in lowering your sense of self-value. It pushes your tendencies to partake in self-sabotaging behaviors and self-harm, which often instigates more negative self-talk, perpetuating a negative cycle. Would your best friend speak to you in the same way?

In her research, Neff found that people who are compassionate to themselves are less likely to be stressed, insecure, depressed, and anxious and more likely to be resilient, optimistic, motivated, and happy. The key is to be kind to *you*, and you can start by practicing the Loving Kindness Meditation.

Practice: Loving Kindness Meditation

PLAY THIS

The Loving Kindness Meditation (LKM) is based on Buddhist philosophies and is embedded with love, understanding, kindness, and empathy toward the self and others. The meditation integrates four aspects of love: *Metta* or friendliness, *Karuna* or compassion, *Mudita* or appreciation and joy, and *Upekkha* or equanimity.

There is no ultimate goal or destination when practicing this meditation; you're simply meant to experience and enjoy the process of receiving love and compassion, and then letting it flow out to others.

Practicing this meditation can improve emotional regulation, positive emotions, empathy, stress management, and even immune functions according to mounting research. You can carve out a time to do it daily or take a break sometime in your day. There are a variety of versions, but each one has the same focus: generating kindness toward yourself and others. You can find different versions online or on meditation apps like the Insight Timer or Calm.

1. **Find yourself a comfortable position, close your eyes, and take a few nice, long, deep breaths. Allow your body to gently relax.**

2. **Breathe in deeply and exhale completely a few times and then let your breathing assume a natural rhythm.**

   As you do so, allow yourself to experience gratitude for giving yourself the opportunity to give and receive loving kindness today. Express gratefulness toward yourself for taking the time to do this loving act.

3. **When you are ready, imagine infinite love flowing your way, flowing in with your breath, filling your chest with love and peace, as you inhale. Imagine you are letting go of tension as you exhale.**

   With every inbreath and outbreath, allow yourself to feel grateful for all that you are right this very moment. Breathe in this love and peace, exhale and let go of tension.

4. **When you are ready, say a loving and positive phrase to yourself.**

   You may say one of the following phrases or any phrase of this nature that you like:

   May I be healthy, peaceful, and strong.

   May I be filled with happiness and joy.

   May I have the strength and resilience to overcome any obstacles.

   May I always be surrounded by people that I love.

5. **Soak in the feeling of loving kindness. Let the feelings envelop you in warmth like an embrace.**

   If you find your mind wanders, take notice and gently bring your focus back to the feelings of loving kindness.

6. **Stay in this space as long as you like.**

TIP

If you want to continue this meditation to include others, you can imagine send-ing this loving kindness to anyone you want: to one person, to several people, to the entire human race, or to the entire planet or universe. You can start with a focus on someone you love and feel your love and gratitude for them, envisioning them with perfect strength, resilience, and happiness. You can then branch out to friends and family, co-workers and acquaintances, groups of people, and so forth.

Recognizing common humanity

Feeling isolated and alone in your suffering is normal when you feel burned out, anxious, depressed, or strung out. The truth is that suffering is universal. All humans suffer in one shape or form. We are all imperfect, and being flawed is part of our humanness. Neff says the second component of self-compassion is recog-nizing common humanity — that you are not alone and that others are likely feel-ing the way you feel. By recognizing common humanity, you broaden your perspective to the human condition, which enables you to better overcome your own shortcomings, mistakes, and hardship, and to be better able to accept your limitations with kindness and compassion.

Neff's premise is that the term "compassion" is based on the recognition that we are all fallible and that the human experience is naturally challenging and imper-fect, and that we suffer together. It's because we *know* that feeling inadequate or experiencing disappointment is universal that we adopt the phrase, "It is only human," when someone makes a mistake. We all do it. Neff also explains that self-compassion differs from self-pity because the latter involves feeling sorry for oneself and feeling separate from others, whereas self-compassion involves knowing that suffering is part of our shared humanity. The beauty of the Loving Kindness Meditation is that it reminds you to fill yourself up with love and com-passion and then enables you to share it with those you love and eventually, with all of humanity, reminding you that we are better off existing in the world as a united "we" than as an individual "I."

Once again, the concept is simple but not easily employed, because the tendency is often to feel inadequate and isolated in your suffering, pain, or shame. By shifting your focus to recognizing humanity, acknowledging the similarities between yourself and others, and extending compassion to yourself and all of humanity (and all living creatures for that matter), you can truly free yourself from this prison.

Practice: Just Like Me

PLAY THIS

The following exercise draws on a meditation created by Sean Fargo, a former Buddhist monk. It is aimed at helping you develop a sense of compassion by becoming connected to the shared sense of experience with all human beings, including those people you may not like or with whom you are in conflict.

1. **Settle in.**

   Find a comfortable position, close your eyes, and take a few nice, long, deep breaths. Allow your body to gently relax.

   Breathe in deeply and exhale completely, gently and slowly for three or four cycles of breath.

   Scan your body and notice any sensations or emotions that arise, accepting whatever you notice without judging anything as good or bad. You are simply witnessing.

2. **Recognize humanity.**

   When you are ready, bring someone to mind whom you just met or don't know well. As you do so, notice any changes or sensations that arise in your body. Notice any changes to your breath.

   With this person in mind, say to yourself, "This person is human, just like me," and take about five to ten cycles of breath to let this statement sink in.

   Do the same with the following statements:

   "This person has a body, just like me."

   "This person has emotions and thoughts, just like me."

   "This person has feelings, failures, and successes, just like me."

   "This person wishes to be loved and fulfilled, just like me."

   "This person wishes for health and happiness, just like me."

   Take a moment to appreciate and notice any changes or sensations that arise in your body now, as you hold this person in your awareness.

3. **Extend loving kindness.**

   Breathe in loving kindness, and as you exhale, let it flow through the rest of your body. Take note of how you feel for three to five cycles of breath.

   When you are ready, send this person loving kindness. You may create your own statements or use one or more of the following:

   "May you be happy."

   "May you be fulfilled."

"May you be healthy."

"May your life be filled with ease and joy."

4. **Settle back out.**

Bring your awareness back to your breath as you gently breathe in deeply and exhale completely.

Notice your body, becoming aware of your body's weight on the chair and your feet connected to the earth.

Take note of your entire self, present, alive, breathing, right here, right now as you open your eyes.

Clear seeing with mindfulness

Neff's third component for self-compassion is mindfulness, which as you discover in Chapter 8, is the practice of moment-to-moment awareness of your experience, including your thoughts and feelings. Mindfulness, Neff believes, rounds up self-compassion because it allows you to be present with your negative emotions and thoughts without getting caught up and lost in them. Being more removed then allows you to "clear see" the situation for what it is and self-comfort more easily with compassion, acceptance, and understanding, like you would for someone you care for.

Clear seeing means that your vision isn't muddled by your emotions or thoughts. It means that the path has been cleared, and you can now be a witness to your experience — the pain, hurt, sadness, or confusion — and allow room for compassion and care. If you've been working through this book from the beginning, you have already done several mindfulness practices that can be done anywhere, anytime, including, "Where are my feet?" in Chapter 8. These exercises can shift your focus to noticing and being a witness rather than being intertwined with a given situation, thought, or emotion.

Facing the Challenges of Self-Compassion

When you open your heart to receive compassion, you may also awaken painful memories of times when compassion was lacking in your life in one form or another. Painful memories are suppressed for a reason — you may not have had the tools to handle such pain in the past. Shutting the memories away likely enabled you to survive and keep functioning. The problem is that now this same hurt may be exacerbating your sense of being alone or unworthy today. The key is to slowly build a cushion of compassion, which can provide you with the ability to be present with all of your feelings. If you do have deep-seated traumas or feel that for any reason practicing self-compassion is too uncomfortable, I recommend working with a clinician who can guide you, help you feel safe, and work with you to enhance your sense of safety and self-worth.

Of course, rekindled hurt, fear, or sadness isn't the only challenge to cultivating self-compassion. Many people believe that self-compassion is a sign of weakness, that it can lead to forgiving yourself too easily, or that it is selfish or self-centered.

Common misgivings about self-compassion

As Neff often explains, the concept of self-compassion is commonly misunderstood, and it's important to clear the air to better understand what self-compassion is *not*.

It is not being weak

Jamal wanted to stop feeling angry. He had just gone through a contentious divorce and felt his anger was negatively affecting his ability to work as a surgeon, be patient with his kids, and have positive relationships. He also felt like he was on the verge of burning out. When I asked him who or what he was angry about, Jamal explained that he was not angry at his former wife, even though she had an affair and was shirking her parental responsibilities, nor his colleagues, who would regularly offload their responsibilities on him knowing that he would never refuse. Rather, he was angry with himself. "I should have known better. I never should have gotten married. It is my fault. I shouldn't be crying like a baby over this and a little hard work. I need to be tougher, like my mother."

Can you tell where I am going with this story? Jamal had a very challenging time with self-compassion. He truly believed that crying, expressing his emotions, being vulnerable, and especially having compassion for his plight and own hurt, was showing weakness.

REMEMBER

Indeed, evidence is telling us that self-compassion is empowering, as it helps you be more resilient and improve your adaptive coping abilities. It enables better psychological flexibility and enables you to feel more like a victor than a victim when facing hardship.

It is not being too forgiving

I used to think that if I didn't beat myself up, I would stray and not continue to excel. I also had an easier time forgiving other people than forgiving myself. I often understood why a person behaved the way they did and that they suffered, and I would choose to forgive them. But then I would end up feeling worse and demoralized. I didn't realize that by having compassion and forgiving someone else without first offering the same to myself was leaving me feeling empty and less valued.

To forgive another person and show them compassion is to understand their plight and to know that they have their own path to follow and their own imperfections to deal with, just as you do. This doesn't mean that their behaviors or actions are appropriate or right, or that you don't have the right to be angry or upset. It simply means you understand. Self-forgiveness involves doing the same for yourself. In doing so, you improve psychological flexibility, your ability to cope and effect positive change going forward.

It is not being self-centered

When you feel centered, you are less bothered by other people's actions and behaviors, or your own mistakes or foibles. You have a higher sense of self-worth, are less likely to become angry and resentful, and are more likely to be compassionate and forgiving.

Take note that being centered and being self-centered are two different things. When you are centered within yourself, you know your value and have self-esteem, and therefore don't crave attention. When you are self-centered, the likelihood is that you do not know your value, need to find ways to build your self-esteem, and therefore tend to demand attention and compare yourself to others. As Neff explains, cultivating self-compassion is not the same as building up self-esteem. She writes, "Although they're both strongly linked to psychological well-being, self-esteem is a positive evaluation of self-worth, while self-compassion isn't a judgment or an evaluation at all. Instead, self-compassion is a way of relating to the ever-changing landscape of who we are with kindness and acceptance — especially when we fail or feel inadequate."

It is not being selfish

Many people often confuse self-compassion with being selfish, thinking that if you focus on yourself, it means you are not focusing on other people who are in need. If you are constantly giving everyone the water from your glass and not filling it back up, what is left in the end?

Self-compassion helps you fill up so that you can actually *give more* to others. With self-compassion you recognize that you are human like the people you care for and that when you treat yourself with loving kindness, you have more resources to help others.

It is not self-pity

Last (but not least, as there are undoubtedly many other misconceptions), it is important to note that when you choose to fill up your cup or be kind to yourself, it is not because you are feeling sorry for yourself. There's a difference between pity and compassion. With pity, it's as if you are high up and looking down, feeling sorry for the sorrowful and miserable state of life another person is in. With compassion, on the other hand, you are aware of another person's sorrow, feel it as your own, and want to help.

So, too, when you partake in self-pity, you are essentially condescendingly looking down at yourself and your predicament, without understanding or knowing that what you are experiencing is shared by other people. When you practice self-compassion, in contrast, you understand your humanness, and you extend love and forgiveness toward yourself and look for ways to help yourself.

TIP

You may find it helpful to do Neff's Self Compassion Test (`self-compassion.org/self-compassion-test/`) to give you an idea of where you stand. Answering the questions may also shed light on your own beliefs and attitudes, and perhaps, misconceptions when it comes to self-compassion.

Experiencing the backdraft

Sometimes, practicing self-compassion may hurt. The reason is that when you open yourself up to feeling, you open yourself up to feeling everything — both positive and negative, joyful and painful — including feelings you may have buried long ago. You may find that as you practice self-compassion, you are reminded of these painful memories, when you felt hurt, abandoned, or unloved, which can in turn cause you to feel that discomfort or pain all over again. Know that this is okay. You are healing.

We all have wounds. We've all had experiences in our lives that taught our hearts to shut down, that it wasn't safe to keep an open heart. We hold onto these experiences in our memories, and as we go through our current lives, situations may stimulate these memories, causing us to automatically react in fear, anger, shame, or another negative emotion.

When you approach these memories with self-compassion, you offer yourself a chance to heal from the experience, so that you no longer are reactive in your current life. Neff and Germer call the experience of old wounds coming forth as "backdraft." They liken it to when a firefighter opens the door while a fire is raging behind it, which introduces oxygen to the fire, causing it to intensify.

The beauty of the backdraft is that it is making old wounds visible so that you can finally heal them in the relative safety of your life, rather than resist them. As you do so, the memories lose their hold on you, and you may find yourself free of them.

Finding the hidden value underneath difficult emotions

Your emotions can have a profound effect on your ability to cope with life's challenges, learn, and store memories. They often fuel your decisions, impulses, and desires. They exist to signal your mind to retrieve memories of what you learned in the past so that you can act accordingly in a given situation.

The problem is that many of your memories were created when you had half a brain or at least one that wasn't fully formed yet. I just got off a Facetime call with my 3-year-old nephew who still believes that I have his nose. The memories that are forming for him right now are based on whether he experiences joy, fear, pleasure, or pain. If his brain didn't continue to develop, he might think that I still had his nose in 20 years. In 20 years, though, he won't remember the game, but he will remember how much fun he had with his auntie as he will remember the experiences of joy and pleasure.

In other words, many of the memories that are tied to your emotions happened when you were very young, before your brain was fully developed, which means your understanding of the situation and of yourself was incomplete. Your emotions, therefore, are often associated with illogical or irrational beliefs that may or may not be based in truth. The stronger your reaction, the bigger the impression the memory had on you, and in the case of negative emotions, the bigger the wound.

The beauty of allowing yourself to experience your emotions is that when you do, you give yourself the opportunity to examine underlying beliefs and hurts and heal something old. Every feeling you experience provides you with another chance to learn, grow, and heal; to discover when and what helps you feel safe and why. Every emotion, especially the difficult ones, thus has value.

Practice: Self-compassion break for burnout

Perhaps right this moment you are feeling exhausted, unmotivated, and maybe depressed or anxious. It's a perfect time to take a self-compassion break. Well, really any time is a good time for a self-compassion break, a tool designed by Neff that you can use anytime and anywhere that incorporates self-kindness, common humanity, and mindfulness (not necessarily in that order), as well as soothing physical touch. The latter aspect is important as it acts to calm the stress response, letting the brain know you are safe, much like you would do for an infant, holding and soothing them when they are crying.

One of the reasons I like this simple and effective practice is that it has a softening effect. In both my clinical and personal experience, when you are burned and stressed, it feels as if you are surrounded by a hard shell and on the inside, you are empty. The self-compassion break helps to soften that shell while also filling up the inside so that you feel increasingly less empty and more fulfilled.

1. **Recall stress.**

   The first step is to think about a situation that is causing you stress. It can be any stressful situation that comes to mind that causes a negative emotional reaction, but for purposes of this exercise, choose a situation that is relatively minor so that you are not totally overwhelmed and upset, and you can get more comfortable with the exercise.

   As you recall the situation, notice the physical sensations that arise in your body. Mindfully notice where tension, contraction, or other discomfort arises.

2. **Bring in mindfulness.**

   Rather than getting caught up in the story and letting your emotions take over, instead, allow yourself to step back and observe *that* you are hurting. You may say to yourself statements like: "I am hurting" or "This is a moment of suffering" or "Ouch, this hurts!" or "This is what stress feels like."

3. **Bring in common humanity.**

   Our tendency when hurting or feeling stress is to isolate and feel alone in our struggles. So at this stage, you want to shift out of that tendency and connect with common humanity by remembering that you are not alone and that all of humanity struggles with imperfections. You can say to yourself statements like, "It's challenging to be human" or "I am not alone in this" or "This feels sucky, but I know others feel this way too."

4. **Bring in self-kindness.**

   Now you want to self-soothe with self-kindness through physical touch and intention. You can place both your hands over your heart, give yourself a hug, place one hand on your heart and one on your lower abdomen (my prefer- ence), or even just rest your hands on your lap. Then think about what you might tell a dear friend who is struggling and say those same words to yourself. You may choose statements like, "I completely understand, and I am here for you" or "You are not alone. I have your back" or "I am so sorry you are going through this." Germer and Neff also recommend such statements as, "May I be patient," "May I live in love," "May I forgive myself," or "May I learn to accept myself as I am."

Meeting the Suffering of Burnout with Loving Kindness

You did not get to burnout overnight, which means that you have been suffering, feeling wounded, and likely very much alone in your struggles for a long time. Keep in mind that you are not alone in this. There is a rising amount of uncertainty in the world, and the lines between home and work have become fuzzy. Many people are overworked, irritable, and unhappy, and even if they do like their work, they are unsure whether they can keep going because they are physically and emotionally exhausted. The suffering you are experiencing is real and prevalent.

Healing from burnout takes time, and doing the self-compassion breakout practice can help afford you a bit of patience as you embark on the journey to recovery, as well as help you have more trust in yourself and your body.

TIP

The more you approach yourself and this process with kindness, the less you will push yourself to be perfect, meet deadlines, or take care of everyone else at your own expense.

When you meet the suffering of burnout with kindness, you essentially fill up your proverbial gas tank so that you can make the drive to heal from burnout and find your bliss.

The three stages of self-compassion progress

You may find, as you proceed on this journey of mindful self-compassion, that you go through the three stages of progress: striving, disillusionment, and radical acceptance.

The early stage: Striving

In the early stages of cultivating mindful self-compassion, you may find yourself "trying" hard and striving to do self-compassion right, as you might with any endeavor to improve yourself. In this phase, it's common to be full of hope and excited to finally feel better.

You can perhaps think about other situations in life when you were striving, looking forward to achieving something, perhaps feeling better or doing better. Remember how motivated and excited you were?

The "muddy middle": Disillusionment

The next stage of progress in mindful self-compassion is often the disillusionment phase, which arises as you begin to work with painful parts of yourself or wounds that have lain dormant. The process of dissolving old and painful wounds can be difficult and confusing. Who are you without this pain? During this phase, it's not uncommon to experience fear and doubt, which is in stark contrast to the "feel good" feelings you may have felt initially.

Know that experiencing disillusionment is normal, and it's often a necessary phase to be able to deepen your awareness and healing journey. The key is to be present with these feelings and to accept them, while staying connected to yourself and your body with loving kindness. You get comfortable being uncomfortable and let go of trying or striving to feel anything in particular. You "non-strive" to simply be present with the experience, being with your emotions, feelings, and thoughts, whether painful or joyful. Rob G. Nairn, a Buddhist teacher, says, "The goal of the practice is to become a compassionate mess," by which he means that the aim of self-compassion is to allow yourself to be fully human — struggles and imperfections and all — with love and compassion.

The later stage: Lightness through radical acceptance

The moment you accept with openness and interest that you are striving or in disillusionment is the moment you also reach radical acceptance. When you accept what is without judgment or wanting it to be something else; when you love what is, who you are, and how you feel in the moment, including your striving and disillusionment, you "embrace life with the heart of the Buddha," as Neff writes. This is where your freedom lies.

Meeting the difficult feelings of burnout in practice

The more you build your self-compassion, and therefore self-love and mindfulness, the closer you will find yourself getting to feeling a better sense of control. Dislodging yourself from your emotions and thoughts with the mindfulness practice is a big step. Adding self-compassion into the mix enables you to meet these difficult feelings without them having control over you. The snafu (also known as confusion in the mix) is that when you are feeling down and out, bringing in self-compassion can create a backdraft, opening the gateway for many of these difficult feelings and beliefs to be awakened from their dormancy.

Accepting that self-compassion can be difficult

PLAY THIS

With love and patience, your way through burnout involves accepting where you are right now and accepting that self-compassion can be difficult. Here is a practice you can do to help yourself cultivate acceptance.

You may want to start doing this practice for five minutes and perhaps set a timer to do so. You are also welcome to reflect as long as you want to.

1. **Reflect.**

   Bring your awareness to your body and notice any sensations you may be experiencing.

   Notice your emotions and thoughts. How are you feeling about this self-compassion journey? Allow yourself to be present with thoughts, emotions, or physical sensations as they arise.

2. **Label.**

   Give your experience a label. You might say, "Feeling butterflies in my stomach. Feeling nervous," or "Noticing resistance, chest is tight," or "Feeling hopeful, shoulders relaxed."

3. **Center with loving kindness.**

   Bring your awareness to the center of your chest, the part of your chest known as the heart center. Imagine you are breathing in loving kindness into your heart center. With every breath, you are allowing loving kindness into your heart. As you do so, your heart may begin to open and relax.

   Keep breathing loving kindness into your heart and allow yourself to witness anything that transpires. There is no right or wrong, good or bad.

   When you do notice something, label it as if you are the observer, noticing or watching it happen. You might say, "Feeling the chest open," or "Feeling a tightness in my chest," or "Feeling sadness," or "Feeling joy," and so on.

4. Soothe and accept.

Keep breathing in loving kindness and at all times remember to speak to yourself as if you are speaking to a dear friend who is struggling.

You can also place one hand or both on your chest to provide you with a feeling of safety and comfort, and say these words to yourself, "I accept my experience as it is right now. I accept myself where I am right now and as I am right now."

Reflect and soothe as long as you want or until the timer goes off.

When you are ready, feel free to journal about your experience.

"This being human is a guest house": Managing self-doubt

Part of the process of self-compassion and, therefore, self-acceptance is remembering that you are human, and like all humans, you are inherently imperfect. I know, thinking of yourself as imperfect and being okay with it is truly challenging. And if you are like many people, focusing on your flaws does not lead to joyful feelings of love and peace, but rather pain and heartache. As such, you're likely to wade through the muddle of disillusionment as you go through the progress of self-compassion. For this reason, you may find it helpful to read inspirational literature or listen to inspirational talks.

"The Guest House," written by the 13th century Persian poet Rumi, is a wonderful poem that many mindfulness and self-compassion practitioners recommend, as it reminds you to let go of your resistance to your thoughts and emotions, the guests in your house, and to instead, meet them with warmth, respect, and courage, as you are being given the opportunity to truly heal. I love that he refers to the emotions and thoughts as "guests" because guests eventually leave!

Perhaps you can take a moment to sit quietly and just breathe naturally in and out for a moment. Then, when you are ready, read the poem.

The Guest House

This being human is a guest house.
Every morning a new arrival.

A joy, a depression, a meanness
Some momentary awareness comes
As an unexpected visitor.

Welcome and entertain them all!
Even if they're a crowd of sorrows,
Who violently sweep your house
empty of its furniture,
still, treat each guest honorably.
He may be clearing you out
For some new delight.

The dark thought, the shame, the malice,
Meet them at the door laughing,
And invite them in.

Be grateful for whoever comes,
Because each has been sent
As a guide from beyond.

Pocket Practices to Get Started with Self-Compassion

You may notice nowadays that it doesn't take a deep gaping wound to cause you to scream high holy murder when someone taps you on the shoulder because you are so tapped out. A simple request can turn into a huge burden fairly quickly, especially when you are running on empty. For this reason, you may find it helpful to regularly take brief breaks to fill up your proverbial gas tank with some easy self-compassion exercises. You can think of them as practices that you can keep in your pocket, which can be retrieved anytime and anywhere.

Remembering you are a miracle

I strongly encourage you to reflect on how difficult it is to be human. First, the notion that when an egg is fertilized it can eventually become a living breathing human being is quite amazing. Then, consider that we have little to no capacity to care for ourselves as infants and that we are completely dependent on other human beings to survive. It is a wonder how we even made it to adulthood. Consider what you have been through, what you have done, and all the adversity you have managed to survive and overcome by the mere fact that you are here, right now, reading this book.

I also encourage you to reflect on nature and life itself. How the sun rises and falls, how the seasons automatically change, that the waves of the ocean move in and out, or that the roots of trees intertwine and communicate with one another underground, without us seeing it.

When you connect with awe, while also recognizing your own humanity and the presence of miracles all around you (including you), you get closer to cultivating self-compassion. You can take it a step further by doing the "I Am a Miracle" exercise:

1. **Contemplate what a miracle is.**

Think about the definition of a miracle: a surprising and welcome event that is not explicable by natural or scientific laws and is therefore considered to be the work of a divine agency.

Then think about your favorite person and how grateful you are to have them in your life. Consider all the ways you view this person as a true miracle, especially in your life. If you can't think of a person, think of something that happens in nature.

Allow yourself to rest in this state of awe for a bit, witnessing how your body reacts or the sensations that arise in your body, emotions, or thoughts.

2. **Turn and tune in.**

Imagine turning this awe inward.

If your eyes are open, close them, and place one hand or both hands on your heart.

Say: "I am a miracle."

Smile.

Say it again. "I am a miracle."

Smile even wider.

Say it again. "I am a miracle."

Imagine you are smiling inside your heart.

Say the phrase again and as often as you like.

Drawing it and putting it in your pocket

For the following exercise you will need two sheets of paper.

1. **On the first sheet of paper, draw an image of yourself (it can be a stick figure if you like) and write thought bubbles next to the image, reflecting what your inner critic is thinking, especially about yourself.**

    Take a moment to honor the way you feel and acknowledge that this drawing reflects your inner-critic's point of view, and that most people have an inner-critic and have these thoughts and feelings too.

2. **Put the drawing that depicts your inner-critic's point of view aside.**

3. **Do the "I Am a Miracle" exercise as explained in the preceding section.**

4. **When you are ready, create a drawing of yourself, this time reflecting your feelings and thoughts as your miraculous and resilient self.**

    Take a moment to honor the way you feel and acknowledge that this drawing reflects your inner resilient self and shared humanity.

5. **When you are done, place the two sheets side by side and take a moment to accept that both points of view co-exist, neither defines you, and you have a choice as to which one you want to give more attention to.**

6. **Fold up the sheets of paper and put them in your wallet or a journal that you plan on carrying around with you everywhere.**

    Whenever you need reminding, you can pull the papers out of your pocket and remember that neither drawing defines you and that you have a choice to decide which voice you want to listen to at any given moment. Regardless of which you choose, you are a miracle.

REMEMBER

Whatever practice you choose, remember to be kind to yourself. The kindness will help you to ultimately heal.

Chapter **10**

Cultivating a Safe and Brave Inner Space for Change

Focusing on healing when you feel like you have little time for yourself can be difficult. It can also be anxiety-provoking to embark on a road to change when the future is unknown and filled with uncertainty. Just the thought of change can be frightening and overwhelming.

REMEMBER

You are not alone if you feel overwhelmed, scared, or simply too tired. As miserable as you may feel, at least you know where you stand right now and that you do have a desire to get better.

Is the desire to get better going to be enough for you to challenge your fears around change? It certainly is a good start, though desire alone may not be enough to sustain the ongoing process of change. If it were, I might be a rock star (the fact that I can rarely remember any words to any songs may have something to do with it too) and people would stick to their diets. The key is to find a way to make the process a little less difficult and overwhelming, so that with your desire in tow, you can embark on the healing journey with more ease, courage, and confidence.

Finding the Will and Way for Change

Have you heard the phrase, "Where there's a will, there's a way?" If you break the sentence down into two parts, you may note that the first part of the phrase is asking you to reflect on whether you have the will, strength, courage, and desire to push forward. The second part of the phrase, "there's *a* way," implies that the pathway ahead may not be clear, but rest assured that if your desire or *will* is strong, you will find the path to traverse and will ultimately be able to achieve your goals.

The *will* is represented by your inner desire to truly heal. In the case of burnout, however, your *will* may be feeling too exhausted, frightened, or beaten down, especially if the path ahead appears mired with obstacles. So, though it is often true that where there's a will, there's a way, in the case of burnout, sometimes it's necessary to strengthen your *will* so that it can indeed lead the way.

In Daoism, an ancient Chinese belief system, the *Dao* means *the way,* or the way of all things that exist in a given pattern, in harmony with the natural and balanced order of the universe. The philosophy lays down the framework for living in harmony with the world and creating ease, so that life can be easier as you go with life's flow. Using nature as a guide, the philosophy says there exists a rhythm and flow to life that you can either resist or accept. You can resist that the temperature is about to drop and go outside without warm attire, for instance, or accept that you can't control nature or the changes that nature brings and put on your winter coat. So, too, you can accept the nature of your situation or resist it. Your ability to be in acceptance of the nature of burnout, and the nature of the change itself, can ultimately influence the degree to which you experience ease or suffering.

As you build up the strength of your *will*, of that inner voice inside you that wants to heal, you discover that you possess more courage and resilience to meet any challenges ahead. So, too, as you learn to accept that which you can change and that which you cannot, and learn to "go with the flow," your *will* finds more ease along the way. This isn't to say that simply accepting your plight and finding courage will fix everything. It just means that you can experience more ease and less suffering as you embark on your path to healing burnout.

The tricky path between acceptance and change

You can accept that you can't change your past, how other people behave, whether pandemics happen, or when the seasons will change. You can accept that you have reached burnout, that your boss has narcissistic tendencies, or that you are juggling your job and caretaking for an ailing parent. That's the way it is. But does accepting these things mean that you are helpless in the face of change? The path between acceptance and change can be tricky. Often, people accept their situation believing that change isn't possible, and they do nothing. Know that just because you accept what is, that doesn't mean that you're powerless to effect change.

Take your job, for instance. If your job serves as your major source of stress, you have the option to leave. The idea of doing so may riddle you with fear because you need the money and are worried that you may not find anything else. The option, however unideal as it is, still exists. Another option is to discover ways to create more ease and gather more support *so that* you can stay. In either case, your choice is to take care of your needs so that you can build your sense of safety, ease, and courage. Do you feel safe and courageous to leave? Then leave. If you don't, you may need to figure out what it will take to help you feel safer or stronger. You want to stay? Then stay. What resources and support do you need to create more ease and fulfillment?

REMEMBER

Know that when you accept something (or someone), you are acknowledging that it exists as it is; you are not condoning or even liking it. You are just taking a pause to acknowledge and accept your given reality without trying to change any of it right now.

In that moment of acceptance, you allow for a shift — a shift out of the dynamics of fear, worry, or struggle toward a better sense of ease and calm. With more ease, the path ahead will appear clearer, enabling you to view more options and better make decisions.

Psychologist Carl Rogers once said, "The curious paradox is that when I accept myself just as I am, then I can change." The point here is that when you accept yourself, flaws and all, you clear the way for change because you are no longer holding on to the past, how you should be, or who you think you have to be. Rather, you are accepting *what is*, and in so doing, clearing the way for adopting behaviors and making choices that will support you to thrive.

Adding mindfulness and compassion into the mix

Looking at yourself, your patterns, your tendencies, and your own role in burnout can be upsetting or frightening. It can also lead to feelings of shame or self-blame without proper care and compassion. If it were easy, well, I wouldn't have a job! Having said that, it is possible for you to move toward acceptance by operating from a place of love and mindful compassion.

When you focus on moment-to-moment awareness, you don't think about the past or worry about the future, as you exist only in the now. When you add love and compassion into the mix of being mindful, you are better able to accept yourself, your flaws, and your strengths and be honest with yourself regarding what needs to change. You soften your lens of perception and view yourself and your reality without fear or blame, seeing the whole picture more clearly.

I know. Simply focusing on the present moment instead of worrying or thinking is easier said than done. It may even seem impossible, given your daily commitments and workload. It can be done, however, and you can start slowly by giving yourself opportunities to pause for short periods throughout your day. Use those moments to shift your focus to the present moment, even if briefly, to allow yourself to be present with what is — with your feelings, your tendencies, your situation, your likes and dislikes, and so forth — without judgment.

Cultivating the capacity to savor the moment

I know when I reached a state of burnout, it was close to impossible for me to appreciate any joy around me. I had *anhedonia,* if you will, which essentially means I had difficulty feeling pleasure because the world around me, and especially within me, was so dark. As I started practicing mindfulness, I found the darkness lifting for moments at a time, and during those moments, I was able to experience a sense of joy and appreciation. When these moments happened, I would savor them, bathing myself in the delight of that sense of lightness that seemed so rare. I then found that the more I savored moments, the more I began to discover things I appreciated about myself and my life. The darkness began to lift more easily as I found myself experiencing true joy and the lightness of my being.

The capacity to notice, appreciate, and savor positive experiences has been linked to helping people cope better with life's experiences. Savoring also takes up more space in your mind so that you have less room to ruminate or focus on negative things. New research is now empirically finding that savoring can improve positive emotions and life satisfaction. Fred Bryant, Ph.D., coauthor with Joseph Veroff of *Savoring: A New Model of Positive Experience* (Psychology Press), says, "Savoring can help us counteract the natural human tendency to focus more of our attention on negative things in our lives than on positive things." He points out that life is full of trials and tribulations, and they are not going to go away. It is therefore important that we prioritize savoring, even in the face of adversity, to help counterbalance the negative effects of stress and suffering.

Alas, if you are finding it difficult to move into acceptance or see the possibility of change right now, that's okay. You can build up to it. First focus on finding small things to appreciate and savor. You can look up at a blue sky and savor the ray of sun shining down and warming your skin. You can inhale the aroma of your favorite dish and savor the smell or the luxurious flavors with each bite. In other words, you can practice mindfulness with appreciation in small bursts throughout your day to start helping yourself connect with more positive emotions, reduce some of your suffering, and build up some resources for times ahead. Every puff will fill up your tank to strengthen your will to find the way!

TIP

One of my favorite things to do is to stare at something I adore while squinting my eyes and appreciating it through the slits. Then, I open my eyes wide and appreciate that much more, savoring the experience.

Perhaps you can take a moment to do so with your favorite person or object, like a beautiful flower, a loved keepsake, or even your favorite food.

Think about everything you adore about this person or thing as you gaze lovingly at it. If it's an object, perhaps you can hold it in your hands and appreciate the texture, shape, or sound and your connection to it or its connection with the earth, like your "here and now stone" (see Chapter 8). If you're savoring food, appreciate the aroma, colors, textures, and tastes. Appreciate the farmer who may have grown the produce or how far it may have come from where it was harvested. Immerse your senses in the experience.

Identifying core values as a compass to guide you

Your core values reflect your fundamental beliefs and what is important to you, and they act like a compass that can guide you on your life journey. They provide direction when you feel confused or lost, or when you meet obstacles or challenges. Your core values are your own unique imprint that help you decide what is right or wrong, help dictate your behavior and choices, affect how you treat and interact with other people, and choose the causes that are important to you.

Say that you want to leave your job right now, but you have no idea how to go about doing so. The path isn't clear just yet. What do you focus on to begin the journey? Do you focus on your goal to make more money or on the value you place on your personal physical and mental health? If you use a higher salary as your compass, you may end up taking a job that pays well but requires long hours that prevent you from truly taking care of yourself.

I'm not telling you to ignore your goals, but rather to choose your goals with your core values in mind. For instance, as part of your value to enhance your health, you may want to ensure that you have a higher salary. You won't, however, compromise your health for a higher salary. In other words, shoot for your goals without compromising your core values.

Practice: Uncovering your core values

When assessing your core values, you want to think about what is important to you, not someone else. Your core values are unique to you, as they have developed over time, from your own experiences, social conditioning, family patterns, cultural background, and even your genetic makeup.

In this light, it can be challenging not only to elicit what is important to you, but it can also be hard to realize that you may have been compromising your fundamental belief system all this time. As you go through the process of uncovering your core values, you may find yourself experiencing feelings of hurt or pain, hearing the voice inside your head that says that you are not worthy of attaining this value or that it simply isn't possible. It's okay if you do. You are getting real with yourself and viewing yourself without a filter. These feelings are your inner self letting you know that you do want to be aligned with your own fundamental beliefs because you do want to live your life going forward with more intention and meaning. Allow yourself to be vulnerable for this process. If you find it too difficult, you may want to think about working with a trusted coach, counselor, or therapist.

Step 1: Self-reflection

I have created the following chart with a sample of values that you can choose from (there are many more than what I have listed). You can choose words from the list to answer the following questions, but also take some time to contemplate your answers and figure out what is true and authentic to you.

>> What do I value?

>> What is meaningful to me?

>> What values to I believe have helped me succeed? What values influence my behavior?

>> What values drive my ability to take care of my health?

>> What values influence my relationships at work? At home?

>> What values drive the relationships to be positive?

>> What values come naturally to me? What are examples?

>> What values are harder for me to align with? Why?

>> What values feel misaligned with me?

>> What values inspire me?

>> What values upset me?

>> What values do I admire in others?

Accountability	Adventure	Advocacy
Appreciation	Being the Best	Boldness
Caring	Challenge	Charity
Collaboration	Commitment	Compassion
Consistency	Contribution	Cooperation
Creativity	Credibility	Curiosity
Decisiveness	Dedication	Dependability
Diversity	Empathy	Enthusiasm
Ethics	Excellence	Fairness
Family	Friendship	Freedom
Fun	Generosity	Growth
Happiness	Health	Honesty
Honor	Humility	Humor
Inclusiveness	Individuality	Innovation
Inspiration	Intelligence	Joy
Kindness	Knowledge	Leadership
Learning	Love	Loyalty
Mindfulness	Motivation	Optimism
Originality	Passion	Peace
Performance	Professionalism	Recognition
Relationships	Reliability	Resilience
Responsibility	Security	Service
Simplicity	Spirituality	Stability
Success	Teamwork	Thoughtfulness
Tradition	Trust	Uniqueness
Versatility	Vision	Wisdom

Step 2: Whittling down your list

The next step is to compile a list of all the core values you wrote about when answering the questions. Then choose the ten values that are most aligned with you and how you want to live your life going forward. You may want to ask yourself a variety of questions in the process of choosing. For instance, you can ask yourself which of these values will support you in the following endeavors:

>> Taking care of your health and well-being

>> Building positive relationships

>> Feeling more balanced

>> Upholding your moral beliefs

>> Feeling happier and more content

>> Making sounder decisions

>> Succeeding professionally

Step 3: Making your statement

The next step is to create your core values statement. You can think of it as a mission statement that is timeless. You can carry it around with you everywhere or post it all over your house to remind you of what is important to you and what you want to live by. It will serve as your compass wherever you are and wherever you go.

>> **Recall feeling good:** To help you along with this process, you may want to think about a time when you felt happy, loved, valued, optimistic, or successful. Perhaps you can think of an accomplishment you are proud of and think back to the moment of success.

>> **Find themes:** Once you have given yourself a bit of time to remember a positive experience, consider what the themes may be. Review your list of values and see if you can choose three to six values that will serve as themes in which to place your other values. For instance, say you note that you were happy and had fun in your story. Happiness, fun, and joy may fall under the value of *optimism*, which now becomes one theme. Or you note that you enjoyed the process of learning and using your intelligence and knowledge to solve a difficult problem. Knowledge, learning, and intelligence can then fall under the theme of *wisdom*.

>> **Write a statement:** Once you have created three to six themes, see if you can form a statement with the values, comprised of one to three sentences. For example, some of my values include integrity, joy, service, sharing knowledge,

wisdom, optimism, and growth. As such, I created the value statement: *I choose to live my life with integrity, so that I can stay whole and balanced, and with optimism so that I can spread love and joy. I seek opportunities for growth and learning so that I can gain wisdom, and in service, I share that knowledge.* My statement helps remind me of how I want to live my life so that I don't make compromises.

It may be helpful to write a sentence for each of the values you have chosen first. Once you have done so, you can either put them all together in one paragraph or see if you can create a summary.

TIP

Take a moment to connect with your value statement. Perhaps you can close your eyes, take a few deep breaths, focus on your heart, and repeat the statement a few times. Mindfully take note of how and what you feel. There is no right or wrong, good or bad, to this process. The goal for you is to simply be authentic and present with yourself so that you can truly connect with what is important to you and for you. When you do, you can use this information to motivate and guide you along the way.

Dark night and dark clouds: Wisdom gleaned from being burned out

When you are burned out, it can indeed feel like your world is filled with darkness, both inside and out. It can be confusing, and you may feel lost, as if there is no foundation beneath you, and almost everything that used to give you a sense of yourself and how you fit in the world is obsolete.

In his book *The Dark Night of the Soul: A Psychiatrist Explores the Connection Between Darkness and Spiritual Growth* (published by HarperOne), psychiatrist Gerald G. May writes:

> For all of us, however, there are moments of dawning awareness, little cracks in our armor that reveal glimpses of our deeper longing and our true nature. . . . We begin to see that the results of our efforts are not quite as perfect as we had hoped for. Perhaps the career we worked so hard to achieve is not as rewarding as we'd expected. Maybe the love relationship we thought would make us complete has become timeworn and frayed. Things that gave us pleasure in the past may now seem empty.

It may be that much of what you believed to be serving you in the past has had little to do with your core values and who you truly are. So even though you may want to cocoon yourself away, you are invited now to come home to yourself. Choosing to face your darkness now can provide you with the opportunity to gain wisdom, discover who you truly are, and find a path forward that involves authenticity; more joy, love, and satisfaction; and less suffering. Just like the puffs of appreciation, you can create more ease on your path by finding silver linings, the nuggets of wisdom that start letting your light shine through.

Exercise: Finding the silver linings in burnout

You do not *have to* find any silver linings right now. Just know that silver linings exist somewhere behind the dark clouds. It may take some time for you to see them, and that's okay. Also know that just because you have found something positive to focus on, it doesn't negate that you are feeling burned out or the real suffering that you have been experiencing. Simply know that if and when you do take a moment to find or focus on a silver lining, you create the opportunity to connect with your positive emotions and shed a bit of light on the dark time.

You can, for instance, look for small things that you can feel grateful for (like choosing to read this book!). My client Ella realized that all her life she thought she was an extrovert. When she no longer felt pressured to go out socially because of the COVID-19 pandemic, she found her lifelong anxiety dissipated and that she was indeed quite introverted. This realization has relieved much of her anxiety.

Here are five methods to find silver linings:

>> **Honor the way you feel**. Your body is brilliant in letting you know what it needs.

>> **Practice self-compassion.** Imagine you are speaking to a dear friend who is struggling.

>> **Connect with your core values.** Focus on sticking to what is important to you.

>> **Look for the blessings in disguise.** Consider what you can be grateful for.

>> **Remember the Serenity Prayer.** Ask for courage to change and wisdom to accept what you can change and what you cannot.

And here's how you can practice looking for silver linings:

1. **Write down all the reasons today or another day went badly.**

You can write about how you felt — angry, frustrated, overwhelmed, and so forth. It's important to validate how you feel, so be authentic and honest. Let it all out!

2. **Now put the paper aside for a moment and do a short breath focus.**

   Shift your mind away from thoughts and instead pay attention to the flow of your breath as you breathe in, counting 1-2-3, and as you breathe out, counting 1-2-3-4-5-6. Follow the breath as it moves in and out for five or six cycles of breath. Imagine you are letting tension and negativity flow out with your breath, just for this moment in time.

3. **Go back to thinking about the difficult day. Contemplate what you may have discovered about yourself.**

   How did your core values come into play? Is it possible to find at least three things to reflect a little brightness on the situation?

Were you able to find any bright sides to the situation? If so, how do you feel having done so? Did you have resistance when identifying silver linings? Some of you may find the silver linings exercise challenging to do as it may feel that looking on the bright side would devalue the real suffering you are experiencing.

REMEMBER

Keep in mind that you are not negating your suffering. Rather, with self-compassion, you are honoring *all* your feelings and the situation — the negative and the positive. You are being invited to identify silver linings to brighten the path ahead so that you can see more clearly and hopefully cultivate a more positive outlook.

As Thich Nhat Hanh wrote in his book *Anger: Wisdom for Cooling the Flames* (published by Riverhead Books),

> When it is raining, we think that there is no sunshine. But if we fly high in an airplane and go through the clouds, we rediscover the sunshine again. We see that the sunshine is always there. In a time of anger or despair, our love is still there also. Our capacity to communicate, to forgive, to be compassionate is still there. You have to believe this. We are more than our anger, we are more than our suffering. We must recognize that we do have within us the capacity to love, to understand, to be compassionate.

Making Change and Listening to Your Voice of Compassion

The voice of your inner critic is often the background negative chatter that accompanies you throughout the day. It questions your decisions, undermines your success, disapproves of your behavior, and essentially helps to exacerbate feelings of inadequacy, guilt, or shame. You may think thoughts like, "I can't do this. I am not smart enough," or "I'm never going to learn this new technique," or "I don't have enough knowledge or strength to deal with that client," or "I'm such an idiot, I should have known better."

I don't know about you, but such statements usually entice me to feel worse and less motivated. Thinking you are "not smart enough" may motivate you to give up on learning. I mean, why bother if you are so dumb? So, too, if you keep calling yourself an idiot, then how are you ever going to know better? The point is that your inner critic mostly talks about ways that you are not good enough or ways you don't have enough for any given situation. You may even believe that it is this voice that motivates you to push harder, and perhaps without it, you would be a slug and never accomplish anything. Though this may be true at times, your inner critic can keep you stuck in a loop of suffering and stress, feeling unfulfilled and averse to taking risks or seeing new opportunities for yourself.

If you live your life looking through the lens that leads you to see yourself as not enough, you have a higher chance of being more triggered and stressed by life events. When you turn up the volume of your voice of compassion, you don't necessarily silence your inner critic. Rather, you accept that the inner critic exists, offer yourself more love and compassion, and perhaps give the inner critic a new job description, one that supports you to know your value and to create opportunities for healing, change, and growth.

Exploring the function of the inner critic

The beauty of the human design is that every emotion or feeling has a purpose to support human beings to survive. The inner critic also has an evolutionary purpose — to keep us human beings in check so that we instinctively behave in ways that ensure survival of the species. The emotion of guilt, for instance, is meant to keep us aligned with social norms and sticking to a given moral code.

Say that you behave in a way that hurts someone's feelings. Now this person is angry with you and is not going to help you the next time there is a shortage of food. This may not seem like a big deal nowadays, when we have access to grocery stores and restaurants. But during the earlier times of human history, getting along with your neighbor and the people in your community was a necessity if you were to survive hard times. As such, guilt triggers instinctive corrective reactions so that you conform your behavior. Can you imagine then how the inner critic served a great purpose in ancient times?

If you feel embarrassed about a certain behavior, the chances are that you won't repeat the behavior again. In this way, the inner critic can be motivating and protective, as it is preventing you from feeling vulnerable again. The problem is that most of us internalize the messages the inner critic is sending. Rather than understanding that a given *behavior* is "bad" or not beneficial for survival of the species, we believe the message is saying *we* are "bad." Rather than understanding that the inner critic is trying to protect us from feeling vulnerable, we interpret the message as meaning we're inadequate. In other words, your inner critic is meant to alert you to where you may have gone wrong with your behavior and to protect you so that you can survive, not shame you for existing.

REMEMBER

When you pay too much attention to the inner critic and internalize the messages, you can end up feeling knocked down, like you are a "bad" or an unworthy person, inadequate, and never enough. The inner critic then loses its job as a protector and turns into more of a destroyer of your human self.

Your inner critic is simple, but it can fill up your head

Keep in mind that your inner critic doesn't consider the big picture or think rationally. You can think about how you may have viewed a situation at the age of 5 versus the age of 50. At 5 years of age, you don't have a fully functioning brain, and your tendency is to instinctively react to situations rather than think or rationalize before responding. You don't form a fully functioning brain until you are in your late twenties. Your 5-year-old brain is not capable yet of understanding nuances or subtleties, let alone why people behave the way they do. Your inner critic is simple minded, if you will, like the scared younger version of yourself, trying to protect you, even though it doesn't understand the whole picture.

Despite lacking a complete brain, you developed belief systems, assumptions, perceptions, and habits at a young age that continue to drive your behaviors today. Say when you were in grade school, a few children made fun of you for speaking up in class, calling you "a teacher's pet." Wanting their approval, you stopped speaking up. Your inner critic now tells you that you hate public speaking, or perhaps it judges others for talking too much in public. Either way, the judgment protects you from feeling exposed and vulnerable again, and you cannot remember a time when you liked public speaking.

Giving your inner critic so much power is like giving your younger, immature self the ability to make decisions for you. The more you listen to the inner critic, the stronger the nerve pathways to the inner critic become, so that it becomes the loudest voice in your head.

Finding your more compassionate voice

You have another voice within you, one that is nurturing and compassionate. Rather than putting you down, this voice lifts you up. It understands your plight while also offering you comfort. If your inner critic is your scared 5-year-old self, you can think of your compassionate voice as representing your older and wiser self, who is patient, loving, rational, and kind. This voice can see the bigger picture, is protective and encouraging, and raises you up instead of shutting you down.

Your compassionate voice is also intricately wired in the human design and represents the part that is deep within you which holds your sense of integrity, love, and positive belief. Your compassionate voice has been there since the day you were born. Depending on your life experiences, especially in childhood, your compassionate voice has either been supported to grow strong or unsupported. If you were surrounded by nurturing parents, friends, and teachers, for instance, your compassionate voice is likely quite formidable. On the other hand, it may be quieter or weaker because of the absence or compromise of external nurturing in your early life.

REMEMBER

Whether your compassionate voice is currently strong or weak, know that it exists and that you can strengthen it now, despite what may have transpired throughout your life.

The wolf you feed

An old Cherokee legend tells the story of a wise old grandfather who is speaking to his grandson about cruelty in the world. He says, "In each human heart, there are two wolves battling one another. One is fearful and angry, and the other is understanding and kind." The grandson then asks, "Which one will win?" Upon which the grandfather answers, "Whichever one we choose to feed."

The two voices, your inner critic and your compassionate voice, will always co-exist. The question is, which voice will you feed?

The voice that you do feed will influence how you perceive yourself and your world, and therefore, how you handle uncertainty and adversity. If you perceive yourself as "broken," sick, or as a victim, you are less likely to handle adversity and trauma effectively or adaptively. You are more likely to succumb to an over-active stress response, having negative emotional, psychological, and physical complaints and thoughts, and giving your inner critic more power. The louder your inner critic, the more limited you become to reason (as the inner critic is simple), make meaning, allow in compassion, and discover the blessings in disguise or silver linings. You become more of a victim in your life rather than a victor.

In contrast, when you feed the voice of compassion, you lift yourself up and connect with positive emotions and more rational and logical thinking, redefining your strengths and understanding how to find support for your weaknesses. You are more likely to align with your core values; look upon challenges and adversity as opportunities for growth and learning; and ultimately, take better care of yourself. Which do you want to choose?

Giving the inner critic a new job without silencing it

Choosing to feed your voice of compassion doesn't mean you silence your inner critic, but that you love and accept your inner critic for wanting so badly to protect you from harm. It has good intentions, and after all, it is a part of you. When you feed your voice of compassion, you offer compassion to all parts of yourself.

You do not banish your inner critic to a dark jail cell. Instead, you choose to thank your inner critic for its service in keeping you safe, and that now that you are safe, it can step back and relax. You might say, "Thank you so much for working so hard to ensure my safety. You can take a break now. How about you just let me know when I am feeling vulnerable, and then I will take over from there." Or you might thank your inner critic and then see if together, you can come up with a new way of thinking that will support you to thrive instead of dive.

REMEMBER

Don't judge yourself or your inner critic for being good or bad, right or wrong. There is value in everything, and the value of your inner critic is to let you know when you are feeling vulnerable and in need of care. This may sound hard to do, and it can be challenging to shift out of the habit of automatically reacting when the inner critic speaks. It is possible, however, to form new habits with practice, especially when you give your inner critic a new job description.

Exercise: Creating a new job for your inner critic

In the following exercise, I invite you to get to know and accept your inner critic through a process of self-compassion. In so doing, the aim is to discover ways you can give your inner critic a new job description.

Step 1: Accepting

The first step in this process is accepting — accepting exactly where you are and how you feel at any given moment. Accept that you have an inner critic and that it's doing its job, protecting you from feeling vulnerable and inadequate.

Take a moment to honor the way you feel in this moment and to accept that your inner critic is present and speaking. You may want to place a hand on your heart and say, "I accept you, inner critic. Thank you for working so hard to protect me all these years."

Step 2: Listening mindfully

Next, close your eyes and mindfully tune into your body. Notice sensations, feelings, or thoughts that you may be experiencing. Bring your awareness to the soles of your feet and be aware of the connection your feet have with the earth.

Imagine that you are now talking to your inner critic, ready to listen mindfully and without judgment to the message the inner critic has for you. What is the message? When you hear it, label it. You might say to yourself, "The message is that I am inadequate," or "The message is that I am not good enough." Allow the thoughts in, without trying to suppress or judge them.

Notice how you feel as you listen to the message. How does your body react? What are the sensations that arise in your body? Mindfully observe your experience. Note or label what you are feeling. You may state, "Feeling a pit in my stomach when I hear I am inadequate."

Step 3: Breathing in space for compassion

When you are ready, breathe compassion and love into your heart. As you exhale, let go of tension or whatever it is your body feels like it is holding onto. You may want to count 1-2-3 as you breathe in, and 1-2-3-4-5-6 as you breathe out. The longer you exhale, the more air you let out of your lungs and the more tension you release from your body, creating more space for compassion to come in.

Breathe in love and compassion and as you exhale, let it flow out to the rest of your body, easing the tension away.

Do this for at least ten cycles of breath, letting in compassion and letting go of tension.

Step 4: Being a lovingly kind friend or parent

When you are ready, imagine that you are speaking with loving kindness to a friend or child who is struggling. As you do so, notice how you feel. Notice the sensations that arise in your body, especially what you feel in your chest and the movement of your breath.

Then direct this loving kindness toward yourself and the little child within you who feels vulnerable or inadequate. What might you say? Perhaps you can say, "I see you. I hear you. I feel you. What you feel is valid. I am here for you."

Appreciate how and what you feel, mindfully observing the sensations in your body, the movement of your breath, and so forth.

Step 5: Embracing your inner critic

Take a moment now to thank your inner critic for protecting your younger self.

Imagine that you are embracing your inner critic for keeping you safe up until today and offer thanks by saying, "Thank you so much for protecting me. I truly appreciate your efforts."

Again, take note of how and what you feel.

Step 6: Creating a new supportive role

After honoring your inner critic, acknowledge that now that you are older, wiser, and stronger, you would prefer the inner critic to take on a different role, one that supports you to stay strong and resilient. Use this time to contemplate what other roles your inner critic can take on from here on, going forward. As your great protector, what other job title could the inner critic have? Coach? Chief Encouragement Officer (CEO)?

Think about how the message you received earlier can be restructured to support you rather than diminish you or your efforts, given the new job title. For instance, the statement that started out as, "I am not good enough" now becomes, "You go, my friend! You are enough and have enough, and no matter what, I trust you to figure it out."

Again, take note of how and what you feel.

Connecting to your story of greatness when you feel burned out

It's normal to have difficulty accessing your voice of compassion when you feel burned out and miserable. Most of us have spent our lifetime identifying with our inner critic. It is what we know or who we think we are. You are not your inner critic, however. You are a human being who has both an inner critic and a voice of compassion *within* you. And perhaps you haven't received the nurturing you needed in your life for the latter voice to be the stronger of the two.

The beauty of the brain is its plasticity. It is able to grow new nerve connections and pathways, meaning you have the ability to rewire the brain, reprogram the experience of being and feeling nurtured, strengthen your voice of compassion, and connect with a story of greatness and resilience. As with most things, it takes time and a lot of love.

When I first met Susan, she complained of exhaustion. With tears running down her face, she told me she felt lost and depressed, that her 25-year marriage was on the brink of collapse, that she felt she was at a dead end at work, that her menopausal symptoms were keeping her from sleeping, that she was the heaviest she had ever been, and that every muscle in her body hurt. It sounds like a mouthful, but unfortunately, such complaints are not uncommon for people experiencing burnout. Together, Susan and I worked through her deep-seated negative beliefs by cultivating mindful compassion, being more self-aware, and enhancing her self-care habits.

Susan quickly learned to recognize that her feelings of low self-worth and inadequacy were keeping her stuck in the same maladaptive habits, preventing her from pursuing other career opportunities, and perpetuating unhealthy patterns in her marriage. She was able to uncover what happened in her childhood that led to these assumptions, and we took steps toward healing these assumptions through self-compassion exercises. Within a month's time, Susan's energy improved, and her pain diminished. She began to accept the existence of the voice that said she wasn't worthy and gave it less power. She also paid more attention to the story of her greatness, one that was filled with new possibilities. She created healthier boundaries in her marriage and spoke with her boss at work about pursuing new opportunities within the organization, which were welcomed with enthusiasm. As her confidence grew, her self-care habits improved, her weight started coming down, her fatigue and pain disappeared, and she and her husband began communicating better. This all happened over a three-month period.

It may sound like a pipe dream right now where you stand, but this truly did happen, and I have witnessed many clients and patients alike do the same when they put in effort and a lot of love and self-compassion. It takes longer for some than others, of course, and not everyone is lucky enough to work for an organization that supports their career goals. However, when you tap into your sense of confidence and self-value, you are better able to make decisions that are right for you, become less stuck, and find opportunities, even in the face of adversity. With time, patience, a lot of love, and connecting with your voice of compassion, you may find that you, too, can emerge out of burnout into your story of greatness.

Chapter **11**

Cultivating the Infrastructure That Supports Your Life Force

If you are feeling burned out, overwhelmed, and distressed, my telling you that you need to up the ante when it comes to your self-care may cause you more frustration. You may be thinking, "If I wasn't so tired and overworked, don't you think I would find the time to exercise and eat right?" I am not going to preach to you that you *must* exercise or that you *must* do anything for that matter. I do, however, explain the concept of your life force, explain how to connect with your energy, and provide you with a variety of self-care practices that you can employ to enliven and strengthen the force or power with which you can live your life.

When you take small steps to take care of *you*, your energy can flourish, which improves your capacity to manage everything else. Sleep, nutrient-rich food, movement, spending time in nature, laughter, social support, spirituality, and meditation are all examples of what I call "infrastructure," the system of support for your body, mind, and life. This system of support helps you manage adversity as well as luxuriate in moments of joy, and you do have the ability to cultivate and build it to suit you. This chapter shows you how.

Your Body (and Mind) Are Brilliant!

Your body-mind complex is brilliant! The body communicates with the brain and informs it through your senses. Trillions of cells, living and breathing, eating, and generating energy, let you know what they need and what you need. Your brain takes in these messages and commands action that help you adapt, live, and thrive. The messages let you know when you are tired, cold, or hungry; when you need to move; and when you need to rest. They let you know when you need to act if injustice is present, when you need to be scared and run away from a predator, and when you need a bit of TLC.

As most of us tend to be busy "doing," we tend not to listen to the body's whispers. We drink coffee when we are tired, eat when we are anxious, or berate ourselves when we need love and care. The beauty of cultivating mindfulness and compassion is that these practices teach us how to listen again, to remember that the body-mind complex is truly brilliant, and that it behooves us to fuel this amazing vessel in order to flourish. Do you not put fuel in your car when you need to drive it long distances?

REMEMBER

Everything you put in your body, surround yourself with, think, or do for yourself is either fuel or, well, it isn't. Your thoughts, the food you consume, environments that you are exposed to, relationships you have, movement that you do (or don't do), and rest and recovery (or lack thereof) either fuel you to thrive or drain your resources, causing you to dive.

Connecting with Your Life Force to Find Ease

In Traditional Chinese Medicine, the word for vital life force is Qi (also known as Chi). Qi represents the energy you have in your body as well as the energy that binds you to all things in the universe. It represents both the fuel you put in your body, such as air, water, and food, and also the vital energy and fluid that flows *through* your body that is in coherence with the flow of life.

Take a moment to think about it:

Think about your own energy as something that is fueled by the sun, moon, earth, and stars, and envision yourself intricately connected with all things. You are not separate from your environment. You are not different from the flower or tree that is nurtured by the sun in the sky, the rain that falls, bees that enable pollination, or the sustenance that the roots deliver from the earth. You, too, gain energy and vitality from the environment. Your energy and how you go about living your life in turn affects your environment, including other people and the planet itself.

Ideally, the energy moves smoothly, through you and through everything else, nurturing, sustaining, and replenishing itself, like the rainfall replenishes bodies of water and rivers.

Why am I telling you about Qi? I'm introducing this concept so that you can mindfully start paying attention to how you feel, so that you can better assess which activities, thoughts, or behaviors enliven your energy or zap you dry.

As you enhance your self-awareness, you get to know yourself better and uncover what your body is asking for. You enhance your knowledge of the different self-care practices that you can engage in, which can enrich energy and life force. You find out more about healthy nutrition, exercise that may benefit you, ways to get more sleep and rest, how to cultivate loving relationships (including with yourself), and ways to enhance your spiritual connection to all things, such as meditation, spending time in nature, or taking care of the planet.

PLAY THIS

The following exercise helps you observe how and what you feel mindfully, connect with your brain, and understand the concept of energy and how it can flow through your body.

1. **Settle in.**

   Find a comfortable position in which to sit or lie down. Close your eyes and just breathe naturally. If you find your mind is active with thoughts, simply notice them and allow them to come and go with your breath. You may say to yourself as you notice the thoughts, "thinking, thinking, thinking," and then gently bring your focus to your body.

   Take a moment or two to scan your body from head to toe, just noticing any sensations that you may be experiencing. Notice where you may feel sensations of ease or tightness, or any other feeling. Notice without judgment. You are simply observing and getting to know your body.

2. **Focus on the breath.**

   Bring your awareness to your breath. Observe the breath as it flows in and out. Notice what you experience or any sensations that arise.

   Next, count 1-2-3-4 as you breathe in, then pause for a count of 1-2, then breathe out on a count of 1-2-3-4, and then pause. Do this for four or five cycles of breath, and then notice how you feel and what you feel.

3. **Gather and release energy from and to the earth.**

   Now bring your awareness to the soles of your feet and take note of any sensations you are experiencing. Note the connection your feet have with the earth. Note the support the earth provides your body. Note the immense life force that exists in the earth.

   Imagine that as you breathe in on the count of 4, you are breathing in the life force from deep within the earth, up into your feet. On the pause count of 2, allow the energy to fill your feet. When you exhale on the count of 4, imagine your breath is helping you release toxins, tension, or anything that no longer serves you from your feet. Do this for two to three cycles of breath.

   Shift your awareness to your calves and knees, allowing anything that no longer serves you to flow out of these areas of your body into the earth when you exhale, while absorbing the vital life force of the earth as you inhale for another two or three cycles of breath.

   Continue shifting your awareness upward, doing the same with your thighs and hips, pelvis, abdomen, and so forth, as you move up your body.

4. **Connect with universal energy.**

   When you are ready, imagine that the energy within you is moving through the crown of your head to the sky or heavens above.

   Take a deep breath in, and as you exhale, imagine that the life force of the universe is shining down, moving into the crown of your head. With every breath that you inhale and exhale, this life force flows through your body, all the way down to the soles of your feet.

5. **Circulate the energy.**

   Next, when you inhale, imagine the life force is moving up through the back of your legs, up your spine and neck, and all the way to the crown of your head.

   As you exhale, the energy moves down the front of your body, all the way down to the soles of your feet.

   The orbit of your breath mirrors the orbits that circulate in the universe. Circulate the energy with your breath for at least ten cycles of breath.

6. **Settle back out.**

   Allow your breath to move into its natural rhythm. Observe how and what you feel.

This exercise shares some similarities to many Qi Gong (translated as "Energy Work") exercises from traditional Chinese medicine and is meant to help you strengthen your life force and vitality. Notice if or how your energy level shifts, as well as your mood or your ability to think more clearly as both your body and your brain will benefit.

Minding Your Nutrition

Though burnout stems from a multitude of factors, many of which are not in your control, you do have control over what you put in your body. In my almost 30 years of experience, I have found that when my patients eat more nutrient-rich food and eat *clean*, avoiding processed and fast foods and eating mostly plant-based foods, their energy and mood improve, and brain fog lifts.

Food is meant to nourish and fuel, not necessarily to calm down emotions, though it can — especially if you find yourself eating foods that are not entirely, or at all, nutritious — because it helps us feel better. Comfort foods are so-named for a reason. The problem is that that "feeling better" is temporary, and it often leads to feeling worse, because you feel either guilty about your food choices (and fat as a result) or achy, tired, and moody from the inflammation that the food creates in the body and brain.

What you choose to eat is an individual endeavor, and I don't propose here that you follow any specific diet. I don't believe in diets per se. I believe in eating nutrient-dense or rich foods, versus nutrient-poor foods, that fuel your life force or energy. I believe in choosing foods that feed the "pit crews" that exist all over your body, paying attention to what your body needs and whether you are enjoying the flavors, textures, and experiences. I recommend eating mindfully, in other words, and enjoying a variety of plant-based foods, including vegetables, fruits, whole grains, nuts, and seeds, as well as lean meats and fish — foods that come from the earth that your body can recognize and digest. In addition, if you do want something that is not on this list, eat it in small amounts and most importantly, enjoy it with gusto!

The reason I don't like to focus on "diets" is because the term implies that you are going to deny yourself something and that food is somehow evil or bad. Your brain interprets "I am going on a diet" as "I am going to starve you," which is hardly a nurturing and kind thing to do to your pit crews and neurons. If our ancestors were given the heads up that they were about to be starved, they would have gone and gathered whatever they could, as much as they could, and as fast as possible. If and when they did see food after a period of forced fasting, they would jump on the food like ravaged animals might.

REMEMBER

Food is not evil or bad. Food is fuel.

Your mood and food: Understanding the gut-brain connection

Up through my residency in medicine, I certainly ate my share of pizza, French fries, and baked goods (my weakness), especially at stressful points in my life, which were often and many. I can tell you that I felt bad afterwards, physically, mentally, and emotionally. Sure, I still accomplished a great deal, and the food helped me cope with my stress levels and anxiety. But my mood and energy also suffered as a result. It wasn't until I was long into practicing medicine that I learned more about nutrition, mood, and the brain. Believe it or not, we didn't learn about nutrition in medical school or even residency — well, at least we didn't back in the '90s. I found out because I had to figure out ways to take care of my mental health and my own energy levels. Since then, the field of nutritional psychiatry has burgeoned, and we understand a lot more about the gut-brain connection.

It is often said that the intestines are the road to a healthier, happier you, and this saying isn't wrong. What you eat not only affects your physical health, but also your mental health, thanks to the gut-brain axis, the millions of nerve cells (the same cells that are in your brain!) and the millions of microorganisms living in your gut lining. Did you know that hundreds of million nerve cells line your gastrointestinal tract that don't just help you digest food, but also guide your emotions?

Have you ever experienced a "pit" in your stomach when nervous, feel "butterflies" when excited, or feel sick to your stomach when upset? There is a reason for this! Your gastrointestinal (GI) tract is considered to be a "second brain," whereby the cells that line the GI tract can act independently of the brain and account for 95 percent of the production of serotonin, the "happy" neurotransmitter that feeds your brain. Ninety-five percent of the serotonin that courses through your brain and helps your mood, perception, and attitude is produced in your gut! What's more is that the function of these neurons and the production of these neurotransmitters is highly influenced by the billions of microorganisms and "good" bacteria, or *microbiota*, that make up your intestinal microbiome and form the gut-brain axis.

You may be thinking that it's gross to have bacteria and other microorganisms inhabiting your digestive system, but in truth, you wouldn't be alive and functioning without them, much like the vegetation and soil of the earth requires its ecosystem for life to grow and flourish.

Recommendations for minding your nutrition

I generally recommend simple guidelines when it comes to minding your nutrition, and most importantly, to avoid judging yourself. Instead, remember to honor your brilliant body and show love to your pit crews. Following are some tips to consider.

Think nourishment

Before eating, you may want to ask yourself, "Is this fuel that will nourish me?" Foods high in sugar, many baked goods, fast food, alcohol, excessive caffeine, or anything processed can wreak havoc on the digestive system, as well as your brain. You can think of such foods as nutrient poor. In contrast, foods that are high in nutrient density and quality provide the natural multivitamins and antioxidants your digestive system needs to function well, which means your brain also wins. Nutrient-rich foods include multi-colored fruits and vegetables; fish; grass-fed lean meats; grains such as quinoa, gluten-free oats, or rice; healthy fats like fish oil or avocado oil; and nuts and seeds.

Take good care of your microbiome

A healthy gut means having trillions of happy microorganisms living, digesting, absorbing, and promoting a healthy immune system and a happy mind. Focus on increasing your intake of food groups that contain live cultures of bacteria like Lactobacillus and Bifidobacterium, or *probiotics,* as well as the foods that help feed them, or *prebiotics. Fermented* foods have been "cultured," and therefore enhance the amount of "good bugs" in your gut. Such foods include pickles, sauerkraut, tempeh, kefir, and miso, for example. Examples of foods that feed the microbiome, or prebiotics, include onions, garlic, leeks, legumes, asparagus, and artichokes.

Add balance

The microbiome in your gut thrives when you bring balance into your life, not just to your meals. You can add balance by increasing positive social interactions, times for rest and relaxation, and stress reduction activities, such as spending time in nature, meditating, speaking to a counselor, relaxing with your pet, or getting a massage.

Slow down

A hectic lifestyle and high workload can take a toll on your gut, health, and mood. How do you slow down when there is so much to do? Practice mindfulness when you can, as it will at least slow down your brain chatter and help you be present in the moment. Steal brief naps when possible or take little meditation breaks. Chew slowly (try counting to 40 when you chew). Eat mindfully. Appreciate the food on your plate — colors, smells, where it comes from, how lucky you are that you are about to be nourished, and so forth. Stop when you notice that you feel full. Appreciate again.

Get colorful

Because your gut makes up a large part of your defense system against disease and pathogens through its physical barrier, its ecosystem (friendly microorganisms), and the immune cells that live there, you want to help your gut along by living an anti-inflammatory life when possible. You can provide your body with ammunition and necessary antioxidants by consuming colorful fruits and vegetables such as kale, raspberries, string beans, sweet potatoes, avocado, spinach, apples, and cantaloupe, for example. Keep in mind that there are trillions of microorganisms in your gut, and they don't all prefer the same foods. The key, therefore, is having a variety of plant-based foods to keep them, and therefore your mood, happy.

Think about adding, not taking away

When you diet, you are essentially telling the brain that you plan to starve, which can trigger the fight or flight response. Denying yourself nutrition is therefore not the way to get healthier. Try not to focus on weight or how you look but on healing burnout and thriving. You are rebuilding your system. Focus on adding a variety of hopefully delicious, nutrient-rich foods rather than dieting. Make it a goal to eat at least 30 different kinds of plant-based foods throughout your week. You can easily do this by making a salad with mixed greens (you've already gotten to three or four out of thirty in one meal when you take into account the different lettuce types), avocado, berries, cucumbers, corn, sunflower seeds, and some cold-pressed olive oil and lemon. You can add other spices or herbs like oregano or cilantro, which offer more flavor as well as antioxidant properties. Make your plate colorful and filled with variety. Most importantly, enjoy it!

Remember to hydrate

Many of us often forget to drink enough water throughout the day. The cells of your brain and body require a great deal of hydration to function well. Depending on your activity level (if you are sweating, for instance), you generally want to think about getting half your body weight in ounces of water a day. For instance, if you weight 150 pounds, aim to drink about 75 ounces of water a day.

If you are going to eat it, do it with mindful gusto

Bringing shame and guilt into the mix when you are meant to be nurturing yourself is not helpful. When in doubt, try to follow an 80/20 plan, whereby 80 percent of your food intake is nutrient rich and plant based, and 20 percent can be your "what the heck" food. Odds are that with this type of ratio, your body can handle what you take in, so if you do eat food that isn't particularly nutrient rich, at least enjoy it. Eat it mindfully and savor every delicious bite. Then, at least, you get in a mindfulness, savoring practice. At the same time, you can also notice how you feel after you eat such foods, perhaps later in the day or the next day. The key is to pay attention without judging yourself so that you can make mindful choices and prepare yourself. It is also important to note that when you are burned out, you may want to stick more closely to a 90/10 plan or even a 100 percent clean eating plan the first couple of weeks, just to reset your system and build up your wiggle room so that any nutrient-poor food you ingest doesn't have such a big impact on you.

REMEMBER

Again, don't judge yourself — or food, for that matter — as being good or bad. Think of nurturing your body, your brain, and the beautiful ecosystem that exists within you. Eating mindfully enlivens your experience of eating and helps you remember how to really appreciate and enjoy your food. It helps you make healthier choices and eat slower, and it can also improve your mood while you're at it.

Why You Want to Get Your Move On

It's well documented that exercise is good for your mental and physical health. Aerobic exercise can boost mood, including anxiety and depression; lower stress levels; and improve memory, self-esteem, and cognitive functioning. The exact mechanisms as to why moving your muscles can have such a significant effect on mental health aren't fully clear, but scientists do know there is a process of *neuroplasticity*, the release of neurotransmitters like serotonin and endorphins, and changes in the stress response system. It's also thought to be partially due to the notion that you are moving and exercising, which enables you to feel better about yourself, feeling more self-efficacy and confident.

Another reason exercise may influence mental health is that when you move different muscles, you activate the corresponding neurons in the brain to come alive. When those same muscles are inactive, the neurons can become dormant and may even, in some cases as we age, wither away. It explains the saying that "if you don't use it, you lose it." The good news is that because of neuroplasticity, even if you don't use your muscles for a long time, when you start using them again, the brain cells can be reactivated to form new connections again.

Indeed, the body was designed to move, not to sit for long periods in a chair or in front of a computer. Perhaps you can observe for yourself if your energy improves when you make a concerted effort to move your body for a few minutes or more every hour on the hour, versus sitting at your desk for seven or eight hours straight.

Exercising for stress relief

The beauty of exercise is that it helps move your energy and relieve tension. As you are likely aware, mental stress can lead to physical tension, and physical tension can lead to mental stress. Moving your body can release both physical and mental tension. Exercise is a stress-buster for even more reasons, including the following:

>> **It boosts your endorphins.** Physical activity may help bump up the production of your brain's natural painkillers and mood elevators, chemicals called *endorphins*. Endorphins are responsible for "runner's high" and for the feelings of relaxation and optimism that accompany many hard workouts — or, at least, the hot shower after your exercise is over.

>> **It reduces levels of stress hormones.** Physical activity reduces levels of stress hormones such as adrenalin and cortisol.

>> **It provides positive stress to the body.** Exercise can imitate the effects of stress and help your body and its systems practice working together through those effects.

>> **It improves self-image and confidence.** Behavioral factors also contribute to the emotional benefits of exercise. As your strength and stamina increase, your self-image also improves. You may feel a sense of mastery and control.

>> **It improves your mood.** Regular exercise can increase self-confidence, improve your mood, help you relax, and lower symptoms of mild depression and anxiety. Exercise can also improve your sleep, which is often disrupted by stress, depression, and anxiety.

>> **It helps you lose your worries for a while.** Exercise and sports also provide opportunities to get away from it all and either enjoy some solitude or make friends and build networks, letting go of thoughts and worries for a bit.

All of these exercise benefits can ease your stress levels and give you a sense of command over your body and your life. The tricky part is either finding the time to exercise or, especially when you're feeling burned out, finding the energy.

Exercising when you feel burned out

When you feel burned out and fatigued, or even just crunched for time, the notion of exercise can be overwhelming. It may be hard to get motivated, or you may feel more achy and tired when you push yourself physically. If you have physiological burnout, it could mean that your adrenal glands can't mount the proper response to stress, and exercising, at least at high intensity, can make you feel worse. Feeling tired after a good, vigorous workout is normal. But when you have physical or physiological burnout, symptoms can be more severe. You may feel utterly drained, have intense body aches, have trouble sleeping, and experience changes in your appetite that can last for days on end. You may feel exhausted all the time, drained, and ultimately, uninterested in doing anything, especially anything related to moving your body.

Because every *body* is different, it's important to be mindful of what movement supports and enlivens your mood and energy, and what drains it. The exercise that works for someone else may not work for you. It's a matter of finding the right balance between when you move, how you fuel yourself, and how often you take time to rest and recover. As you build up your resources and energy over time, the type of movement or exercise you can partake in will improve. The first step is to enhance your sense of interest and motivation to *want* to move your body.

Building exercise into your life

If you find you need help implementing an exercise program, the following sections provide some tips to get your started.

Take it slow

This is not a race. More is not better. Start with simple movements like walking or a slow bike ride. You can turn on some music and dance for ten minutes or less. Whatever you choose to do, keep the movements light and slow, and if you need to, short. You may want start with a five-minute daily walk, for example, and increase the time you spend walking by one to five minutes each week, gauging how you feel. Or you may start with five minutes two or three times a day. You can do body weight movements like air squats or lunges, perhaps five to ten, once a day and slowly increase the number every week. If you are unsure how to proceed, you can consider working with a trainer who is knowledgeable about burnout symptoms.

Focus on fitness, not on your weight, how you look, or how much you are doing

If you focus on being thinner or looking better, lifting more weights, or running as fast as you ran in high school, you may find yourself stuck in a cycle of shame, blame, and often, failure and inadequacy. Negative self-image is not a great motivator, at least not in a sustainable way, and it's a primary reason many people get to fitness burnout. The key is to have compassion for yourself and focus on enlivening your energy. Concentrate instead on providing your brain and body with plenty of love and support, which includes proper fuel and rest, so that you can be fit to handle your life. The goal is for you to enjoy moving, not hate yourself because of it.

Factor in a lot of rest and recovery time

Again, your life is not a race, nor is the need to exercise. Right now, your body may need more recovery time than other people's. That's okay. Know that muscles repair themselves and grow during the recovery period; therefore, it's essential for any person, including high-level athletes, to sleep and rest when it comes to getting fitter and stronger.

Do what you love with people you love

If you engage in activities that you enjoy, you're more likely to do them repeatedly. So too, if you exercise with a friend, you are more likely to stay motivated and engaged. A myriad of options exists for you to choose from. If you're not enjoying yourself or are bored, you won't do it. Try different movement activities, turn up the music, get out in nature, be mindful of how you feel physically and emotionally, switch it up, get a buddy, and have some fun.

Fuel yourself

Remember, food is fuel. It provides you with the energy your brain and body need to function optimally in life. When you exercise, your body needs adequate fuel to perform. Your muscles need carbohydrates and protein. Your brain likes these too, as well as healthy fats. And all of you requires hydration. Practice being mindful, listening to your body, and noticing what helps you feel more energized.

Tapping into mindful movement to heal burnout

Many wisdom traditions incorporate mindful movement techniques like Qi Gong or yoga. The guiding principle of these practices is the coordination of body movements, focused attention of the mind, and breath control to improve energy and well-being. Also known as mindful movement or meditation in motion, they're the perfect remedy for enlivening your energy, calming your mind, enhancing your mood, and moving your body when you feel burned out. It's not just aerobic exercise that has mental health benefits, after all, but the actual movement itself, especially when combined with a type of meditative practice. You can walk mindfully, stretch mindfully, or dance — you guessed it — mindfully.

TIP

An easy practice to do is the "Where Are My Feet" exercise (see Chapter 8) and add in a slow walk. Focus on how your feet feel touching the earth, how it feels when you shift your weight, the feel of the ground, the texture of your socks or shoes, and so forth, all the while taking nice, slow deep breaths.

Taking Time for Recovery

Your brain and body need a time-out for rest, for quiet, to refuel, and to regenerate. Even your car needs pit stops to refuel, change the tires, and let the engine cool off. When you embrace opportunities to take a time-out — to rest, sleep, meditate, let yourself off the hook, or simply be — you build an even stronger foundation within yourself that supports you to heal from burnout.

Why sleep when there is so much to do?

During sleep, your cells repair themselves, your brain cleans itself of toxins and forms new memories, and the body gets a chance to refuel its resources. Stress hormone levels fall, and other hormones, such as growth hormones, rise. Without adequate levels of sleep, the balance of your hormones, immune system, and virtually every system of your body is taxed. Good sleep improves your brain function, boosts your immune system, helps your weight stay under better control, keeps your appetite in check, regulates your emotions, and much, much more.

To begin the process of improving your sleep, consider following these sleep hygiene guidelines:

>> **Avoid ingested stimulants.** Try not to drink too much alcohol, caffeine, or sugar, especially in the evening.

>> **Implement stimulus control.** Remove all electronics, work, or other objects that stimulate your brain. Your bedroom is a place for sleep and sex only.

>> **Set a schedule.** Go to bed and wake up at the same time every day so that your body gets into a rhythm. Avoid napping unless you have lost sleep time at night and need to catch up.

>> **Exercise your body during the day.** Physical exercise helps regulate cortisol levels and other neurochemicals, helping you get more restful sleep at night. Hard workouts tend to improve deep sleep.

>> **Calm your mind.** It's important for your mind to be calm and quiet so that you can go into deep sleep. You can do a meditation prior to going to sleep. Definitely don't work or watch the news for at least an hour, if not more, prior to going to sleep.

>> **Eat early.** You don't want your digestive system having to work hard while you are trying to sleep. You also don't want your body to be hungry. Have a nourishing meal several hours before bedtime that isn't too heavy.

>> **Optimize your sleep environment.** Make sure your bedroom is quiet and dark and that your bed is comfortable. Disturbances like noise and light may keep you from getting deep and restorative sleep.

Giving yourself permission to pause

Most of us are used to going 100 miles an hour every day, all day. There is always something do and much more to get done. Rather than thinking about not having enough time, perhaps you can consider that you will benefit from taking regular *pauses* throughout the day, so that the time you have is spent well. These pauses can last seconds to minutes, from a few to many. The effects are cumulative. The same goes with sleep. You have a sleep bank, and if you take naps and time to meditate, it adds up, providing your body and brain with time to recover and gain more energy.

You can take short pauses throughout your day. You can pause and do a breath focus, listen to a guided meditation, do a movement meditation, repeat a mantra or affirmation along with deep breathing, bathe your senses in nature, or practice mindfulness. You can do any of the mindfulness practices shared in this book or be anywhere. You can immerse your senses in experiencing the present moment, enjoying a gentle breeze against your skin, the aroma of your food, the temperature of the water and how it feels on your skin when you shower, or the beauty of the blue sky or shapes of the clouds as they pass by. The more frequent or longer these pauses are, the more time you are giving your body toward recovery, being gentler with yourself, and understanding how to better listen to your body and what it needs.

Exercise: Taking a pause in stillness

The following exercise guides you to practice shifting your gaze to focus on details and then on the spaces in between the details, while also having you pay attention to how you feel and what you sense.

1. **Examine with a wide lens.**

   If you can go outside or look out your window, take a moment to gaze at a tree or a group of flowers as if you are looking at the entire flower or tree with a wide-angle lens. See if you can notice the different details — colors, contours, sizes, any motion, the contrast of the sky, sun, or clouds, and so forth.

2. **Examine with a zoom lens.**

   Then imagine that you have a zoom lens and zoom in on one leaf or petal and notice all the details of this one leaf or petal. Trace the shape, contour, color, size, and so forth. Zoom in and notice everything about the leaf or petal.

3. **Shift your gaze into space.**

   When you are ready, shift your lens to gaze at the empty space in between the leaves or petals. Focus on the space in between.

   Imagine that you are floating in this space in between. You are floating in a space where nothing exists, just yet. Notice how and what you feel, floating in the space in between.

4. **Expand the lens.**

   When ready, widen your lens and notice the entire tree or flower again, this time taking in all the spaces in between the leaves or petals.

   Continue to expand your lens even wider to notice the expanse of space around the tree or flower. Notice the vastness of the sky, earth, field, planet, or universe. Notice how space connects all objects, people, plants, and so forth. Gently observe how and what your body feels as well.

5. **Settle back in to reflect.**

   Shift your lens to focus on your own body, noticing how you feel sitting where you are, the weight of your body sitting on the chair or floor, any sensations you may be experiencing, the movement of your breath, and the space around you in the room. Gently bring yourself back into the now.

Being nurtured by nature

If you really want to get the best bang for your buck to gain more energy with minimal movement, take a pause in nature. Did you know that according to new research by Ming Kuo, spending time outdoors in nature promotes health and can improve your mood, vitality, and even immunity?

Any time in nature is beneficial, but if you can, try to step out in nature for at least 15 minutes a day, whether you take a walk, hike, picnic, garden, or fall asleep lying on a blanket in a field. Nature is loaded with unseen elements like negative ions and phytoncides — chemicals that stimulate or relax your brain and benefit your immune system as they lower your stress response. When you are outside, exposed to the beauty of nature, its variability, its smells and sounds, the brain automatically shifts into a positive mental state, as does the body. Note that you can bring nature into your home with plants, photos of nature, and the like, all of which can also improve mental health.

My favorite place to practice mindfulness is in nature. I find that it is easier to engage all my senses in the experience of being in nature, and when I do, I achieve a state of calm and clarity more easily. Scientists have discovered that enjoying a mindful walk in nature reduces stress and improves energy, cognitive functioning, and immunity, especially when the walk involves "forest bathing" (Ye Wen, et al.). Also known as Shinrin-Yoku, "forest bathing" involves bathing all of your senses in the experience of walking through a forest. It was developed in Japan almost 40 years ago and has become an integral part of healing and preventive medicine in Japan. Just 15 minutes of forest bathing can result in the blood pressure dropping, mental clarity, improved concentration, and reduced stress levels.

TIP

Consider getting 15 to 20 minutes of nature time every day, if possible, even if it means taking your work outside. If you can, take a mindful walk in nature and just make sure you leave your mobile phone behind, as well as your camera, so you can walk aimlessly and mindfully. The goal is to have no expectations or goals in mind and to simply allow your body to guide you where it wants to go. Take moments to pause and gaze around you. Sit down where you feel your body wants to sit. Close your eyes and smell, hear, and feel. Do the "Where Are My Feet" exercise from Chapter 8. Notice the sensations you experience in your body as you sit and when you are walking.

Playing is not just for kids

According to Dr. Stuart Brown, play deprivation is a real issue. He says in his TED talk, "The opposite of play is not work; it's depression." Playing is just as important for your health and well-being as exercise, nutrient-rich food, being in nature, and restful sleep.

When you play, you give yourself the opportunity to take yourself or life less seriously and instead focus on allowing yourself to be momentarily carefree, laughing, amused, and simply engaging in something you enjoy. You may choose to play a sport or a board game, watch a funny movie, or play an instrument just for fun. Choose activities that you can do on your own or find playmates to join you, and observe your energy improve.

A myriad of ways exists to play, and of course, the ones that give you joy are the ones you want to partake in. Find activities that you love. Do you enjoy painting, dancing, playing cards, playing an instrument, or singing karaoke? Schedule at least one hour a week to engage in this fun activity. Plan a hike, a treasure hunt, or a game night with friends or take time to watch a funny movie.

TIP

Play dates aren't just for kids. Our lives can get so busy that by the end of the week we aren't sure how time flew by so quickly. Schedule play dates with people you enjoy being around at least once a week.

Allowing Time for Connection and Belonging

Spending time in nature, playing, and pausing in stillness have many benefits in common, one of which is that they can help you experience a greater sense of connection. The sense of belonging and being connected are qualities that support you to bounce back when meeting life's challenges; perform better under duress; have more positive expectations of the future, positive emotions, and better relationships; and pave a path to healing burnout.

Humans have an intrinsic need and motivation to belong. It is internally wired. The desire to belong and connect influences behavior, beliefs, and even your values. It affects what you may do to conform your behaviors to gain acceptance, how you may see yourself in comparison to others, and how you may want to be seen. It influences if and how you seek support from those around you and how you make meaning and find purpose in the face of hardship. The stronger your sense of belonging and connection — to other people, to the larger world within which you exist, and to yourself — the better able you can heal from burnout and ultimately, come out of it happy and thriving.

Why the sense of belonging can help you come out of burnout

Feeling like we belong stimulates dopamine reward systems in the brain, which are what propel intrinsic motivation, according to neuroscientists Stephano L. Di Domenico and Richard M. Ryan. These are the same reward centers that are stimulated when we get high from doing something we enjoy or when we get addicted to a substance. Indeed, there are many rewards when it comes to feeling like we belong to a community or social group. It supports self-esteem, self-efficacy or competency in managing problems, and the belief that we matter, that we have something to offer and something to contribute. These are all traits that positively influence resilience.

Like many young adults who leave school to enter the working world, I found finishing my residency and joining the force of working primary care doctors was very challenging, not because of the job itself, but because I lost my community of fellow residents, interns, students, and fellows, as well as nurses and other hospital staff. Because of the high stress and workload in those days at Boston Medical Center, we had to work as a team, share values, and find ways to get along. We understood one another, shared inside jokes, and bored other people with our conversations when we went to social functions that included non-hospital personnel. I didn't realize how important that sense of belonging was to me until it was gone, when most everyone, except for me, finished their residencies and left Boston to pursue their careers. I remember feeling quite depressed and empty, as if I were going through withdrawal, and I had to make myself seek out opportunities to find a new community. It took time, but it was necessary and worth it in the long run as I, like everyone else, needed the connection, support, and sense of belonging.

Cultivating a sense of connection with a Love Pyramid

When I wrote my first book, *The Love Response* (Ballantine), I wrote about the Love Pyramid, a way you can create a life structure to support you through life's stresses, sustain your needs, and assist your growth, which involved accessing love in its various forms. The Love Pyramid is composed of three layers: The base is comprised of Social Love, or the love and support given and received between yourself and others; the middle is comprised of Self Love, or the love, nurturance, and compassion you provide to yourself; and the top layer, Spiritual Love, is the connection you possess with all of life, the universe, and all that is, seen and unseen.

Each of these layers involves connection and belonging, and each layer is part of our human makeup, which means we need each one to thrive and flourish. When you build stronger and healthier connections with other people, you gain resources and help in times of need. When you are treated with loving kindness by others, you also remember that you are a valued human being yourself and are more likely to treat yourself with compassion and care. So, too, when you feel like you belong to something greater and more profound, you are better able to make meaning from hardship, connect with feelings of awe, and find strength to handle adversity.

The importance of social support

Humans are social creatures. Early in our evolution, our ancestors did not have comfortable homes and readily available food, clothes, transportation, and communication devices. Their lives were hard and often threatened by the environment or predators. It was relatively impossible for humans to exist on their own, let alone a pregnant woman, a child, or an infant. It was imperative that they stuck together, and this bond enabled our species to be resilient.

We are thus biologically wired to bond with one another so that our species can survive, and it is hardly surprising that supportive relationships help us manage hardships, be resilient, and get through burnout. So, too, it is often the lack of such social support that can lead to burnout. The key word here is "supportive." Not all relationships support your resilience and health. In their 2003 study, Kiecolt-Glaser and colleagues found, for example, that couples in troubled marriages produce more stress hormones during conflict, levels of which persist to stay elevated throughout the day and night, than those couples whose marriages are not troubled. Conversely, according to the 2010 study "Social Relationships and Mortality Risk: A Meta-analytic Review" by Julian Holt-Lunstad and colleagues, quality relationships buffer stress, help you live longer and heal faster, and improve behaviors.

Quality relationships involve mutual commitment and support; trust; genuine care; and the willingness to grow, collaborate, and compromise. They involve seeing value in yourself and others, good communication, acceptance, and reciprocity. Numerous studies have pointed to the benefits of social support in helping people manage adversity and get through illness. Not all relationships are created equal, and the next chapter can help you examine your social connections and show you how to improve them so they can support you to heal.

Achieving self-love

Self-love is often the most difficult form of love to achieve, especially when you feel badly, incomplete, less than whole, or burned out. Building self-love entails cultivating self-compassion and self-nurturance. It is based on the principle that you are both part of humanity, and therefore share joy and suffering with others, and that you are also unique and one-of-a kind. Sure, you are flawed, and so is everyone else. Your imperfections are part of your individual makeup and are neither good nor bad. Indeed, your imperfections are part of the perfection that is you!

Building self-love involves learning to perceive yourself without judgment, with openness, interest, and of course, love. By using your tools to take care of yourself, to bring love into your heart and life, and to let go of your fears and shame, you can learn to feel stronger internally, have a better sense of well-being, improve your relationships, and have more faith in your internal and external resources to manage uncertainty.

Self-love is not an option but a necessity if you want to heal from burnout. Fear not if you are having difficulty with the self-compassion practices or self-love. It will come with time.

The more you practice and the more you learn to receive love, the more you will discover that you can reach deep inside of you where your beliefs can shift into viewpoints that support and nourish your life.

Connecting with spirituality

A growing body of literature is showing that a spiritual outlook makes humans more resilient and that people who have a stronger sense of purpose and meaning in their life are more likely to have a higher quality of life, better health and functioning, and greater ability to cope with adversity, including burnout. In his research, Harold D. Koeneg has found that individuals with a strong connection to spirituality have better coping skills, social support, and a higher sense of well-being. It suggests that greater spirituality is also associated with healthier behaviors. Being burned out doesn't mean you are not spiritually inclined. It just means that when you connect to your sense of spirituality, you have a bigger bandwidth to handle challenges in your life. You can think of it as spirituality adding fuel to your tank and supporting your energy or life force.

Connecting with your sense of spirituality doesn't necessarily mean being religious. Religion is only one path to spirituality. Though many perspectives exist as to what defines spirituality, it is agreed that spirituality translates to the sense of being profoundly connected to something larger, a sense of purpose, and a belief that there is meaning to life's experiences. You can pray, meditate, join a spiritual community, follow a religious practice, connect with a sense of purpose, or commune with nature. You can join a spiritual group such as a church or synagogue, have a daily gratitude ritual, spend time in nature, perform acts of kindness, or practice loving kindness meditation. Whether you believe in God, a higher power, or simply feel profoundly connected to nature, there is no right way to connect to your sense of spirituality other than to connect with the way that works for you.

Expressing loving kindness does not mean enhancing intimacy or romantic love but rather choosing to care for everyone, including people you don't know, and especially yourself. Perhaps you can take a moment to practice the loving kindness meditation (LKM) explained in Chapter 9. The purpose of this meditation is to melt down the negativity you may have toward yourself or others, melt down walls of separation, and to open your mind and heart to deeper levels of feeling love and kindness. It is a practice that not only can connect you with a sense of connection and belonging but can also bring you peace and stillness, and ultimately, nourish your life force.

Self-assessing your infrastructure

I encourage you to take some time to reflect on your current infrastructure. In a 2012 study evaluating 7,200 surgeons, Tait D. Shanafelt and colleagues found that the ones who were least likely to be burned out had more strongly positive answers to the following questions. As you read along, reflect on whether the statement is true for you. Write down your answer as well as the reason why it is true or not true.

>> I find meaning in my work.

>> I protect time away from work for my spouse, family, and friends.

>> I focus on what is most important to me in life.

>> I try to take a positive outlook on things.

>> I take vacations.

>> I participate in recreation, hobbies, and exercise.

>> I talk with family, a significant other, or friends about how I am feeling.

>> I incorporate a life philosophy stressing balance in my personal and professional life.

>> I look forward to retirement.

>> I discuss stressful aspects of work with colleagues.

>> I nurture the religious/spiritual aspects of myself.

>> I engage in contemplative practices or other mindfulness activities such as meditation, narrative medicine, or appreciative inquiry, and so on.

>> I engage in reflective writing or other journaling techniques.

>> I have regular meetings with a psychologist/psychiatrist to discuss stress.

Chapter **12**

Establishing High-Quality Connections

S ocial isolation is defined as the quantitative or qualitative lack of interactions with other people on an individual, group, or community level. According to Ruda Clarie and colleagues, social isolation, especially loneliness or perceived social isolation (meaning you feel isolated even though you are around other people), is associated with poor life satisfaction, higher work-related stress, less trust of institutions, increased substance abuse, domestic abuse, worsening psychological symptoms, and burnout, which surged during the COVID-19 pandemic. Indeed, loneliness has been found to be one of the most powerful negative influences on increasing depressive symptoms, and it can be a big factor in pushing someone toward burnout.

On the flip side, strong social connections support human beings to thrive and manage adversity, to feel a sense of belonging and that they're not alone, especially when struggling. To heal burnout, it's important to work toward improving social connections, especially healing those that may be broken, while aiming to cultivate new positive connections. This chapter explores the importance of connection and how to heal and foster collaboration and healthy, strong relationships that support you to thrive.

Connection as the Foundation for Healing, Growing, and Thriving

Positive connection, the sense of belonging, and the love and support that you give and receive throughout your life support your everyday existence. They serve as stimulants for your personal growth, self-concept and identity, and ability to make meaning of the hardships in your life. Just as you need to breathe in and breathe out, you also need positive connections.

Human beings are innately wired to connect, and we are hard-wired with a neurobiological mechanism that encourages us to bond so that a pregnant female isn't left to fend for herself, children are not abandoned by their parents, and communities can pull together during times of adversity and hardship. The foundation of this wiring is love. Love and affection elicit a host of physiological changes that include the release of the hormone oxytocin into the bloodstream, which promotes bonding and attachment and increases sociability. Oxytocin has other beneficial effects as well, such as lowering stress hormone levels, reducing pain, improving wound healing, and enhancing mood and feelings of hope and euphoria.

Positive social connections involve both asking for help and giving help, building community and relying on community, supporting and being supported, and giving and receiving love and compassion. For many, especially people who eventually arrive at burnout, supporting others comes easily, while accepting support and compassion is challenging. The result is that the person who is giving and not receiving can end up feeling burned out.

Building connection through compassion

If you don't feel worthy of love and support, chances are you won't let love and compassion in, even if they are knocking at your door. With less gas in the proverbial gas tank, this can then lead to increasing feelings of overwhelm, fatigue, and ultimately, burnout. Thing is, when you are at your lowest, a caring word or gesture from someone can make the difference between whether you collapse or find the strength to keep moving. The feeling of not being alone in your suffering can transform your pain into something that is more manageable and even uplift you.

REMEMBER

Practicing mindful compassion helps you accept yourself and others as they are; ensure your expectations align with reality; and improve your ability to communicate, resolve differences, and heal. Through compassion you can offset feelings of isolation and loneliness and enhance positive connection as it imparts a willingness to acknowledge and recognize your own and other's suffering, while also having a motivation to alleviate it. Compassion then becomes a two-way street, and you are better able to create and sustain positive connections.

Practice: Giving and receiving compassion

A wonderful mindful compassion practice is called *tonglen*, the Tibetan word for giving and receiving. It involves using breath to fill up with loving kindness and then exhale to share it with others. The element of the breath helps provide the sense of connection with yourself and all things, as the breath is ever present and ever flowing. Because it is a mindfulness exercise, the aim is to be present with your experience, notice any resistance that may arise, become aware of any emotions, thoughts, or changes that occur, and regularly and gently bring your awareness to the present moment of the breath if you find your mind starts wandering. The combination of mindfulness using a breath focus with the element of allowing loving kindness to flow in and out then becomes a wonderful way to achieve more peace and acceptance, while also creating more space within you to foster loving connections with yourself and others.

Whether you do it in the heat of the moment or you have time to step away from a stressful situation, this practice helps you experience love and kindness in the moment. The breath opens you up to hear, listen, speak, and understand, without judgment or negative triggers getting in the way. You create room in your heart so that the space is large enough to hold loving kindness for yourself and your own suffering as well as for other people and their suffering.

The following is a Giving and Receiving Compassion practice adapted from Chris Gerber and Kristine Neff's work on self-compassion.

1. **Get comfortable.**

   Find a comfortable position. Close your eyes and, if you like, place a hand on your heart or abdomen as a way to comfort yourself as you ground yourself in this loving experience.

2. **Connect with the breath.**

   Breathe in deeply; then exhale completely. Gently bring your awareness to your breath as you breathe in and out.

   Notice how your chest rises and falls as you inhale and exhale, or how your abdomen moves.

   Let your breath move into its own natural rhythm. Notice any sensations you may be experiencing as you breathe in and out. Notice the rhythm of the breath. Perhaps it is like the waves of the ocean that flow in and out. In and out. Perhaps you can allow yourself to feel moved by the rhythm of the breath as if you are being gently rocked or cradled.

3. Connect with nourishment.

Consider that every time you breathe in, the breath nourishes you, and when you breathe out, it soothes you and helps remove that which doesn't serve you. Every breath you breathe in is another breath that brings nourishment to your mind, body, and soul. Every time you exhale, your breath moves through you, comforting and soothing, clearing away anything that no longer serves you.

Imagine you are breathing in something nourishing or whatever it is you may need, be it love, guidance, support, acceptance, kindness, or compassion. Allow yourself to receive it as you breathe in and flow through your body as you breathe out. Every breath you breathe in delivers more nourishment and whatever it is that you need into your lungs and into the rest of your body.

As you breathe out, your whole body is just letting go of whatever it has been holding onto. Notice the ease of exhalation and letting go.

4. Visualize connecting with another person.

When you are ready, bring to mind someone you dearly care for or someone you know who is struggling and needs compassion. See this person clearly in your mind's eye.

As you breathe, continue to breathe in loving kindness or whatever else you may need but this time as you exhale, intentionally direct this warmth and kindness to the other person. Breathe in compassion and love, and exhale to share ease and kindness with this person. If you're feeling a little empty, focus on filling yourself up first, and when letting it flow out feels easy, allow it to flow out to the other person.

5. One for me, one for you.

When you are ready, just focus on the sensation of breathing compassion and love or anything good in and out. You may want to say to yourself, *"One for me and one for you,"* allowing the cycle of your breath to mirror the cycle of giving and receiving, receiving and giving; flowing in, flowing out, and flowing back in again.

You may want to create more cycles of breath with other people, a group of people, a country, or every living being, knowing that your breath is ever flowing and ever present.

6. Let it settle in.

When you are ready, open your eyes and allow the experience to settle in. Perhaps take a moment to reflect on the experience.

Managing Difficult Relationships

Not all relationships are created equal. Some relationships are supportive and nurturing, while others can be hostile and destructive. When you are burned out, it may be more important than ever to have more of the former than the latter. When you cultivate healthy relationships that support you to thrive, you are also better able to let go of those that may lead you to dive.

If you find that your goals, expectations, values, and purpose are not aligned with the person you are in a relationship with, be it a romantic partner, friend, family member, or colleague, you may find yourself in constant conflict, falling into negative patterns, trying to fix the other person or help them at your own expense, and overall feeling more drained than invigorated. The impact of such a relationship can be devastating on both your mental and physical health. You may find yourself experiencing more anxiety, insecurity, depression, shame, or guilt, especially if you assume most of the responsibility for the troubles in the relationship and have difficulty expressing or communicating your needs for fear of losing the connection.

Know that if you find yourself in one or more difficult relationships, there are ways to improve these relationships, and if they don't get better, you have the option to leave. The key is to heal your own fears around feeling disconnected, for that fear is usually what drives your anger, anxiety, or subsequent maladaptive coping behaviors. It also involves addressing your expectations.

The pain of feeling or fearing disconnection

When you feel loved, other people's actions and behaviors bother you less, and you are more likely to feel compassion and forgiveness toward their actions rather than anger and resentment. Think about a time when you felt wonderful, perhaps a time when you fell in love or had great success at work or play. Your heart felt open and full, and you seemed to have a permanent smile on your face. Almost nothing bothered you.

Now recall the opposite scenario — a time when you felt tired, overwhelmed, or unhappy about the way you looked or felt. Perhaps this is how you feel right now. Do you have the same capacity for understanding, forgiveness, or compassion?

When you are running on empty, the capacity to connect with yourself and others is greatly diminished. Remember the bonding hormone, oxytocin? When the stress response is activated and negative emotions abound, oxytocin levels plummet along with other neurotransmitters like dopamine and serotonin. There is a biological reason for this. If you are being attacked, it behooves you not to try and hug the massive predator that is trying to eat you or your children. The fear of pain, of being disconnected from life or your loved ones, activates a fight or flight response that motivates lifesaving behaviors. The problem is that even though you are currently running on empty and are miserable at work or in your relationship, it is unlikely that your life is in actual danger (if it is, that's a different discussion). Yet the fight or flight response and associated emotional patterns and behaviors persist.

REMEMBER

The first steps in managing your difficult relationships are — yes, you guessed it — having compassion for yourself and allowing yourself to feel the pain so it can be healed. Without exploring and healing underlying fears and wounds, you may find yourself falling into the same negative patterns in your relationships and not achieving the loving and fulfilling relationships you deserve to have.

The cost of anger unexplored

Anger is a natural and necessary emotion and is meant to protect you. It lets you know when injustice is present, when you are hurt, and when you felt victimized or vulnerable in the past. The problem is not the emotion, but the subsequent reaction or behavior that stems from anger.

Think about a time you were angry — or perhaps you feel angry or resentful right now. It can affect your sleep; cause you to feel like you are on edge all day, argue with your loved ones, and have a hard time appreciating anything or finding pleasure; and lead you to crave food, a cigarette, or a drink. When expressed appropriately, anger can be a useful emotion, as it propagates action and change. When uncontrolled, however, it can lead to a myriad of problems including anxiety, physical ailments, destructive habits, addictive behaviors, crumbling of relationships, other social problems, and even losing your job.

Connecting expectations and unmet needs

If you look closely at your difficult relationships, you may discover that sometimes you see people not for who they are but what you want them to be, and more often, who or what you expect or *need* them to be. Not seeing a person for who they really are, apart from the role they play in serving your needs, can have the unwelcome side effect of leaving you feeling hurt, neglected, disappointed, or angry, as your needs are not being met. This can be a setup for disillusionment and dissatisfaction in any relationship.

I'm not telling you not to have expectations, just as I haven't told you not to feel your feelings. Expectations exist to signal you that something is out of balance within you and that you have unmet needs. Your expectations guide you to better define your needs so that you don't expect a waiter to hand you medications or a pharmacist to serve you a meal. As is true for most people, you may not be aware of your needs, especially your deeper needs.

REMEMBER

If you dig deeply, you may uncover unmet needs, and by identifying them, you are better able to take personal responsibility for them and take care of them. You may find yourself feeling more whole and complete, and, as a result, have fewer expectations of others. You can more easily overcome fear and anger, make rational decisions, and accept the person for their true nature. Then you can decide whether it is best for you to stay and work on the relationship, or leave.

Exercise: Exploring expectations and meeting unmet needs

To begin, spend a few moments contemplating the expectations you place on yourself as well as the expectations you place on others. If you are unsure how to figure out what your expectations may be, think about scenarios that cause you to get upset, anxious, or angry, perhaps more so than the situation may call for.

For example, perhaps you note that you get upset when your partner is not on time, courteous, or clean. Ask yourself why you expect them to be so. Why does it upset you? Why is it so important for you that they meet your expectations? What happens to you when they don't? Did you grow up in a certain way that predicated this expectation? Does their behavior remind you of something?

The key here is free-flow writing. Don't judge yourself; just inquire and see what flows as you engage in stream-of-consciousness writing. You may want to set a timer for five to ten minutes. When the timer sounds, set aside the paper.

1. **Settle in.**

   When you are ready, find a comfortable position and close your eyes.

   Take a few gentle, slow, deep breaths, and then let your breath assume a comfortable rhythm, taking note of how and what you feel after doing the writing exercise.

2. **Remember.**

   Next, bring an old relationship to mind that still elicits negative feelings or emotions, especially anger or resentment, even though you may have "moved on" and the feelings or emotions do not serve you anymore.

   Allow your mind to take you into the relationship, remembering the details, and let your emotions rise up through your body. Feel them without judging yourself or attempting to push any anger, resentment, or bitterness away.

3. **Strip the layers with compassion.**

   Imagine that you are gently stripping the anger or resentment away so that you can see what lies underneath. Is it grief, hurt, loneliness, or fear? Examine what lies underneath your feelings with compassion and care. Notice how and what you feel, becoming aware of any sensations and images as they arise, without judgment. You may want to place a hand on your heart or somewhere on your belly as a means of comfort.

   You may want to label these feelings by saying, "These are my unmet needs."

   Breathe in love and compassion and as you exhale, see if you can release the image of the other person with your breath for a moment in time.

4. **Delve in.**

   Then bring your focus back to delve into your unmet needs further. Ask, "In what way did this situation trigger me to feel that I am not enough? What is it that I really need?"

   Label your experience and what you uncover. You may, for instance, say, "I notice a tension in my stomach and the unmet need of being valued."

5. **Meet the need with love and compassion.**

   Decide now to lovingly meet the need yourself. You may say, "I hear you," "I love you," "I value you," or whatever it is that you need. Meet the need with love and compassion.

   Say these words to yourself as you breathe in love and compassion, uttering the same words you might speak to a dear friend or a child who was struggling.

6. **Settle out.**

   When you are ready, place your hands on your lap and let the exercise fade so that you are now just sitting with the experience and with how you feel, being just as you are.

When being connected to others hurts

Healthy relationships share the characteristics of mutual respect, trust, honesty, good communication, emotional control, fairness in conflict, compromise, under-standing, empathy, healthy intimacy and sexual contact, and effective conflict resolution. No relationship is perfect, of course, as it is comprised of perfectly imperfect humans, but it is possible to be involved in an unhealthy relationship, where pain, disrespect, and hostility are a rule, rather than an exception.

When your relationship is a source of pain, you may become wary, defensive, offensive, more sensitive, or withdrawn. Your behavior, projected at the other person or yourself, may be damaging not only to your relationship and your health, but also to your ability to fully engage in life, including at work. It can drain you physically, mentally, emotionally, and spiritually. As you put a wall around your heart to protect yourself from feeling vulnerable, you become further disconnected from yourself, other people who can support you, and your connection to something greater. The other person in the relationship is also likely to shut down to avoid the pain related to their own unmet needs. To avoid feeling vulnerable, the other person may reject you, push you away, devalue your existence, or take without giving back. The disconnection hurts.

If you don't pay heed to your pain, you deny yourself the opportunity to heal underlying wounds, take care of unmet needs, and meet someone else's pain with compassion. Connecting with compassion doesn't mean you condone hurtful behavior; it just means that you can stand back and observe that the behavior comes from suffering. As you heal yourself, you can better step back and decide whether the relationship truly serves you and whether change is possible. You can then meet the relationship and your needs with compassion and balance, or equanimity.

Practice: Compassion with equanimity

This next practice is a mindfulness exercise that guides you to dislodge yourself from your difficult negative emotions, tap into compassion, and embody a sense of equanimity.

1. **Get comfortable and settle into present awareness.**

   Find a comfortable position. Close your eyes and if you like, place a hand on your heart or abdomen, as a way to comfort yourself as you ground yourself in this loving experience.

   Breathe in deeply; then exhale completely. Gently bring your awareness to your breath as you breathe in and out. Then gradually notice how and what you feel in your body, as you settle into present moment awareness.

2. **Connect with balance and a desire for happiness.**

   Bring to mind a time when you felt balanced, a time when you felt a sense of peace and ease. Perhaps you can imagine being somewhere in nature, experiencing peace and balance, where there is no right or wrong or the need to fix anything. Nature eventually fixes itself.

   Recognize the ability within you to feel equanimity. You may say to yourself, "This is feeling balance and equanimity," or "It is within me to feel balance and equanimity."

Next, reflect on your deepest desire for happiness and freedom. Reflect on how you wish for happiness and freedom for yourself and others. Notice how you feel in your body.

3. **Visualize the challenge and recognize humanity.**

   When you are ready, bring to mind a relationship that is challenging for you, one that makes maintaining equanimity and compassion difficult.

   Notice what happens in your body as you bring this person and situation to mind. Allow emotions, feelings, and sensations to arise without judging or pushing anything away.

   Reflect on how it feels to be unable to fix or control this relationship.

   Now reflect back on your feelings of equanimity and remember that like you cannot control nature, you cannot control the other person's journey nor are you responsible for their actions. Everything has its own balance. You may want to say, "I recognize that we all have our own journey. All beings are responsible for their own actions. I am responsible for my own happiness and shining my light so other beings can find their own light switch."

   Allow yourself to connect with the balance between the desire to see yourself and others happy and the knowing that your own happiness is the only thing that is in your control. You may say to yourself, "I can be with things as they are with compassion, without trying to change things or fix things that are not in my control."

4. **Let it settle in.**

   When you are ready, open your eyes and allow the experience to settle in. Perhaps take a moment to reflect on the experience.

Mending Your Relationship with Yourself

If you find yourself in an unhealthy relationship, it's important to ask yourself why you may be hanging on to a situation that is hurting you. Is the fear of being disconnected or alone stronger than the hurt? The inquiry starts with you, uncovering your unmet needs, examining your expectations and behaviors, taking responsibility for your role, and working toward mending the relationship you have with yourself. Having a loving relationship with yourself means being on a continual path of self-discovery, one that is filled with love, respect, and commitment.

Here are eight tips to improve your relationship with yourself:

- » **Embrace and accept yourself.** Embrace and accept yourself as you are, with faults, failures, weaknesses, and strengths.

- » **Practice self-care.** Practice self-care and nurture your body, mind, and spirit by making sure you get restful sleep, move your body as it is meant to move, eat nutrient-rich food, and meditate regularly. Make self-discipline self-love, not denial or restriction.

- » **Respect yourself.** Respect and find value in yourself. Self-respect and value show up in the way you treat and accept yourself and how you end up relating to other people.

- » **Know your core values.** Assess your core values or the beliefs that you live by, that guide your behavior and moral views. Understanding yourself better allows you to find people who share your values.

- » **Take time to reflect.** Take time for quiet and self-reflection, to understand yourself better or your connection with the larger universe that you exist within.

- » **Make a commitment.** Make a commitment to love yourself even at the times that you don't. Commit to staying true to your core values, beliefs, and path to self-discovery and resilience. Be your own best friend.

- » **Be grateful.** Take time to appreciate the ways you are blessed or lucky. From the small things to the big ones, find gratitude in what you get to do and be.

- » **Ask for help.** Allow yourself to be vulnerable and ask for help when you need it. Allowing yourself to receive love and kindness reflects your willingness to admit that you are worthy of this love and support, not that you are weak.

REMEMBER

Creating quality relationships takes time, and it takes self-discovery. You will have moments of elation and moments of sorrow or discouragement. The key is to remember that you are on a journey and that your relationships help you discover more about yourself. The quality ones provide you with people to share your journey with.

Improving connections with the five R's

So how can you go about improving your connections? One way is through a tool taken from the social justice movement called the five R's of restorative justice: relationship, respect, responsibility, repair, and reintegration. The concept was originally identified by Beverly Title, the founder of the Resolutionaries Inc, an organization that aims to integrate restorative practices into schools. It was designed to be a collaborative process to help people take responsibility for their behavior while also remaining connected to one another.

Relationship: Mending what is broken

In the "relationship" part of the restorative process, you consider that your connections are important for your well-being and fulfillment, and that it is not just you whose heart may be broken. Everyone hurts. For relationships to prosper, all parties must take responsibility for their part and make amends. This doesn't mean blaming or shaming, but rather being open to your own healing process as well as that of the other person and being accountable for your own behavior and the choices you make because ultimately, you recognize how important the relationship is. All parties, in other words, need to be willing to work toward healing.

Being accountable for your role in hurting someone else without shame, blame, or justification when you are hurting yourself can be extremely difficult. Beginning the process with self-compassion and improving your relationship with yourself can make it a bit easier. When you do so, you may find you can more readily take responsibility for choices or actions that may have inflicted pain on someone else.

Respect: Listening deeply

Positive connections exist because the parties involved have mutual respect. Respect enables each person to feel safe, as each person is recognized for having their own beliefs, values, or points of view. You don't have to agree with someone's belief system to respect them. So, too, when you respect someone else, you don't assume that you know what or how they think or understand something. Upholding respect in your relationship involves deep listening, where you listen to what the other person is saying rather than jump to conclusions or stick to preconceived assumptions. Your intention is to respect and understand, even if you disagree.

Think about a time when you felt that you were not being listened to or your thoughts were dismissed or diminished. How did that feel? How do you feel about that person or that relationship? You may note that a sense of trust is lost when you don't feel truly heard and valued. On the flip side, how did it feel to have an open conversation where all parties had the chance to share their unique perspective?

It feels good to be heard! You can practice listening and being heard with someone easily. The practice is called listening deeply. The aim is to remain open, present, curious, receptive, empathic, and compassionate.

1. **Choose a subject.**

   Choose any subject that the two of you (or more) want to talk about. You may want to start with a subject that isn't too emotionally charged. You could be simply relaying "news and goods," or what happened during the course of your day.

2. **Assume a position.**

One person is chosen to speak first, and the other person or people then become the listeners.

3. **Set the intention and the time.**

Set the intention to be mindful, open and curious; that if thoughts or assumptions come into mind, you will allow them to flow on by and always direct your focus to hearing and listening to what is being said. You may want to take three or more cleansing breaths and place your hands on your heart and state: "I set the intention to be fully present and deeply listen." Set a timer for five minutes or simply be aware of the time.

4. **Listen mindfully.**

Listen with openness and curiosity. Allow space for the other person to speak and share their views. When the speaker is finished, allow a pause of silence to appreciate that you have either been able to speak or been given the gift of hearing the other person's story or point of view.

5. **Reflect and ask.**

Reflect back what you have heard, asking questions with genuine interest.

6. **Reset and go.**

Switch roles, set the timer, and do it again.

Responsibility: Searching inside your heart

When you take responsibility for your behaviors and words, you act honestly and authentically, which opens the door for the other person to do the same. Keep in mind that being accountable for your part doesn't mean taking responsibility for things that you did not do. You can't force someone else to take personal responsibility, nor can you be forced to do so, especially for something you *did not* do. Taking ownership for everything that you *do* say and do, however, is the foundation upon which healthy relationships and connections are built and healed. It also serves as a reminder that you are the co-creator in your relationships; therefore, how you act and what you say influences the trajectory of the connection, for better or for worse.

Taking personal responsibility for your mistakes and actions can be challenging, especially when you are in pain. On the flip side, because of your pain, you may be taking on responsibility for actions that you didn't do. This can happen when you justify the other person's behavior and instead take the fault upon yourself.

Here are three rules for taking personal responsibility:

>> **Commit to honoring and honesty:** Notice how you feel. Be honest with yourself and practice self-compassion. Doing so allows you both to be witness to how you may be feeling hurt or why you may have hurt someone else, honestly and authentically without exacting shame or blame.

>> **Seek balance and equanimity:** Take slow deep breaths, do a mindful grounding practice, or take a mindful walk. Allow the stress response to quiet so that you have access to rational thinking and feel less emotionally charged. Connecting with equanimity helps you be open to viewing the bigger picture, which includes how the other person may feel, enabling you to respond appropriately rather than be reactive.

>> **Choose forgiveness and learning:** With self-compassion and equanimity, you are better able to forgive yourself as well as the other person without condoning behavior. Choose to learn from mistakes and learn how to create healthier boundaries and develop better trust and pathways for communication.

Repair: Moving positively past harm

Sometimes so much harm has transpired in a relationship that there is too much water under the bridge for that relationship to heal and move forward positively. In many cases, however, the relationship is repairable, but it requires all parties to take responsibility for their role, act with respect and positive intention, and commit to healing the broken connection so that trust can be rebuilt. It is only possible to move forward positively after harm and rebuild trust and faith in the relationship when the desire to heal is mutual.

Here are some guidelines to help you repair a relationship:

>> **Mutually commit to healing.** The only way to heal from hurt is to move through it. Know that the path is not easy. It is possible, though, when all parties are committed to healing the relationship.

>> **Apologize and back it up.** If you are the one who inflicted harm, it's important that you commit to the relationship and not only apologize for your behavior and your role, but be consistent in your actions, ensuring that the behavior is not repeated.

>> **Listen, accept, and be thoughtful.** If it is the other person who has done harm, listen to their apology openly and compassionately. Keep in mind that everyone is human and makes mistakes.

>> **Communicate and value.** Communicate and express your feelings and validate the other person's feelings and words on a regular basis. Keep the dialogue open, stay open and respectful, and regularly assess and find solutions for triggers or when you feel your buttons are pushed.

>> **Find a way to forgiveness.** Forgiveness is at the foundation of rebuilding trust and moving forward. The way to forgiveness is also the pathway to emotional freedom as you no longer allow past mistakes to dictate your feelings.

>> **Seek help.** It can be challenging to truly move past hurt, so you may want to seek help from a counselor or coach who can facilitate the conversations and help guide you to forgiveness and healing.

Reintegration: Returning to collaboration and co-creation

With mutual commitment to heal and forgive, you can deepen your connection, reintegrate your lives to be on equal footing, and see one another as co-creators of the healthy relationship. This means knowing your own value and being able to see the value in the other person. It involves sharing tasks and interests and the capacity to continually work together and connect with one another in an open and respectful way. When you do so, the relationship becomes collaborative, and it evolves, strengthens, and deepens.

Remember, you are the co-creator of this relationship. How you act, speak, or behave influences the trajectory of the connection one way or another.

Here are tips for returning to reintegration:

>> **Support one another.** Value each other's thoughts, interests, fears, and hopes. Listen openly and curiously, ask questions, and find ways to support one another.

>> **Share responsibilities.** Share responsibilities, roles, and decision making so that the process is collaborative.

>> **Stay self-aware.** Work to maintain equanimity by staying self-aware, taking care of your unmet needs when you can, and communicating your needs clearly. In this way, you can work collaboratively and compassionately to ensure needs are met together.

>> **Seek spiritual connection.** Find ways to connect on a deeper level, discussing beliefs, dreams, and hopes. Spend time in nature together, appreciating

your connection to all things and to one another, or join a spiritual community.

>> **Share in the fun and love.** Enhance your bond by keeping joy and love alive. With pleasure and the experience of love, oxytocin (the love and bonding hormone) levels rise, strengthening the social bond. Creating new memories of love and joy also helps remind you why you are connected in the first place. Share interests, spend time with friends, and engage in fun activities together.

Practice: Ho'oponopono, the forgiveness prayer

One of my favorite practices is the Hawaiian teaching for forgiveness called Ho'oponopono, which translates to "make things right." The prayer encourages you to forgive yourself for any mistakes you may have made and to forgive another person, opening pathways for love and balance as well as reconciliation and communication. Repeating the prayer can be extremely powerful, as it requires you to acknowledge your own role in hurting someone else and therefore acknowledge feelings of shame or guilt that exist within you, while also acknowledging love both for yourself and others. It supports you to be with your feelings, be accountable, recognize humanity, and heal on the deepest of levels.

The prayer itself is extremely simple and goes like this:

"I'm sorry. Please forgive me. Thank you. I love you."

Give it a try and repeat the forgiveness prayer ten or more times: "I'm sorry. Please forgive me. Thank you. I love you." Then, notice how and what you feel.

4

Beyond Burnout and Toward Resilience: Flourishing and Thriving

Harness your innate ability to heal and begin to chart a course to healing burnout and finding resilience.

Improve resilience by improving conditions that help you get there.

Maximize your ability to flourish by taking care and being self-aware.

Cultivate a culture of care so everyone can flourish.

Chapter **13**

Charting the Course from Burnout to Resilience

rriving at burnout means that you have already traveled an extremely difficult road. You may be finding that your self-care has fallen by the wayside, your ability to feel engaged and work productively is flailing, and your personal relationships are strained. Yet, you are here, reading this book, and this means you are already resilient. It's just a matter of fostering your resilience so that you are no longer barely keeping it all together, but flourishing.

You didn't arrive at burnout because of some sort of failing on your part. Even the most resilient person can be knocked down by repetitive external stress and toxic environments. As you discover in previous chapters, burnout happens because a plethora of internal and external factors get mixed together to create a perfect storm. Some factors are not within your control to change, but others are, and you can use the latter to chart a course to flourishing and better resilience. This chapter shows you how.

Setting the Stage for Resilience

Resilience confers the ability to bounce back and thrive in the face of life's *many* inevitable challenges. Some people are naturally more resilient than others, meaning that they are better able to see challenges as opportunities, maintain a positive outlook despite hardship, find meaning in the struggle, and successfully adapt to adversity. Most of us vacillate between feeling optimistic and being adaptable, and feeling hopeless and helpless, depending on what is happening in our lives, the hardships we experience, the support we have, and how we are feeling about ourselves. With burnout, most people face continuous negative and uncontrollable hardships and their efforts at effecting change fail. They eventually stop trying and give up believing they have any power to improve their circumstance, causing their resilient traits to go dormant. Perhaps you can think of burnout as the dark side of resilience, where it feels like your ability to bounce back has taken permanent leave and you feel helpless to effect change. *Dormant* is the operative word here. You can awaken and ignite your personal resilience, which can support you to chart a course to fulfillment and freedom.

In my book *Resilience For Dummies*, I detail how to build resilience through cultivation of six pillars: physical vitality, emotional equilibrium, mental clarity and toughness, spiritual connection, loving relationships and strong social connections, and understanding your influence as a leader within your community. Though the path toward optimal resilience differs from one individual to the next as we all have different tendencies, backgrounds, and life circumstances, cultivating these pillars can help you get there.

Going Inside to Find What Makes You Tick

Aside from having clarity about who and what you need for support, being clear about what matters to you also helps you know where and how you want to focus your time and energy. It adds meaning to everything you do, improving both your professional and personal life. According to researcher Carolyn S. Dewa and colleagues, healthcare providers are less likely to experience burnout when they allocate at least 20 percent of their time to focusing on what they most value.

To chart a course to fulfillment and freedom, you need to know what makes you tick and what truly drives you. You want to uncover what really feeds your soul, passion, or sense of purpose, because if you get the fuel you need, you will have a bigger bandwidth to handle pretty much anything. Purpose and passion do not have to be about saving the world or feeding the poor. Knowing that you have a purpose means knowing that your existence here on this earth is valuable. You were born with gifts, interests, abilities, and insights like no other person. How can you share them and show up in the world? You may find purpose by healing others; seeking knowledge; being a parent; or living a life of compassion, collaboration, or generosity. Whatever you do, you can do it with passion.

You do not become valuable because of what you may do, who you may know, or the possessions you may have. Rather, it is because of your value that you seek out certain actions, people, or objects to deepen your experience. As important as it is to align with your core values to serve as your compass on the path through and out of burnout, so, too, is connecting with your self-value and what makes you tick.

Awakening your story of resilience

How you perceive yourself influences how you experience your life and more so, how you handle uncertainty and adversity. If you perceive yourself as "broken," inadequate, hopeless, or helpless, your ability to manage difficulty diminishes and you are less likely to handle adversity and trauma effectively or adaptively. You always have a choice about how you want to perceive yourself, even when bad things happen. You have a choice to either listen to your inner critic, believing that you are a victim who needs protecting, or recall your story of resilience and remember how strong you are and how to look for opportunities for growth.

Of course, this is easier said than done when you've been hit by so many challenges that you literally do not have the strength to keep going. At such times, the inner critic truly wants to protect you from further harm. It's not unusual for this voice to get louder such that you end up identifying with the story of suffering more strongly than the story of resilience.

Exercise: Identifying with self-value

PLAY THIS

The goal is for you to become more accustomed to listening to your own story of resilience. You can do so by learning to connect with your sense of self-value. The following is an exercise that guides to reflect on feelings of gratitude and on positive memories and experiences.

1. **Settle in and reflect.**

   Close your eyes, take three or four deep cleansing breaths, and allow your thoughts to float out with your breath.

   Bring your awareness to the soles of your feet and the connection your feet have with the earth. Observe the rest of your body, aware of the weight of your body sitting on a chair or the floor. Notice any sensations you may be experiencing.

Reflect on the breath as it moves in and out. Notice your chest rise and fall, the rhythm of the breath, and how and what you feel.

Reflect and appreciate that the breath connects you with the air and the outside world, brings nurturance into your body, and then shares a part of you with the world.

Reflect and appreciate that your breath connects you to everything and that you are a human being who breathes and lives right here, on the earth.

2. **Remember value.**

Take a moment to bring back a memory where you felt successful, lucky, fulfilled, connected, blissful, or like you were on top of the world, even if only for a moment.

Allow the details to come to mind and see yourself in that experience. Allow yourself to experience the feelings and take note of them.

3. **Journal.**

When you are ready, write about your experience, including the sensations or feelings you experienced, what made you feel such bliss, the hardship you overcame, and so forth. Write a letter to yourself or even your inner critic, noting how proud you are of your success, what you are grateful for, and perhaps how you would like to set the intention to remember these feelings and experiences in the future.

4. **Settle out.**

When you are done, fold the paper or papers and place them in an envelope that is stamped and addressed to yourself (you will mail it to yourself).

Then sit quietly for as long as you like, reflecting on how you feel and your experience.

Exercise: Connecting with your gifts

By identifying your self-value, you can better uncover your gifts and delineate what is important to you. For example, I value the sharing of knowledge and I have discovered that I have a gift of translating complex information and sharing this knowledge in practical and tangible ways.

1. **Make a list of the gifts you believe you have.**

Here are some examples:

- I have a gift for connecting people to one another.

- I have a gift for solving problems.

- I have a gift for simplifying things and making things easier.

- I have a gift for nurturing other living beings (including plants or animals).

- I have a gift for desiring to contribute to something greater and to help others.

- I have a gift for taking care of details.

- I have a gift for organizing.

- I have a gift for being fair.

- I have a gift for making something out of very little.

- I have a gift for telling stories.

- I have a gift for making people laugh.

2. **Rate each gift on a scale of 1–10 for each of the following questions:**

- How important is this gift to you?

- How much do you enjoy using this gift?

- How gratified do you feel when you share this gift?

- How often do you get to use this gift in your current life?

- How well does this gift align with your core values? (You may want to review your list from Chapter 10.)

TIP

Consider asking a friend or close colleague to write a letter of recommendation for you, describing your qualities, gifts, and capabilities, as if you were applying for a job. Other people who know you well can offer wonderful insight when it comes to appreciating your gifts. You never know, the letter may also come in handy someday!

Connecting with meaning and purpose

Consider taking the time now to contemplate meaning and purpose in your life. Note that I didn't ask you to consider reflecting on *your* meaning and purpose, or *the* meaning and purpose of your life, though you are welcome to, as long as you keep in mind that the meaning and purpose for every human being is to be a human being. In other words, reflecting on meaning and purpose isn't meant for you to try to label yourself for who you are or who you are not. It's meant to help you seek meaning and purpose in things that you do or situations that arise so that you can discover more about yourself, life, your gifts, your flaws, human nature, or anything else that helps you grow and flourish.

For instance, contemplate how differently you approach and answer these two questions:

>> **What is the purpose and meaning of life?**

Take note of how and what you feel in your body when contemplating these questions, and journal your response.

>> **How can I bring more meaning and purpose into my life?**

Take note of how and what you feel when contemplating this question, and journal your response.

See, the first question asks you to give an absolute answer in a way, much like asking, "What is my purpose or meaning for existing?" The second question is open ended and paves the way for exploration, curiosity, and creativity.

Mindfully getting to know your unique situation

Gordon came to me feeling completely burned out, depressed, in constant physical pain, and disconnected and disengaged in his relationships. He also came with a desire to heal, develop better habits, clarify his purpose, and "find his calling," which would be "best if it generates income." He felt like he was a shadow of who and what he was a year and a half prior, when he had the energy to participate in extreme sports, put in long hours at work, and as he put it, "thrive on chaos." As it turned out, Gordon grew up in a chaotic household. His mother had physical and mental illness, while his father's extreme moods vacillated between kindness and rage, and he was so opinionated that Gordon frequently doubted his own opinions and decisions, especially because of his dyslexia.

Through self-examination, mindfulness, and self-compassion, Gordon was able to identify his caregiver and perfectionist tendencies, as well as the inner critic that spoke often of his inadequacy — not being good enough or being of any value. As he focused more on knowing his self-value, he took better care of himself, eating nutrient-rich foods, improving his sleep hygiene, meditating regularly, getting out in nature, and being more present in his relationships. His brain fog lifted, his energy improved, and his sense of self evolved to one of value rather than inadequacy, though niggling self-doubt often reared itself. Gordon dug deeper to uncover his core values, self-value, and how he found meaning and purpose, and realized that he wanted to teach and go back to school to get a degree to do so. He wrote in his email, "I am matching my perception of myself with reality. Whatever negative stories my inner critic has told me might have gotten me where I am, but that inner critic is getting a new job description and title. Something like coach or advocate or Chief Empowerment Officer (CEO)."

My hope for you is that you, too, can transform your view of yourself and the possibilities that may lie ahead, as your inner world truly grounds you and acts as your compass, guiding you through life's ups and downs.

Keep in mind that everyone has a unique situation. By connecting with your values and compassionate voice, you can mindfully assess your unique situation, and hopefully feel ready to effect change, whether you discover a newfound passion for your current job or that you are ready for a complete change.

Getting into a place of acceptance for change

One of the hallmarks of resilience is being able to adapt to a given reality, even when that reality involves hardship. The key to this adaptability is accepting reality for what it is, taking care of your own needs, and letting go of expectations. Keep in mind that accepting reality doesn't mean giving up on what you want, but rather, acknowledging the situation for what it is and believing in your ability to figure things out and thrive. You remember the serenity prayer: "Grant me the serenity to accept the things I cannot change, the courage to change the things I can, and the wisdom to know the difference."

Exercise: Mindfully getting to acceptance

Are you ready to get into a place of acceptance for change? Take these steps.

1. **Settle in.**

   Assume a comfortable position and close your eyes.

2. **Mindfully connect with the breath and your feelings.**

   Breathe in deeply; then exhale completely. Gently bring your awareness to your breath as you breathe in and out. Count 1-2-3 as you breathe in, and 1-2-3-4-5-6 as you breathe out. Use your breath to help you clear out tension or anything that no longer serves you. Imagine that the breath is releasing it out into the wind, ethers, down a river, or into the earth.

   Observe your feelings, thoughts, or bodily sensations. You may want to start with focusing on the soles of your feet and move your way up the body. Witness your experience and anything you feel as an observer, without judgment. Notice discomfort or comfort.

3. **Mindfully connect with self-compassion.**

   Acknowledge your feelings with self-compassion, treating yourself as if you were listening to a dear friend who is struggling. Remember you are human, and everything you are feeling is valid. Accept, honor, and allow whatever you are feeling or thinking to exist.

Acknowledge that your feelings and expectations may be pointing to unmet needs and honor those needs.

4. **Mindfully connect with the way of nature.**

Consider nature's wisdom and resilience, how it doesn't judge and how it continues to bring life forth, even after devastation. Nothing is good or bad, right or wrong. Nature takes care of its needs.

Consider how you can't make the waves of the ocean go any faster than they do or make a flower bloom before it is ready. Everything has its time and place as nature takes care of its needs.

Consider that in nature, everything has a cycle and a rhythm and flow. Night and day co-exist, as do life and death, and earthquakes and blooming flowers in the spring. Nature takes care of its needs.

Consider that you are also part of nature, that you are able to adapt to the changes in nature, you are also resilient, that you have cycles and a rhythm and flow, and that you, too, can take care of your needs.

5. **Mindfully connect with acceptance and let go.**

Just like you can't hold onto your breath even if you try, let go of expectations or whatever is not in your power to change right now. Give yourself permission to accept your situation as it is right now.

Perhaps you can repeat the serenity prayer: "Grant me the serenity to accept the things I cannot change, the courage to change the things I can, and the wisdom to know the difference."

Take as long as you need to sit with this experience of surrender and acceptance.

6. **Settle out.**

When you are ready, reflect on how you feel.

Charting a Custom Course of Action

Hopefully, you now feel grounded enough in your core values and self-value to be able to chart a custom course to navigate, plot a personal strategy, be cognizant of any pitfalls or patterns, and ultimately craft a job and life that are right for you. The first step is to explore the contributing factors and sources of stress, which you do in Chapters 4 and 5. The next step is to acknowledge what you can take responsibility for that is in your power to change. You can identify immediate changes you can make, and then the ones that will require some time, strategy, and patience.

What is your responsibility and in your power to change?

Many factors that influence burnout are not in your power to change, such as institutional support, an elderly parent who needs caregiving, global pandemics, or even the fact that a project is time consuming. There also exist factors that you do have the power to change, even if they're seemingly minor or small. With mindful, nonjudgmental, and compassionate awareness, you can evaluate sources of stress, personal commitments, time spent in self-care, and ways to change personal tendencies or patterns.

TIP

The key is to accept where you are right now, start small, and take care of what you can. Once you have gathered all the data, you can plot your personal strategy to heal burnout. Remember that small changes can go a long way!

Plotting a personal strategy with patience

Following are seven steps you can take to navigate your way through and hopefully out of burnout. To plot out your personal strategy, read through and reflect on each step and write out a list of action steps that can help you.

1. **Accept with self-compassion.**

   As you go about plotting a personal strategy, it is vitally important that you accept your predicament with compassion and understanding. You will not be able to fix everything right away, and some things may not be fixable at all. The desire to get stuff done, fix things, be perfect, and be efficient may be partially responsible for how you got to burnout to begin with. Accept the latter fact too.

2. **Explore your role.**

   Explore the various factors of burnout and identify where you may be over-committing or pushing too hard, or where work or caregiving supersedes your ability to engage in self-care practices or recovery.

   Explore your core values and self-value and in what ways your actions support or deny these values.

   Explore your tendencies, inner critic, and beliefs and the ways they influence you to put aside your values.

3. **Refuel your life force.**

   Your brain and body require high-octane fuel and time for rest and recovery to function at full capacity. Perhaps you can make sure you get better quality sleep, change up your nutrition, and spend time in nature.

   Explore when and where can you initiate little breaks, move your body, practice meditation, engage in a playful activity, or *do absolutely nothing* in order to refuel your reserves.

4. **Seek support and connection.**

   Navigating through burnout is more possible when you have support from others. Explore who you can turn to for support and how to improve existing social connections or let go of the ones that are not amenable for mending.

   Lean on your friends or family, or work with a therapist, coach, personal trainer, or spiritual healer. The key is to decide to allow yourself to be vulnerable and reach out for help, which may even include talking to human resources or your boss at work.

   Consider reaching out to a trusted advisor, counselor, or coach who can help you. Make sure it is someone who has the capacity to understand you and your particular needs, given that the course you take will be unique to you.

5. **Prioritize action lists with what matters to you most in mind.**

   Connect with your core values and self-value, and identify what really matters to you personally and professionally.

   Organize your time and create a schedule that includes prioritizing what is important to you so that you have the fuel you need to take care of everything else.

   Figure out what your true duties are, as depicted by your job description, and what is expected of you, as well as what you are actually doing that you may not be enjoying or that is causing you a lot of stress.

   Consider your to-do list and think about what can be delegated to someone else.

6. **Set healthy boundaries.**

   The better you know yourself, your self-value, and your core values, the greater your ability to set healthy boundaries that enable you to take time to fuel yourself so that you are not helping everyone else at your own expense perpetually.

   You can create a healthy boundary between work and home, for example, in that you stop working the minute you leave the office, be it an office building or your desk at home. The minute you cross the threshold, it becomes *your* time for healing, joy, and relaxation.

You can also set healthy boundaries with people. Take yourself, your energy, and your time into account before you take on anything, and don't be scared to say "no."

7. **Craft the job to suit you.**

   Though not always possible, there may be ways for you to effect changes in your job or situation that enable you to find joy in what you do again. As you refuel yourself, create healthier boundaries, and get the support your need, you can better assess your career and work environment to figure out where and what you have the power to change.

Anticipate the pitfalls and patterns of being you

As you embark on this journey, aim to accept and be compassionate with yourself. Patterns and habits don't change overnight. Your habits have become your habits because they have helped you cope in one way or another. In other words, they have served a purpose. Coping is coping, maladaptive or not.

The problem with maladaptive coping is that you are coping with stress at the expense of your health and well-being because you are not truly addressing the underlying source of stress. The other problem is that the coping behavior has become a habit; it's your go-to, especially when you are feeling stressed, and is easy to fall back on when you are trying to develop new, adaptive coping habits.

If sticking to healthier habits was easy, most of us would not be making the same New Year's resolution year after year. You start out strong and then in a month or maybe two, you find yourself slipping back into old patterns. Know that this is normal and something to anticipate. I encourage you not to get upset with yourself. Anticipate that these pitfalls may happen and have self-compassion.

REMEMBER

Repetition of positive coping habits will eventually lead to the reprogramming you seek.

Here are some tips to anticipate and manage pitfalls:

>> **Do one thing at a time.** The key is not to try and change everything at once. Choose small goals and take small steps that will actually show up as big changes in your life.

>> **Choose the habit that, if changed, will fuel you most.** For instance, you might focus on improving your sleep quality and quantity. This one change of habit could create a world of difference in your life. My client Jenna cleaned up

her nutrition first and noted that her brain fog lifted, her body aches eased, and her mood improved. Focus on the goal until it becomes habit and then move on to the next one.

>> **Avoid choosing the habit you have a lot of resistance to.** Another client, Michelle, hated exercising but knew she had to move her body. Every attempt she made to tell herself to exercise was met with feelings of inadequacy and a desire to eat instead. I had her focus on employing meditation and mindfulness into her day instead, which has successfully become part of her daily routine. The point is that you don't want to set yourself up for failure.

>> **Slow and steady wins in the end.** Avoid going all out when you start. Many people want to put in the maximum effort, expecting results to occur more quickly. This is a surefire way to burn out on making a change. Take it slow. Meditate or exercise for five minutes a day and then increase the amount to a few times a day or a few minutes a day.

>> **Seek support and buddies of accountability.** Changing habits is much easier when others do it with you or at least support you to do so. Let one or more people know of your intentions and ask them to support you in the process through reminders, text messages, or joining you on your endeavors.

>> **Write down your plan and create reminders.** Write out your goal and create a plan, noting how much time you will spend to do the habit on a daily basis. Know that the key to changing habits is to actually do the new habit you want to acquire consistently. Organize your day in such a way that the habit is programmed into the schedule and set yourself reminders on your calendar, phone, or even sticky notes.

>> **Plan for pitfalls.** Know that you may fall back into old patterns and remember, that's okay. You are human. Have a plan for when this happens: You can have a little pep talk with yourself, up the ante when it comes to your support team, or revise the original plan if necessary to get back on track.

Getting crafty with your job

For many of you, it may be possible to make the job you have more worthwhile, meaningful, and satisfying, a concept called *job crafting* in that you *craft* the *job* you want. Justin Berg, Ph.D., an assistant professor in organizational behavior at Stanford University says, "Job crafting captures the active changes employees make to their own job designs in ways that can bring about numerous positive outcomes, including engagement, job satisfaction, resilience, and thriving." The process involves actively taking steps to redesign what you do at your current job, whether this means improving relationships, modifying workflow processes, changing tasks, or enhancing your own perception of how you approach your work so that you can gain more meaning and enjoyment.

Before you decide to up and leave your current job, consider the possibility of crafting the job you want where you are. When you do, you want to ensure that your job involves these four main factors that have been shown to increase an individual's ability to feel happier and more engaged at work:

>> **Control and autonomy:** In a healthy workplace, you should have autonomy, set schedules and goals, and create strategies to meet those goals. You should feel supported to customize processes, give feedback, have flexible schedules, and be creative.

>> **Meaning:** When you can find meaning in what you do, the chances of being more engaged and fueled by your work are greater. You're more likely to experience a sense of fulfillment and purpose, and feel happier, more committed, healthier, and more engaged.

>> **Connection:** Improved social connections in the workplace are associated with enhanced motivation and engagement, lower stress levels, and improved mental and physical health. Having strong and positive work relationships fosters better trust and improves the quality of the work done.

>> **Order and healthy boundaries:** A sense of order as well as having more order can help alleviate feelings of overwhelm and contribute to a healthier and more fulfilling work experience. Having more order might mean clearing out your desk, changing workflow processes to improve efficiency, enhancing clear communication and cooperation, having a clear delineation of what your job is, or being able to delegate responsibilities to those you trust.

Understanding ways to get crafty

Keep in mind that knowing how to get crafty with your job can also give you tools to get crafty with your home life and personal responsibilities. To better understand how you can get crafty, Professor Amy Wrzesnieski and colleague Jane E Dutton in their article, "Crafting a Job: Revisioning Employees as Active Crafters of their Job" in the *Academy of Mangagement Review*, say there are three ways you can employ different behaviors to optimize the job you have. These include task crafting, relationship crafting, and cognitive crafting, as follows:

>> **Task crafting** involves changing, adding, or dropping responsibilities that are outlined in your job description so that you can shape your job into one that better suits you. It may mean that you decide to allocate your time differently or change the nature of different responsibilities. With task crafting you are given the opportunity to focus on tasks that you enjoy doing, find resources to

support you to perform certain tasks, change what you are doing altogether, or take away responsibilities.

>> **Relationship crafting** involves changing how, when, and whether you interact with other people. You may choose to work with new people on certain tasks, find better ways to communicate and collaborate, and form relationships with co-workers for the purpose of learning and growth, not to mention improved social connections.

>> **Cognitive crafting** involves changing your mindset about tasks and responsibilities so that you can find more meaning and fulfillment. As an accountant, for instance, you might be bored with doing spreadsheets all day but are able to change perspective by remembering that your findings help people feel more at ease about their finances. Is there a way to reframe your job so that you can find more meaning in your daily experience?

Whether your ideal work situation involves staying put or leaving, you want to ensure that you have clarity regarding what you need and want. Once you do, it may be possible to redefine and establish the right job for you.

Optimizing the job you have

The current aim is to optimize your current job to align with your ideals. You may find, as you delve into this process, that you have more support than you realize to effect change, or you may find that the culture of your workplace is simply not amenable. Either way, you will have clarity about what is best for you. I recommend starting by taking note of the different tasks you do, your responsibilities, how much time you delegate to these activities, and how you feel when you partake in them. Separate your tasks into three categories:

>> The tasks that consume the most attention, effort, and time

>> The tasks that require minimal effort and time

>> The tasks that fall in between

Keeping your ideal work situation in mind, consider these tasks and responsibilities and answer these questions:

>> When you engage in this task or responsibility, how and what do you feel?

>> Does the way you spend your day align with your values?

>> Are one or more tasks leaving you drained and unfulfilled?

>> Is there opportunity to play to your strengths and passions?

>> Is there opportunity to learn more or fix your weaknesses?

>> Is there a way to reallocate your time and energy?

>> Is it possible to do more of the tasks that lift you up?

>> Which tasks and responsibilities do you enjoy, and which drain your energy?

You don't have to answer these questions all in one go. Take your time over the next couple of weeks, observe, and take notes. When you are ready, establish five goals that will best serve you most at your workplace. Then aim to set aside time, at least 30 minutes, each day to work toward achieving a goal. For instance, you might research to whom you can delegate the tasks that drain you or don't serve you if possible. See if there is a way to split up the responsibilities or take on those that you truly want to do, and give other responsibilities to people who would excel at them.

Looking at the social side of work

Over the next two to three weeks, you may also want to evaluate your relationships, especially the people you interact with daily, noting who you enjoy collaborating with and spending time with versus the interactions that lead you to feel more drained or exhausted. You can use the following questions to guide you:

>> How do you feel when you spend time with different people at work?

>> Who do you spend most of your time interacting with? Does it leave you energized or drained?

>> What sort of interactions do you enjoy? Is there a way to create better boundaries to protect your energy?

>> Are there new sources of support and collaboration you can connect with?

>> Are there more social activities you can take part in to feel better connected with your colleagues?

>> Are there people you trust that you can delegate or share responsibilities with?

Set intention every morning before leaving for work to spend your day connecting with the people who best support you. Clarify your boundaries from the get-go and ensure that you are spending time with the right people for you.

Boosting autonomy and sense of control

Aside from evaluating tasks, responsibilities, and relationships, you also want to examine your level of autonomy and sense of control. Take note of workflow, your schedule, whether you feel safe to provide feedback, and whether your input is heeded. Inquire about the following:

>> Are you supported to have autonomy to make decisions?

>> Is your role clearly defined?

>> Do you have the ability to have a flexible schedule?

>> Do you have time to focus on what is more interesting to you?

>> When are you most productive?

>> Do you have the ability to organize your time so that you can do certain tasks when you know you are at your best and more productive?

>> Do you have the ability to provide feedback and to feel heard?

>> Are there ways to allocate your time to be more efficient?

>> Are there ways to delegate responsibilities to improve workflow?

>> Are there other processes that can be implemented to improve organization and workflow?

If you find that you are safe to provide feedback and the organization that you work for is open to listening to your ideas regarding the flexibility of your schedule or ways to improve workflow, take advantage of it. You may want to engage a team of people to evaluate processes and workflow that will benefit everyone. On your own, you can always take measures to organize your schedule to best suit you.

Communicating openly and honestly

As you are observing your relationships, workflow, efficiency, and sense of autonomy, examine closely how people and the organization operate. Is there open collaboration and communication? What is your contribution? You can use the following questions to guide you:

>> Do you feel heard when you speak, especially offering feedback?

>> Do you listen or interrupt when others speak?

>> Is the process of communication effective?

>> Do lines of communication get crossed often?

>> Is poor communication an obstacle to success and a source of stress for you?

>> Is empathy and sensitivity present in workplace communication?

>> Are there ways to improve communication?

>> Is there a way to increase the sense of value and respect in order to enhance communication?

>> Is there a better way to document and streamline communication?

>> Is there a way you can be more honest and transparent?

Begin to establish new ways of communicating. Practice deep listening. Create rituals or routines in your workplace where people are encouraged to be mindful and to show value and respect to colleagues. Can you lead by example?

Extracting more meaning

If you can extract more meaning at work, chances are you will feel more fueled. Observe ways in which you may be able to shift your perception to milk more meaning from your daily experience. Is it possible to recognize that even setbacks provide opportunity for learning and growth, or are there simply too many setbacks to be able to recover? Ask yourself the following questions over the course of the next two to three weeks:

>> What tasks or actions feel more meaningful to you?

>> Does what you do align with your core values?

>> Does a mismatch in your core values and that of the workplace affect your attitude and behavior?

>> What values can you focus on that would influence your behaviors, perception, or plans?

>> Is it possible to be more mindful and find silver linings?

>> Is there a way to foster more optimism?

>> Is there a way to see challenges as opportunity?

>> Is there something bigger that you are a part of?

>> Are there ways to do your work that provide more value to you?

Exploring other options for change: Aspirational crafting

You may discover, as many do, that no matter how good your intention, crafting an ideal job in your current work environment is not possible, either because the company is not the right company for you or the role itself isn't. As such, you can use this time to get clarity about what you truly may want based on what you don't want. This is a good time to review your career assessment (Chapter 6) or take one of the many available online career assessment quizzes. Here are some questions to contemplate:

>> What do you like or not like, want or don't want?

>> Do you want to do the tasks that require so much of your time and energy? Do you enjoy these tasks?

>> Are there tasks that you do enjoy related to your job or simply things you do in your personal life?

>> Does a job or role exist that enables you to do the tasks you enjoy?

>> Does this job position help you feel more energized or more purposeful?

>> Is there something else you always dreamed of doing?

>> Are there people you can speak to who can help you figure out new options?

You can keep a list going over the next few weeks, continuing to examine what you do and don't want, like and don't like. You can then figure out if you are in the wrong position or the wrong organization or both. Once you do, you can explore options for change.

Whatever you do, know that options do exist. Everything may still seem fuzzy and unclear right now, but continue visualizing, taking notes, improving your social connections, and using your core values as a guide and you will find that the course from burnout to resilience becomes clearer.

Chapter **14**

Creating Conditions for You to Flourish

lourishing is a rather hot topic in the field of positive psychology. It has moved beyond the notion of being happy or your general well-being to refer to the experience of being fully engaged in your life, relationships, and career, and also experiencing great energy and joy. Dr. Martin Seligman explains that *flourishing* is the state created when you tend to your positive emotions; engage with the world, your work, or hobbies; forge healthy relationships; find meaning and purpose in your life; and apply strengths and talents to achieve your goals. In his research, he also found that anyone can cultivate flourishing, even those who feel burned out.

What do you think and feel when you think of flourishing? A flourishing garden, a flourishing waterfall, or maybe a flourishing business? What would it mean for you to flourish? This chapter reviews what it means to flourish and how you can cultivate flourishing as you heal from burnout.

What It Means to Truly Flourish

Researcher Corey L. M. Keyes notes in his article, "Promoting and Protecting Mental Health as Flourishing: A Complementary Strategy for Improving National Mental Health" in *American Psychologist*, that flourishing is associated with fewer missed workdays, less feelings of helplessness, better resilience, enhanced intimacy, and clearer life goals. Indeed, Keyes says that flourishing has been linked to fewer missed workdays, less limitation in daily activities, and fewer physical ailments as evidenced by lower healthcare utilization and positive mental health. When you flourish, you truly experience greater life satisfaction, feel more present, consciously connect with positive emotions, find meaning, find gratitude everywhere, celebrate your life, feel energized, and essentially thrive. You feel as if you are in flow with life.

I imagine that scenario is quite different from the way you are experiencing life right now, and it may seem like flourishing is a foreign concept since you may feel as if you can barely function. But know that it is possible for you to get there. Flourishing is not something that only certain people are born with. Rather, it is accessible to everyone.

Using PERMA to flourish

In his book, *Flourish*, Seligman created the PERMA model, which is comprised of five factors which, when tended to, can help you flourish:

Positive emotions: The consistent presence of feelings of gratitude, joy, hope, amusement, awe, love, inspiration and serenity

Engagement: Feeling in a state of *flow*, becoming "one" with a given task with complete engagement

Relationships: Having healthy and strong social bonds

Meaning: Having the sense of belonging and connection to something greater.

Accomplishments: Feeling masterful in achievements and accomplishments

Seligman explains that each element contributes to your ability to flourish, and one builds on the other. How much you need of each element differs from person to person, time to time, and situation to situation. The recipe isn't the same for everyone, but the exciting part is that when you tend to each element and develop a recipe that works for you, you can flourish and not only feel good, but also do good for others, helping other people flourish too.

Positive emotions and feeling good

Positive emotions have been described as mental responses that evoke a specific positive feeling. They are, in other words, much more than just feeling happy. Pioneer positive psychologist Barbara Fredrickson has outlined ten of the most commonly experienced positive emotions including joy, gratitude, serenity, interest, hope, pride, amusement, awe, and love. She developed this top ten list after many years researching emotions and coming to understand that positive emotions are our internal signals that motivate us to engage in our environment, explore new ideas and people, and essentially encourage "approach behavior" (versus withdrawal) that enables better learning, growth, and ability to stay open, which have a positive impact on our lives.

Regularly striving to experience positive emotions calms the stress response, enables you to access more rational and positive thinking, motivates more adaptive coping and healthy choices, enhances relationships, improves performance and engagement, and ultimately supports resilience and flourishing. It can, of course, be difficult to connect with feeling good when you are feeling so bad. The key is for you to build your positive emotion capacity and reservoir.

Here are five simple tips to build positive emotions:

>> Spend time with people you love and enjoy being around.

>> Engage in activities that bring you joy and are fun.

>> Start a gratitude practice. This can mean keeping a journal in which you write down things you feel grateful for daily, or you can sit in meditation and focus on feeling gratitude.

>> Practice mindfulness. Take note of your feelings without judgment and allow yourself to feel.

>> Watch, listen, or engage in something that makes you laugh and provides amusement.

Engagement and being in the flow

In his book, *Flourish,* Seligman refers to the element of engagement as "being one with the music." It occurs when you are completely absorbed in a given activity without being self-conscious, employing the perfect combination of skill or strength and challenge, a concept known as "flow," as described by Mihaly Csikszenmihalyi in his book, *Flow: The Psychology of Optimal Experience.* In the state of flow, you are moving smoothly through life, without any obstacles in site as the path is open and your mind is clear. You are fully engaged without being self-conscious, fully present in the moment and completely focused. It can truly feel exhilarating.

Being engaged and in the flow involves not being caught up in your thoughts, but instead being present and fully focused. In this way, you can accomplish more with less effort.

Here are some tips to improve engagement:

>> Practice mindfulness throughout your day, being fully present and nonjudg-mental even while doing daily tasks like brushing your teeth, eating breakfast, or getting dressed.

>> Fully engage in activities that you love and enjoy without focusing on time or how you are doing them.

>> Immerse your senses while walking in nature without a specific destination or time frame in mind. Be fully present and engaged in the process.

>> Pay attention to your energy level. Take note of your nutrition, sleep, or need to move and what helps your brain stay more alert and focused.

>> Identify things that you excel at, including your character strengths, and look toward learning and developing these traits and skills.

Relationships and having healthy connections

The PERMA model takes into account that the ability to flourish is dependent on how supported, loved, and valued you feel. Chapters 11 and 12 delve quite deeply into improving your mental and physical health and the importance of building healthy and loving social connections for cultivating resilience. You can now add the intention of wanting to flourish.

The key is for you to have healthy and loving connections surrounding you per-sonally and professionally.

The following are six tips to improve relationships:

>> Choose to be curious about people by asking questions to find out more about them and listen attentively.

>> Regularly connect with your friends and colleagues on a social level.

>> Reestablish connection with friends you haven't spoken to in a while.

>> Join a group or take a class in something that interests you so that you meet people of like interests.

>> Be consistent in your relationships and show your commitment.

>> Celebrate successes and share good news with your connections.

Meaning and finding value

Seligman says meaning refers to having a sense of belonging, to serving something greater than ourselves, and/or having a sense of purpose. You may discover meaning through your job, a spiritual belief, a hobby, volunteering, a creative endeavor, or a social cause. You can milk meaning from eating your lunch or in joining a protest rally.

Here are some easy ways to enhance meaning and value:

>> Regularly connect with your core values and let them be your compass to help guide you toward the activities and behaviors that are most in alignment with them.

>> Practice mindfulness and self-compassion to discover meaning in your own experiences, even the negative emotions and habits, instead of beating yourself down.

>> Join an organization, group, or cause that matters to you.

>> Volunteer and consider using your skills or passions to help other people, animals, or the planet.

>> Savor moments doing things you love or being with people you care about.

>> Regularly ask yourself how you can create more meaning in your life.

Accomplishments and feeling masterful

Being able to look at yourself with a sense of pride is an important contributing factor to flourishing. In Seligman's PERMA, the last element represents accomplishment or achievement, or your ability to achieve mastery and competence in a given endeavor. Feeling that sense of mastery and competence can improve your sense of well-being and self-value.

Here are some tips to help you feel accomplished and masterful:

>> Celebrate your achievements, especially in new and creative ways, whether big or small.

>> Set measurable and achievable goals, both extrinsic (like getting to the gym once a week) and intrinsic (like feeling a stronger sense of connection with your colleague).

>> Start small with your goals and celebrate each success. You will find more encouragement and motivation to keep going.

>> Start a new challenge that involves something you are passionate about.

>> Reflect and journal regularly on your successes, recognizing the work you put in and your self-value.

Connecting to flourishing

PLAY THIS

The following is a mindfulness practice meant to guide you to envision extending loving–kindness to yourself so that you can experience flourishing and share it.

1. **Settle in and focus on breathing.**

   Find a comfortable position, preferably a quiet place, and close your eyes.

   Take a moment to bring your awareness to your body as it is right now, noticing how and what you feel.

   Bring your awareness to your breath. Count 1-2-3 as you inhale and 1-2-3-4-5-6 as you exhale, noticing sensations in your body all the while. Recognize that the breath enhances your life force, providing nourishment and love and helping you let go of whatever no longer serves you. Appreciate the breath, its movement, how you feel, and the life force that fills you for a few cycles of breath.

2. **Reflect and connect.**

   Now reflect on what it feels like to flourish. You might think back to a time when you felt full of joy and a deep sense of contentment or well-being.

   Breathe in deeply, drawing the idea of flourishing in with your breath, and exhale completely, letting it flow through your body as you exhale.

   You can imagine that you are absorbing the flourishing life force from the earth and the universe at large as you inhale and letting it energize every cell of your body as you exhale.

   As you breathe in, imagine you are being given everything that you need to flourish. You may want to say to yourself, "I am open to receiving everything I need to flourish; I welcome the support" as you breathe in and let the energy and loving kindness flow through your body.

3. **Imagine overflowing and sharing.**

   Imagine being so full of energy and loving kindness that it is overflowing out into the world. It may seem that it or you are radiating flourishing with every breath that you exhale while taking in loving kindness as you inhale. Imagine yourself sharing your loving kindness, skills, and passions with others.

4. **Settle back out.**

Allow the images to fade and settle back in to being present with your body, noticing the weight of your body sitting or lying down, any sensations you may be experiencing, how you are feeling now, and the movement of your breath.

Take a deep cleansing breath and then let your breath assume a natural rhythm, gently bringing yourself back and opening your eyes.

Take some time to journal your thoughts and reflections. Consider then creating a list of intentions or simple action steps you can take to support your ability to flourish.

Building Your Recipe for Flourishing

There is no one-size-fits-all recipe for flourishing because everyone is different. There is only the perfect recipe for you. Flourishing may sound like a pipe dream, and the process is not always easy, but when you follow the steps in your particular recipe, one at a time if you have to, you may find, without realizing it, that you have begun to flourish.

Here are the seven basic ingredients to flourish. Each is covered in the subsections that follow.

>> Staying mindfully present, patient, and kind

>> Minding your energy and fuel

>> Leaning on your unique character strengths

>> Nourishing relationships and seeking trusted support

>> Milking situations for meaning, including at work

>> Igniting curiosity and embracing ambiguity

>> Tuning into gratitude and something greater

Staying mindfully present, patient, and kind

I know flourishing may feel too far away from where you find yourself currently, but the aim is for you not to focus too much on the future, but rather to stay present with where you are right now, just knowing that it is possible to feel better than you do. Every moment is a new moment to provide yourself with self-compassion, seek meaning, or investigate ways to improve, imagine, develop, or grow. If you focus your attention toward the future — the what-ifs, worries, or perceived obstacles — you will find your energy drained, and this certainly is not going to support your progress. Instead, you want to focus your attention on the present moment and engage in the experience of being in the here and now.

Following are guidelines to keep in mind to help you build a daily practice for flourishing:

>> **Start simple with a daily routine:** Choose one routine to do daily and focus your attention on the experience, engaging all of your senses in the moment-to-moment details. You might choose to mindfully brush your teeth, eat breakfast, or wash the dishes.

>> **Take mindful mini-space breaks:** Choose to take 10 seconds or 10 minutes at a time that you mindfully breathe and practice being present. A break period includes any time that you are shifting from one task to the next. Stop, mindfully breathe for ten breaths first, and then go.

>> **Create reminders to ground and breathe.** As it is easy to get caught up in the day's activities, worries, or stress, consider setting reminders in your calendar or phone to take a pause to mindfully breathe and ground yourself. I usually recommend setting the reminder to go off every hour on the hour.

>> **Lean toward curiosity.** The key to making mindfulness into a daily habit is to lean toward being curious about everything and use your senses to investigate. When you find yourself frustrated or overwhelmed, imagine saying to yourself, "Hmm . . . how curious? What an interesting feeling I am having. I shall observe it further."

>> **Above all else, be kind.** As you engage in more mindful practices, remember to be present with loving kindness. This will better allow you to be with the experience as it is, and to be more accepting of yourself and your situation. Find different ways throughout the day to offer yourself self-compassion.

Minding your energy and fuel compassionately

As discussed in Chapter 11, one of the pillars of resilience is physical vitality. The stronger your energy and life force, the more wherewithal you have to manage life's curveballs. As such, the next ingredient in the flourishing recipe book is to understand your body, how it speaks to you, and how to discern your energy, noting how full or empty your fuel tank is. With better self-awareness, you can intentionally make choices to better take care of your needs. You may decide, for instance, to up the ante when it comes to meditating or putting nutrient-rich food in your body on days that you know will be more challenging. You may also choose to put off a conversation if you know that you do not have the bandwidth just yet to communicate effectively with that particular person who has a tendency to push your buttons.

Here are three simple steps to listen to your body and discover how to flourish:

1. **Mindfully observe.**

   Do a mindful body scan, noting how you feel, your energy level, and what you may need. You can do so on your mini-space breaks, when your timer goes off, or around the times you eat and refuel.

2. **Ask yourself the following questions.**

   How am I feeling right now?

   What is my energy level right now?

   How do I feel compared to an hour ago (or another frame of reference)?

   What does my body need? What does my mind need? What does my heart need?

   What emotions am I feeling right now? How are they affecting my energy?

3. **Take care and fuel.**

   Once you have completed your self-inquiry, choose to take care of yourself and your needs. As you do so, continue to be mindful of your energy.

Leaning on your unique character strengths

Seligman says that character strengths represent the compilation of positive qualities that you possess, which enable you or a community to flourish and thrive. Dr. Seligman and his colleague Peterson studied and identified 24 character strengths that exemplify positive value traits that can support an individual or community to experience better emotional well-being, face hardship, and cultivate resiliency. Indeed, much of the research on these 24 character strengths has served as a foundation for the PERMA concept and is the basis for the Values in Action (VIA) classification on character that Seligman and Peterson created as a means to evaluate the strength of each character for a given individual, as presented in their book, *Character Strengths and Virtues: A Handbook and Classification.*

Know that every individual possesses these traits in varying degrees. You may be high in some character strengths and lower in others. This does not mean you have weaknesses, but merely that these character strengths are not your highest. The purpose of the VIA classification is to identify which traits you can lean on and which you may want to strengthen to enable you to better flourish and thrive. Psychologists Claudia Harzer and Willibald Ruch believe that building these character traits is associated with lower work stress and burnout and better adaptive coping strategies. Researchers Hadassa Littman–Ovadia and Michael Steger have also that found that being able to use your character strengths in the workplace has also been positively correlated with improved well-being.

To better appreciate and understand the character strengths, later studies divided the 24 character strengths into six virtues. I provide the six virtues for you here and include some questions to contemplate to help you assess your own signature strengths:

>> **Wisdom:** The cognitive strengths that propagate you to seek knowledge, love learning, be curious and open-minded, and gain perspective (Character strengths: creativity, curiosity, judgment, love of learning, and perspective).

- Do you enjoy coming up with new ways to do things or think?

- Do you tend to employ critical thinking, examining something from all sides to gain perspective?

- Do you like taking an interest in a variety of topics?

- Do you enjoy learning new skills, researching new topics, or developing a new mastery?

>> **Courage:** The emotional strengths that support you to meet challenges and obstacles, forge ahead, and accomplish goals (Character strengths: bravery, perseverance, honesty, and zest).

- Is it important to you to speak the truth?

- Is your tendency to be authentic and genuine?

- Do you embrace challenges, difficulties, or pain rather than withdraw or avoid them?

- Are you known for your zest as your tendency is to approach everything with excitement and gusto?

>> **Humanity:** The interpersonal strengths that lead you to care for the well-being of others (Character strengths: love, kindness, and social intelligence).

- Do you enjoy doing nice things for others?

- Do you get value from doing favors for or taking care of other people?

- Do you value your close relationships?

- Do you tend to be empathic or aware of other people's feelings and needs?

>> **Justice:** The civic strengths that guide you to take care of your community (Character strengths: fairness, leadership, and teamwork).

- Is it important to you to treat people with fairness and inclusivity?

- Do you tend to take on a leadership role when organizing activities and ensuring things happen?

- Do you enjoy working with others, forming a cohesive team?

>> **Temperance:** The balancing strengths that enable you to have balance and moderation in a world of excess (Character strengths: forgiveness, humility, prudence, and self-regulation).

- Do you generally have the capacity to forgive others, even when they have wronged you?

- Do you tend to deflect praise and prefer to let your accomplishments speak for themselves?

- Do you think before you act and avoid doing things that you may regret later?

- Do you tend to have good self-discipline, whether it comes to your diet, habits, or emotions?

>> **Transcendence:** The spiritual strengths that help you find meaning, connect with something greater, or find purpose (Character strengths: appreciation of beauty and excellence, gratitude, hope, humor, and spirituality).

- Do you have the propensity to appreciate beauty and excellence in everything?

- Do you often express gratitude and contemplate what you are thankful for?

- Do you tend to believe in positive outcomes, that they are possible, and it is worth working to making them happen?

- Do you believe you have a profound connection with something greater, have a purpose, or have a sense of meaning in life?

TIP

You can find the VIA Inventory Strengths (VIA-IS) assessment tool online if you want to identify your signature strengths.

Nourishing relationships and seeking trusted support

Improving your social connections is another main ingredient in the recipe for flourishing. Close relationships offer you emotional and material support, help you feel accepted and more connected, and give you a sense of belonging — all qualities that can boost you up when times are tough. Different people may serve different purposes in your life, as you may turn to one friend for practical advice and another for emotional support. The goal is to expand and enhance your support system, both personally and professionally, making new connections and strengthening the ones you already have.

The following sections present ways to improve relationships.

Consider what rewards you want and need

Take into consideration what sort of support you may benefit from right now and in the future, both personally and professionally. You can start by identifying the goals you seek and then figure out what or who can support you to achieve these goals. Do you need someone to guide you professionally? What rewards do you need to receive from your work relationships? What would you offer someone at work in return?

Take some time to evaluate and review your notes from the job crafting exercises and self-inquiries. Create a list of rewards or goals that you seek and prioritize the kind of social connections that can help you achieve them.

Do an inventory

Conduct an inventory of your top ten social connections. If you would like to add more, you can if you feel these connections are important to you or beneficial for workplace success. You can use this list to help you determine which relationships are most meaningful to you and which bonds you would like to build as you go forward. Write down the name, the category of association (family, work, client, friend, and so on), the basis of your relationship, and the average amount of time you spend or interact with them during a normal week.

Determine commitment

Once you have compiled your list, the next step is to think about each relationship and how committed you are to seeing each one grow and deepen, keeping in mind that strong bonds take work and dedication. Do you want to improve this relationship? Does this relationship add value to your life? Is this a temporary social connection or do you see yourself being connected to this person for the long haul? This part of the evaluation can propel you to dig deeper into each relationship to help you determine where you may want to put your focus while also showing you what aspects of your relationships can be improved upon to strengthen the bonds.

Determine mutual investment, rewards, and trust

Next evaluate what sort of rewards are shared in each of your connections. What do you acquire and what do they acquire by being in the relationship? Is there trust? How well do you communicate? In this way, you can better assess the value of the relationship and whether the investment by each person is equal. The goal is to examine whether you each feel safe, respected, and valued and what you each get out of the relationship.

Put in the effort

The next step is to set intention to strengthen the bonds you have and put in the effort by

>> **Communicating with presence and curiosity:** Aim to be mindful and fully present when communicating. Ask questions and be curious.

>> **Building trust and reliance:** Say what you mean and mean what you say. Be consistent, show up when you say you will, be true to your word, and keep your promises.

>> **Supporting and being supported:** Avoid making assumptions, be clear about your needs and ensure you understand the other person's needs, check in regularly, and offer support and advice when asked.

>> **Accepting and acknowledging:** Accept and acknowledge humanness, imperfections, and differences in points of view and opinions. Release expectations and seek value wherever you can.

>> **Settling differences.** Work toward navigating differences and disagreements with compassion and mindfulness. Respect and value one another and your beliefs, and aim to learn and grow from one another.

>> **Investing in "add ins":** Add meaning to the relationship through meaningful conversations. Add lightness through fun and laughter. Add in celebration for successes. Add in support for setbacks and downturns. Add in thoughtfulness and compassion when deliberating. Add in personal space for taking care of yourself.

Create new connections and seek support

Support exists everywhere if you choose to access it. Whether support comes from experts, friends, colleagues, or your neighbors, there are likely people around you who have been through something similar or at least understand you and what resources you may need. Consider reaching out to a coach, therapist or counselor;

a wiser person who can offer meaningful words of wisdom, comfort, and advice; or a support group that meets in person or on the internet.

Milking situations for meaning, including at work

Another major ingredient in your recipe to flourish is discovering ways to enhance meaning and meaningfulness. Researcher Stacey M. Schaefer and colleagues believe that the ability to find meaning from life's experiences, especially the challenging ones, supports resilience. You can milk situations at work for meaning as a means to grow and better understand your gifts, values, or passions.

The following tips can help you enhance meaning to flourish:

>> **Mindfully intend to create meaning.** Every morning, spend a mindful moment offering up this question to yourself: "How can I fill my day with more meaning?" Sit with the experience of asking the question.

>> **Seek inspiration and opportunities to learn.** You have set the intention; now keep your mind, heart, and senses open to notice nuances, feelings, and details as you proceed with your day. You may notice a strength you didn't realize you had or gain a deeper understanding of a person, situation, or yourself. Take time to reappraise your story, reflecting on a given chain of events, what proceeded or led to what, who was involved, or why you think something happened. Note your own assumptions, beliefs, and contributions. Examine your reactions, feelings, and emotions. Listen deeply and observe.

>> **Look for silver linings.** Looking for blessings in disguise or silver linings can help you find meaning whenever you are going through difficulty or looking back in hindsight. You can examine what you have discovered or you can contemplate a what-if situation, or you can consider how an experience could have been worse. Examine in what way you may be lucky. Dig deep and uncover your strengths or opportunities for growth and learning.

>> **Find equanimity by looking to nature.** When you get caught up in the mundane aspects of life, especially when you're overwhelmed and over-worked, the tendency is to have a narrow perspective of life and yourself. It can help sometimes to step back and remember that in nature, opposites co-exist. Allow yourself to take a step back every so often to view your environment as if you were walking through nature, appreciating the balance within the conflict and looking for patterns.

>> **Have a meaningful conversation.** Especially during difficult times, turning to other people for help and support can enable you to face your own fears. It can also help you gain new perspectives from people who aren't standing

so close to the situation. The best part of having a meaningful conversation with someone else is that you also end up forging stronger bonds.

>> **Consider everything as fuel for your energy.** When you take a step back to consider whether a thought, situation, or conversation is fueling your energy, much like the food you eat, you assume a more mindful stance and approach, giving you the opportunity to act with meaning and intention. You can then eat, move, choose your words, or nurture your relationships with purpose.

>> **Connect with love and awe.** When you connect with love and awe, neurochemicals like oxytocin, dopamine, and endorphins fly through your brain, affording you sensations of pleasure and euphoria, lowering the stress response, and broadening perspective. You can think of a situation of awe or reflect on miracles that happen all around you.

Igniting curiosity and awe

Growing personally and professionally involves engaging on a path of continual learning and discovery, and for this reason, it often entails being comfortable not knowing or having answers. Whether you're dealing with loss, adversity, or change, you choose the path of inquiry and curiosity, desiring to learn more about yourself or a situation, challenging your assumptions, and choosing to be open to growth.

Here are six ways to ignite curiosity and awe to flourish:

>> **Practice mindfulness and self-compassion.** Practicing mindfulness and self-compassion supports you to better examine yourself and control your emotions. These practices also function to reduce the stress response, allow you to gain a greater perspective on a situation and be in the present moment.

>> **Keep a notebook.** Write down questions, observations, ideas, and insights throughout your day. Look for signs in unlikely places and be open to having an "Aha!" moment, when all of a sudden, the dots connect and you gain a keener understanding of something.

>> **Ask questions.** Imagine that you are like a 3-year-old child who is constantly asking, "But why?" (though I encourage you to treat yourself with loving kindness rather than annoyance). Know that no "right" answers exist, only great questions. Ask questions that are open ended using such words as "why," "what," "when," "who," "how," "where," and "what if."

>> **Use your imagination and look for patterns.** Most people make connections according to their observations and experiences, but usually leave out their imagination. The stress in your life and fear-based thoughts can lead you

to perceive life in a rather narrow and concrete way, which lacks creativity and doesn't allow you to see the big picture and subtle connections or possibilities. The secret to avoiding narrowed thinking is to soothe your stress, accept that discomfort and paradoxes exist, and step back and engage in *systems thinking,* or the appreciation of the complexity and connection between things. The secret is to look for patterns and connections everywhere.

>> **Connect with awe wherever and whenever you can.** Observe the miracles all around you. Observe rivers flow and seasons come and go, the sunrise and sunset, allowing yourself to connect with the impermanence of nature, and therefore, life. Open your view to see and find silver linings.

>> **Give thanks.** You could be thankful that you have food on your plate, you found a parking spot, you have two feet, or you see a mailbox. It can be something big or small. You can even be thankful for the negative. Even though a situation is hurtful or scary, appreciate somewhere in your mind that there is a silver lining or an opportunity for growth somewhere. Keep a gratitude journal, thank a stranger, or send a thank-you letter to someone else or yourself.

How Do You Know If You Are Flourishing?

You may be thinking at this point that flourishing requires a lot of effort, and you may be wondering how it is possible for you to know if and when you have arrived at flourishing. Well, you will certainly know that you no longer are feeling burned out, so that's a positive promise. You may also discover that your energy is brimming. You may find that difficult situations don't bother you as much and that you can be more in "the flow" as you maneuver through life's twists and turns. You may find yourself caring without caring, in that you will have compassion for yourself and others without also experiencing strong emotional charges that leave you feeling more distressed, helpless, or hopeless.

You aren't going to arrive one day at flourishing and think, "Okay. This is it. I have arrived." Rather, flourishing is an ongoing process that is continuously evolving. It is a journey that will have its ebbs and flows, and you will experience days when you feel energized and others when you feel more depleted. It is a journey that involves cultivating new habits and ways of thinking and being in life, which will continually change, as all things do. The question you may want to ask yourself is not, "How am I going to know that I am flourishing?" but rather, "What can I do today to support my journey of flourishing?" Then, you check your toolbox of tools and figure out what you may need to take with you on your journey each day. Make sure that you pack loving kindness, your core values, your connection to breath and something larger, your loving relationships, awe and gratitude, and ultimately, the choice to heal and flourish!

Chapter **15**

Building a Culture of Care and Flourishing

Whether you consider yourself a leader or are in a leadership position, know that you have influence on everyone and everything around you, positively or negatively as it may be. Your sphere of influence may be wide or narrow, but influence it is, nonetheless. Both a boulder and a pebble create a ripple when thrown into the water. So, too, you create ripples wherever you go, big or small, for better or for worse. The question is whether you want your influence to be positive or negative.

If the leader of a family unit, be it a parent or guardian, is thriving, they have a larger bandwidth with which to care for and nourish their children to flourish as well. The same is true in the workplace. When leaders flourish, they possess more energy, compassion, and ability to genuinely care about their employees. In turn, employees are more likely to care about the leaders, their co-workers, and their job. The culture of the workplace then becomes one of care and one that is more prone to experience increased productivity, engagement, job satisfaction, collaboration, a stronger organization, and most importantly, less burnout.

A culture of care is thus established from the top down. This means it starts with leadership caring first. The problem is that a leader who is burned out, will find it quite challenging to have the bandwidth to genuinely care. Indeed, many of the clients I worked with over the past couple of years were leaders who felt burned out and simply wanted to leave their job. Once they honed their skills in self-compassion, empathy, being better organized, finding meaning and purpose, and upholding self-care, they were then better able to do the same for their employees.

This chapter focuses on how you can create a culture of care in the workplace and lead in a way to create positive influence and flourishing.

What Is a Culture of Care?

In a culture of care, leaders genuinely care about *all* the people who work in the organization and are willing to make meaningful investments in them, whatever the job and however high or low on the rung that job is. They listen, welcome input and feedback; share values; and offer professional development, mentorship, opportunities for growth, and ongoing support. Leaders act with respect, honesty, kindness, compassion, and trust. Everyone benefits. As a result, employees are more likely to be dedicated, engaged, motivated, and invigorated by their work rather than burned out. Indeed, in their article, "Flourishing in the Workplace: A One-Year Prospective Study on the Effects of Perceived Organizational Support and Psychological Capital" in the *International Journal of Environmental Research*, researchers Henry C. Y. Ho and Ying Chuen Chan noted that when organizations provide nurturing and supportive psychological resources, psychosocial functioning improves within the workforce in the long run.

The key is to help people feel a sense of connection, trust, support, and psychological safety. When you care and invest in people, you help them leverage their strengths, develop professionally, feel a sense of purpose and meaning, and have a sense of accomplishment, all of which support flourishing.

Care builds flourishing communities

Humans are social beings who not only desire connection, but thrive on it. Cultures of care are based on this fact. Social support, and really support of any kind, is necessary for employees to be able to manage the very challenging times we live in. The more supported people feel by leadership, which includes the material and financial resources to do their work, the more fuel they have to optimize engagement and performance, and ultimately, to care about their work. Care does the following:

>> **Boosts motivation:** Whether you are motivated to do good for others, eat healthy, or exercise, when the group you admire and respect is engaging in a given activity or behavior, you are more likely to do it too. Your close-knit

relationships motivate you to work harder, cooperate, and support one another.

>> **Improves sense of security:** When you know several people have your back and that resources are available to you to access (emotional, financial, material, and so on), your sense of security in your ability to handle adversity increases.

>> **Encourages reliance and cooperation:** Knowing you can rely on others encourages you to offer the same. Having a shared goal that has benefit not only for you but for the group encourages this mutual reliance as well as cooperation.

>> **Increases trust:** Feeling more secure and knowing you can rely on others increases trust that your needs will be taken care of in the future, and thus in your resources to handle uncertainty. It also increases your need to be trusted, encouraging you to be supportive and more trustworthy.

>> **Fosters commitment and devotion:** Trust encourages stronger commitments, and the more people show up for one another, the more likely they are to be committed and devoted to helping one another during difficult times.

>> **Provides new perspectives:** Having other people to turn to who can add new perspectives enables better problem-solving and creativity.

>> **Enhances learning:** Getting different perspectives and feeling secure to ask for help opens you up to learn and grow. You also learn from the questions, mistakes, and successes of those in your group or community.

>> **Elevates performance:** You only have to look at athletic teams that work well together to note how a team leverages strengths and mines weaknesses, enabling an individual player to shine. In a team, each player has a valuable role that creates the collective. One person doesn't do everything, meaning the responsibilities are shared and success is accomplished through cooperation. Each individual is also inspired to work harder, better themselves, and show up!

Building a culture of care with a code of conduct

Don Miguel Ruiz, in his book *The Four Agreements* (published by Amber-Allen Publishing), offers a code of conduct that can help people create a better sense of connection, happiness, and freedom, which I believe can help foster flourishing in the workplace. The Four Agreements are four promises you can make to yourself:

>> **Be impeccable with your word.** The words you choose are powerful. Be mindful and notice how your words affect you or others, how they can transform your own way of thinking or behavior and also influence others. Being impeccable with your word reinforces being mindful and compassionate, and not blaming or shaming yourself or others.

>> **Don't take anything personally.** When you know your self-value and you are centered in your core values, you don't take things personally because you know who you are. Other people's issues are just that: Other people's issues. They are not yours.

>> **Don't make assumptions.** Rather than make assumptions or jump to conclusions, ask questions instead. Be curious. Don't make assumptions regarding why you think you can't do something or why you believe someone else behaved in a certain way. Let go of the need to be right or wrong, and stay open to learning, deeper understanding, and getting the whole picture.

>> **Always do your best.** Situations change, and you can only do the best that you can in any given moment. Some days will be easier than others to be impeccable with your words, open, and stronger within yourself. Whether you are focusing on your job, leading, or keeping to these promises, be compassionate and forgiving with yourself and aim to do your best.

Setting the Example for Caring

The Four Agreements can serve as a foundation for you to be conscientious and purposeful with your actions and leadership style. It will take a bit more than this code of conduct, though, to follow through on your ability to lead with care. You also want to set the example by doing the following:

>> **Embrace change and seek out opportunities.** Be eager to learn and grow. Don't let the fear of failure get the best of you. Be curious to learn, be willing to take risks, and look for ways to be creative and inventive. Seek new strategies and ideas, and be open to learning a new skill, management strategy, or approach. Your humility and openness will encourage your team to also be innovative, creative, open, and trusting.

>> **Communicate empathically and openly.** When you communicate, be clear while being empathic and transparent. Be distinct about what you want and clear when relaying expectations, goals, and objectives. This empathic, approachable, and authentic nature builds trust and opens pathways for discussion and to receiving feedback.

» **Build healthy networks of support and trust.** Aim to cultivate strong social bonds within the organization, build trust, share goals and core values, and connect through shared purpose. Find out about the people who work with you and for you. Stick to your word, assure fairness and justice, and facilitate the group to work together and collaborate so that collectively, the group can be stronger.

» **Be willing to be humble.** It's important that as a leader you act with confidence, but this doesn't mean you can't also act humbly, understanding that you, too, have much to learn. Stay open to feedback and allow yourself to be coachable, reaching out for advice from trusted sources, counsel, classes, and others.

» **Take care.** Work toward maintaining your sense of calm and emphasize your own work-life balance. Make self-care and self-awareness a priority and encourage others to do the same.

» **Seek purpose and be purposeful.** Seek meaning and purpose in your approach to how you work, communicate, and function as a leader. Act purposefully so that you're driven by the knowledge of the impact your efforts have on others or achieving a purpose rather than just the bottom dollar.

If you are noticing a pattern in everything I am writing, you are correct. Whether your goal is to be happier, more successful, prevent burnout, or find a way to get more people engaged and productive, the efforts you take to help yourself be resilient and flourish are the ones that you implement strategically in your organization to create a culture of care and help others flourish. Everything starts with you, and the more authentically and compassionately you live your life, the more positive your influence will be on others. It starts with you.

Unlocking Resources from Within

Whether you are focusing on yourself or your community, the key is finding a way to nurture signature strengths in each person, showing respect and understanding that everyone has value. When you nurture others, their strengths and value can shine. You see value everywhere, in yourself and the people around you. You focus on believing that it's possible to unlock resources from within and for everyone to flourish.

Making flourishing the prime focus

When it comes to your workplace, you, your co-workers, and direct reports likely feel more motivated by the desire to flourish and thrive than by the fear of collapse or ruin. Studies show that when leaders focus on flourishing and implement flourishing interventions, job satisfaction and happiness at work are more likely, as well as less emotional exhaustion and workplace stress. This doesn't mean that you don't pay heed to problems, especially when burnout is concerned. Rather, it means that you focus on flourishing as a means of enhancing engagement, collaboration, and well-being while also healing and preventing burnout.

Getting to know your people

As a resilient and flourishing leader, you can support your community, co-workers, or direct reports to see opportunities for growth in the workplace, develop their strengths, and focus on what matters to them most. Doing so helps them to flourish and to cultivate PERMA. (See Chapter 14 for more on PERMA.) The key is to invest in people and get to know them. Find out what matters to them and how they see themselves, including their capabilities, what they value, where they have self-doubt, and what makes them tick. This is how you can do it:

>> **Find out why.** When a project goes well, find out why. If it goes poorly, find out why. Have conversations with the people involved. Find out who did what and what the process was like.

>> **Avoid empty praise when something goes well.** Avoid praising people without getting the details. Instead, engage the group in a conversation about how each individual contributed and the cause for success. In this way, not only do you get an idea of where strengths lie in each person, but so does everyone else.

>> **Pinpoint skills.** When given the opportunity, pinpoint the specific skill each person has, commend them for it, and encourage them to harness it as a strength.

>> **Encourage the view that setbacks present opportunities.** When a project experiences a setback, support the team to view it as an opportunity to learn and grow, to uncover where collaboration may be necessary, and to see if someone's strengths were not best utilized or if someone was given a role that they were not best suited for.

>> **Discover strengths as a group.** You may want to have everyone on your team fill out a personality profile or a character strength questionnaire. Find out more about the people you work with and support them to discover more about themselves.

>> **Set people up for success.** Aim to determine personal characteristics of value that help people function and operate at their best. In other words, work toward ensuring that you have the right personalities and strengths in the right roles, setting people up for success and positive self-belief so that everyone flourishes, including you.

Cultivating positive identity in workplace

The narratives in your mind shape your beliefs, the way you think, how you see yourself, and how you act and behave. The story of self-doubt and inadequacy influences a very different trajectory of actions than the narrative of confidence and self-value. Imagine an entire community or team that is being influenced by a story of inadequacy and self-doubt.

For most people, it's relatively easy to fall prey to the more negative of our stories. How many times did you feel good about an accomplishment, but the positive sentiments were short-lived because you soon realized that you missed one small detail? Thus starts the spiral of self-doubt. As a leader, you have the ability to offset this spiral and instead help people cultivate a more positive self-identity.

In the book *Exploring Positive Identities and Organizations: Building a Theoretical and Research Foundation*, Professor Laura Roberts says that the way to generate extraordinary performance and well-being in organizations is to view the individual who belongs to them as a capable and essential resource who creates value for the organization. She says that individuals learn about themselves through their interactions with others and that people perceive their value, character, and competence based on these social interactions. She documents how individuals can discover their strengths, unique contributions, and abilities through positive reflected appraisals, especially done by leadership. Roberts also makes sure to point out that every individual is responsible for their own identity. In other words, they are not victims of the environment or organization, but rather, co-creators and conspirators that can work together to build themselves up or knock themselves down.

As a leader, you can thus be a co-creator with your team, community, or direct reports to help them cultivate positive identities. The process starts with you, meaning you lead by example, practicing self-compassion and mindfulness, and harnessing your own recipe for flourishing (Chapter 14). The next step involves transferring this compassion to how you communicate, see value, and offer praise as well as accountability or constructive criticism; provide opportunities for growth, mentorship, and professional development; and support individuals to discover their strengths.

Overcoming negative attention bias

When asked to describe her experience and how she felt, my client Jade recalled being repeatedly criticized by her former boss and told me that she experienced the sense that her chest was collapsing inwardly and noticed associated feelings of sadness and hurt. She admitted that she was aware that her former boss felt threatened by her and her out-of-the-box ideas because they challenged the legacy of ideas he wanted to be remembered by, which was understandable, given the nature of the industry. Even so, she still felt upset. Despite recalling the many clients and colleagues who sang her praise, Jade still had niggling self-doubt as a result of never quite getting the recognition she yearned for from her former boss.

If you find that you, too, are more drawn to dwelling on negative experiences, criticisms, mistakes, or feelings of inadequacy, you are not alone. The brain is wired to remember negative events more strongly than positive ones, because remembering the negative can help you prepare, avoid, or react quickly if threatening situations were to happen again. The tendency to feel rejection, rebuke, or criticism more strongly than the elation of praise is referred to as "negative bias" and is indeed part of a survival response. For this reason, you are more likely to remember hurts rather than happiness, post-traumatic stress rather than post-traumatic growth, and insults rather than praise.

The problem is that when you hold on to negative bias, you maintain the perception of yourself being inadequate, somehow unworthy, or not enough. This then influences the lens with which you perceive the rest of your world, including your relationships and your job. Negative bias can influence everything you do — how you behave, interact, and perceive yourself and your world, and your ability to make sound decisions. It can affect your work and the people you work with, and ultimately, negatively influence the entire organization.

Though negative bias is part of our human wiring, there are ways to overcome it. As a leader, you can help others shift out of negative bias and into flourishing by implementing a five-step approach. Doing so enables you to communicate mindfully, engage your direct reports with empathy and compassion, celebrate successes and strengths, and regularly discuss errors and setbacks within the framework of learning and growth.

Here are five steps to shifting out of negative bias:

1. **Pause.**

   Do mindful breathing or ground yourself using a here-and-now stone.
   (See Chapter 8 for an explanation of the stone and how to use it.)

2. **Bring in mindfulness and compassion.**

   Approach yourself, someone else, or a situation with honor and compassion.
   Be present and allow in loving kindness.

3. **Thank the negative.**

   Thank your inner critic, any negative feedback, or criticism, understanding that it is just pointing out where you, another person, or the situation are vulnerable.

4. **Remember value.**

   Redirect your focus to the story of value. Celebrate strengths and seek out value and silver linings.

5. **Reappraise setbacks.**

   Reappraise the situation and consider where the opportunity for growth and learning lies.

Activating virtuousness

Happiness can be *hedonic* or *euadimonic*. It can take on the form of immediate gratification, or it can be a deep sense of well-being that you feel at your core. Why am I explaining this to you? The English word that most reflects the meaning of eudaimonia is (you may have guessed it) flourishing, and according to Aristotle, eudaimonia is the highest state of human good, which can be achieved by practicing virtues like being kind, honesty, service, compassion, generosity, good humor, or wisdom. In other words, to flourish and be happy from the core of your being, it may behoove you to live in harmony with your values and morals and "be a good person," at least according to Aristotle.

Now, I am not an advocate of using the labels "good person" or "bad person." The environmental conditions that you find yourself in certainly influence your ability to flourish, whether you are living according to your code of moral excellence or not. However, when you do connect with your core values or virtues such as kindness, honesty, acceptance, compassion, dignity, and so forth, and practice living according to them, you may find yourself accessing a more positive mindset, finding purpose and meaning more readily, being more compassionate, experiencing more richness and joy, and thus flourishing. And of course, when you flourish, others flourish. In their article, "Virtuous Leadership and Employee Flourishing: The Mediating Role of Work Engagement," Martjin Hendriks and colleagues note that evidence does show a positive association between virtuous leaders and employees' engagement and flourishing.

Like anything else, the more you practice your virtues, the more you cultivate them to be more prevalent in your life, which then influences how you show up and influence others. You may find your relationships improving, that you feel more fulfilled by your achievements, and that you can overcome negative bias more easily. You lead a more purposeful life and become more trustworthy and trusting, which strengthens your connections because people trust that you genuinely care and live by your word.

REMEMBER

As a virtuous leader, you don't just commit to being better yourself; you also commit to helping others become better.

Exercise: Activating virtues through mindful contemplation

When I want to fully embody a given virtue, I practice a mindful contemplation exercise, where I sit with the feeling that arises from bringing the given virtue to mind for a moment or more. It's a wonderful practice that you can do in a moment of stress, prior to an important conversation, to start or end your day, or anytime in between.

1. **Choose a virtue.**

   Choose any virtue to contemplate. (You can choose more than one to contemplate in one sitting, but focus on only one at a time.) Feel free to pick a virtue from Table 15-1 or come up with a virtue you want to activate that isn't on the list.

2. **Settle in and focus on your breath.**

   Find a comfortable position, preferably a quiet place, and close your eyes.

   Take a moment to bring your awareness to your body, as it is right now. Notice how and what you feel.

   Bring your awareness to your breath. Count 1-2-3 as you inhale and 1-2-3-4-5-6 as you exhale, noticing sensations in your body all the while. Appreciate the breath, its movement, how you feel, and the life force that fills you for a few cycles of breath.

3. **Breathe in the virtue and reflect.**

   Breathe in deeply and exhale completely. Imagine that you are breathing in the virtue and letting it flow through your body as you exhale. Take a deep breath in, and when you exhale, say the word silently or out loud to yourself, letting it flow through your body with your breath. Do this at least three times.

   Allow your breath to settle into a natural rhythm and let the virtue resonate throughout your body. Take note of the feelings that you then experience. Notice what images or thoughts come to mind.

   As you breathe in and out, imagine the virtue is getting stronger within you as you embody it. Say to yourself, "I like the feeling of being (acting, speaking, or the like) _____" three times, filling in the blank with the said virtue. You might say, for instance, "I like the feeling of being compassionate," "I like the feeling of acting with integrity," or "I like the feeling of speaking with fairness." Say the statement at least three times and take note of how you feel and how your body feels.

4. Come back.

When you are ready, gently shift your awareness back to noticing how your body feels sitting where you are, your feet resting on the floor, the movement of your breath, and any other sensations you may be experiencing.

Take two or three cleansing breaths and then when you are ready, open your eyes.

TABLE 15-1   ## Virtues Word List

Acceptance	Affection	Agreeableness	Amiability	Beauty
Benevolence	Bravery	Care	Charity	Cleanliness
Commitment	Compassion	Confidence	Consideration	Contentment
Cooperation	Courtesy	Creativity	Curiosity	Detachment
Determination	Devotion	Dignity	Diligence	Discretion
Duty	Earnestness	Enthusiasm	Ethical	Excellence
Fairness	Faithfulness	Flexibility	Forgiveness	Fortitude
Friendliness	Generosity	Gentleness	Goodwill	Graciousness
Gratitude	Harmonious	Helpfulness	Honesty	Honorable
Hope	Humanity	Humility	Humor	Idealism
Imaginative	Impartiality	Integrity	Intelligence	Joyfulness
Justice	Kindness	Kinship	Leniency	Love
Loyalty	Magnanimity	Mercy	Moderation	Modesty
Moral	Noble	Openness	Optimistic	Orderliness
Passionate	Patient	Peaceful	Perseverance	Preparedness
Purposefulness	Questioning	Quiet	Reliability	Reputable
Resilience	Resourcefulness	Respect	Responsibility	Restraint
Reverence	Righteousness	Self-discipline	Selflessness	Sensitivity
Simplicity	Sincerity	Spontaneity	Steadfastness	Strength
Sympathy	Tact	Temperance	Tenaciousness	Tenderness
Thankfulness	Tolerance	Toughness	Tranquility	Trust
Truthfulness	Understanding	Unity	Upstanding	Virtuous
Visionary	Vitality	Wholesome	Wisdom	Wonder

5. **Reflect, inquire, and set intention.**

Consider and reflect on what you can do to support yourself to actively embody this virtue throughout your day. How can it show up in your communications, relationships, and professional duties?

Let images and thoughts form and consider writing down your intentions and what you can do to support your ability to activate this virtue, help others, and collectively, help people flourish and thrive.

Building a sense of purpose and meaning to foster flourishing

Similar to core values, a sense of purpose reflects what really matters to you. You experience purposefulness when you strive to create or achieve something that is meaningful to you. In their article, "Purpose of Life Predicts Better Emotional Recovery from Negative Stimuli," authors Stacey M. Schaeffer and colleagues note that evidence tells us that people who have a strong sense of purpose tend to be more resilient and recover better from the negative effects of stress. According to their in-depth report conducted during the pandemic, the management consultant firm Mickinsey & Company found that people who said they were "living their purpose" at work reported a five-times-higher level of well-being than those who said they weren't. Furthermore, they found that purpose contributed to improving employee experience, engagement, and commitment. On the flip side, lacking meaning and purpose had a higher correlation with the risk of getting burned out.

It is challenging to feel purposeful or believe that your job has purpose when the organization that you work for or leadership doesn't provide you with support, positive feedback, or evidence that your contribution is impactful or that you matter. People can take care of themselves, believe in their abilities and in what they do, but it can only go so far if the culture they work in is toxic, uncollaborative, punitive, and unrewarding.

Leadership and organizations can support individuals to find, feel, and maintain their sense of purpose. They can give people something to feel purposeful about and create an infrastructure that values them and their contributions. If you want your colleagues and direct reports to find purpose and feel purposeful, in other words, you can help them do so. It requires you to get to know and understand them, find out what is important to them and what they are proud of, support them to lean on their strengths and find out about their struggles, and empower them to be the unique individuals that they are. This is how you can help:

>> **Help them remember the "why" of their work.** Whether you use outsource inspiration, meaningful conversations, social gatherings, or reward incentives, you want to help others remember why they do the work they do and what and whom their work impacts. People want to know that what they do matters.

>> **Help them remember that they matter as individuals.** Listen mindfully, be open to feedback, reward when appropriate, and support them with their struggles. Consider their input when making decisions and communicate the impact their input has had on the decisions once they are made. Take interest in their hobbies or goals.

>> **Help them grow and learn.** Create opportunities for professional development and mentorship. Meet regularly to review goals, review struggles, and find ways to improve and learn. Invest in their education, training, and future.

>> **Help them collaborate.** Create an environment where people are encouraged to work as a team and collaborate, gain knowledge from one another, and use their individual strengths and skills to achieve a collective outcome.

>> **Help them be accountable.** Communicate and collaboratively create strategies where both leaders and direct reports confirm to one another when action steps are completed, keeping everyone collectively focused and accountable.

>> **Help them celebrate.** Celebrate their successes and the impact their work has on others, including the organization and customers or clients.

When you help, you show that you care, and when people feel like they matter, they are more likely to feel a sense of purpose, have a desire to engage, and help other people.

Creating a Conspiracy of Goodness to Support Flourishing

In the past few months, aside from working on this book and juggling a busy consulting and coaching schedule, I have been focused on caretaking. My father, who is legally blind, has been in and out of the hospital, while my mother has been recovering from a total knee replacement. Despite being diligent about taking care of myself — exercising, eating nutrient-rich foods, and meditating — I still found myself feeling like I was on the edge of having nothing left last week. Having been burned out before, I was able to recognize the signs of when my fire begins to flicker and my patience runs dry.

At one point, I became irritated with my father, and I knew right then and there that I had to take a time-out. I didn't like my behavior or the way I was feeling. I didn't admonish myself, however. Rather, I had compassion for the way I felt and told my family that I needed to take a break and take care of myself. I left their house and walked outside, shed some tears, and the next thing I knew, a close friend called out of the blue; a child in a stroller waved and said "Hi!"; a driver waved at me, letting me cross even though I was jaywalking; and several people walking down the street greeted me with "hellos" and smiles (which is rare in this particular neighborhood. People usually keep their head down and faces turned). As I stood waiting to cross the street, a gentle breeze caressed my skin, bringing with it the aroma from the flowers blooming in the trees. I thought to myself, "I feel like I am in a movie, where everything is in synch and everyone is conspiring goodness. It's as if the world is trying to remind me that I am loved, and that kindness and beauty still exist."

The point of this story is that I didn't fall into my negative bias and was able to shift into a more positive outlook because *other* people treated me with kindness. I was already treating myself with care; I just needed *other* people to remind me that I mattered.

So once again, we live in a time where a vast number of people are burned out or close to it, and chances are this is true in your workplace. As human beings, it is normal and quite easy to slip into negative bias, which means the culture of the organization may be collectively negative. The people in your workplace may be caught up in negative conspiracy theories, especially regarding leadership and reasons to distrust the organization's motives. This doesn't need to be the case.

REMEMBER

You can work toward creating a conspiracy of goodness in your culture. You can create a culture of sharing, learning, kindness, and connection, where leaders communicate compassionately, encourage, and support their employees, and offer opportunities for learning, growth, and mentorship. And again, it starts with you. It is equally as important to ensure that you, as a leader, get the care you need as well.

Did you know that the Latin components of *conspiracy* are *"con,"* meaning "together" and *"spirare,"* which means "breathe"? Together we breathe. And together we can breathe a negative bias, or we can breathe care and flourishing. I don't know about you, but I prefer the latter.

5

The Part of Tens

Use your body to create more ease in your mind.

Discover action steps you can take to flourish at work.

Chapter **16**

Ten Ways to Use Your Body to Ease Your Mind

t has been well documented that physical activity can improve mood and cognitive abilities. It has been linked with a bigger brain size, more endorphins/serotonin, and greater neuroplasticity and has been shown to improve mood, including anxiety and depression; lower stress levels; and improve memory, self-esteem, and cognitive functioning. When combined with a type of meditative practice or breath focus, moving your body or mindful movement can also help create a sense of relaxation and ease, improve sleep, and improve physical and mental health. This chapter offers you ten simple practices that help you use your body to ease your mind.

Enhancing Physical Activity

Exercise is a natural and effective way to reduce stress and lower feelings of anxiety. It relieves tension, boosts physical and mental energy, and enhances well-being largely through the release of endorphins and neurotransmitters. A ten-minute walk may be just as good as a 45-minute workout for helping anxiety and depression. Although the effects may be temporary, a brisk walk or other simple activity can deliver several hours of relief, similar to taking an aspirin for a headache. Being more active helps you be less anxious in general, as well as helps you feel more capable of coping with stress. The more you exercise, the better it gets for you in the long term, with regard to preventing anxiety, not just the short term.

REMEMBER

It doesn't matter which exercise you do, just that you do it. There are a multitude of options to choose from. You can walk, jog, cycle, row, swim, jump rope, rollerblade, dance, or play basketball, tennis, or ultimate frisbee. Weight training is also an option. Be gentle and mindful with yourself. If your body is truly burned out, you don't want to push yourself right from the start. Take it slowly and pay attention to how your body feels during exercise and the next day. Perhaps start with ten minutes and see how you feel.

Breathing with Alternate Nostrils

The beauty of your breath is that you can take it with you everywhere. When you are feeling anxious, overwhelmed, and stressed, you always have the option of creating more ease in your body and mind by focusing on your breath, controlling its rhythm, and mindfully observing it. There is no end to the ways you can use your breath to relax, and one very effective technique is called alternate nostril breathing, or the focused practice of rhythmically breathing through one nostril at a time. This controlled breathing technique can help regulate your nervous system, lower blood pressure, improve oxygen flow and lung health, quiet the mind, create a feeling of balance, and reduce fear and anxiety.

Here is how you can do alternate nostril breathing:

1. **Find a quiet place to sit and close your eyes if you like.**

2. **Inhale through your left nostril.**

   Gently apply pressure with your right thumb on the side of your right nostril, while your index finger and middle finger rest on the bridge of your nose. Press down until the right nostril is closed and then inhale slowly, counting 1-2-3, through your left nostril.

3. **Exhale through the right nostril.**

   Release your thumb from the right nostril and place your ring finger on the left nostril, gently pressing down so that it is closed, and slowly exhale through the right nostril, counting 1-2-3.

4. **Inhale through the right nostril and exhale through the left.**

   Slowly count 1-2-3. Then press down with your thumb on the right nostril while releasing the left nostril by lifting your ring finger, and exhale slowly from your left nostril counting slowly 1-2-3.

5. **Inhale through the left nostril and exhale through the right.**

   Inhale through your left nostril slowly for a count of three, then press your ring finger down on the left nostril while releasing the right nostril by lifting your thumb. Exhale through your right nostril slowly to the count of three.

6. **Repeat the full process for up to five minutes.**

   If you feel dizzy, slow down your breathing or take a pause.

Mindfully Being in Motion

When you focus your attention on whatever is happening within you and around you in the present moment with an attitude of open interest and acceptance, you can calm incessant mind chatter and better achieve a sense of ease and peace. Mindfulness can help you feel less affected by stress, more relaxed, more creative, more open to learning, sleep better, improve your relationships with others, and enable you to feel happier and more satisfied with your life. Combining mindfulness with movement and a breath focus can triple the benefits as you engage your muscles, brain neurons, and other happy neurochemicals.

You can do the following mindful movement practice anywhere, as it involves minimal movement while also helping you feel more grounded and calmer.

1. **Stand with your feet shoulder width apart, keeping your knees slightly bent.**

2. **Keep an upright posture with your head lifted, chin tucked, and back straight.**

3. **Close your eyes.**

4. **Inhale deeply and exhale completely, focusing on the breath as you breathe in and out.**

   Be aware of your chest and abdomen rising and falling, the flow of the breath, and any other sensations you may experience.

5. **Bring your awareness to the soles of your feet and just be aware of the connection your feet have with the earth.**

   Notice sensations and where your weight falls as you stand on the earth.

6. **Breathe in and imagine you are gathering the energy of the earth into the back part of the soles of your feet.**

7. **Exhale, releasing the energy from the front pad of your feet back into the earth.**

8. **Inhale, gathering the energy of the earth in the back part of the soles of your feet.**

   Lean into the back of the soles while allowing the toes to come up slightly.

9. **Exhale, releasing the energy from the front pads of your feet back into the earth.**

   Lean onto the front pads of your feet, allowing your heals to come up slightly (you will be swaying slightly back and forth).

10. **Sway back and forth as you inhale and exhale, connecting with the earth for at least ten cycles of breath.**

11. **When ready, stand still and just be aware of your connection to the earth.**

   Notice how and what you feel.

Stretching and Twisting into Peace

Mindful stretching is a wonderful option to achieve calm while moving when you feel too tired to engage in aerobic physical activity or you don't have the option to get outdoors or to a gym. Practicing yoga, for instance, can help reduce stress response reactivity while also improving your flexibility and strength. A variety of yoga forms exist, including Kripalu, Iyengar, Kundalini, Hatha, or Bikram, to name a few. Kundalini yoga is a branch of yoga that combines chants with breath-work and poses, also known as Kriyas, and has been associated with better mood, cognition, and flexibility. The following is a Kundalini Kriya pose that involves twisting the body along with controlled breathing. I find stretching and twisting the spine to be extremely helpful for creating a sense of calm and improving energy flow.

1. **Find a quiet place to sit comfortably.**

   If you can, aim to sit on the floor in a cross-legged position.

2. **Place your hands on your shoulders.**

   Put your right hand on your right shoulder, and your left hand on your left shoulder, grabbing the shoulders so that the thumbs are in the back and your fingers are in the front. Adjust your elbows so that your arms are parallel to the floor.

3. **Inhale deeply and twist to the left.**

4. **Exhale completely and twist to the right.**

   Keep your spine upright and face forward.

   Continue for 1–4 minutes.

5. **Notice how you feel.**

Smiling to Your Body

In our busy and demanding lives, we tend to forget to appreciate our bodies, the fact that they carry us around all day, put up with our antics, and enable us to live and exist in the world. Taking the time to offer gratitude to your body can have the effect of elevating your mood, calming your stress, and helping you access more positive emotions.

The following is one of my more favorite appreciation exercises. It involves smiling to every part of your body and goes like this:

1. **Find a comfortable position and close your eyes.**

2. **Breathe in deeply and exhale completely.**

   Count to three on the inhalation and six on the exhalation for three or four cycles of breath.

3. **Imagine breathing loving kindness.**

   When you inhale, you are breathing loving kindness into your heart center. When you exhale, the loving kindness flows through the rest of your body. Breathing in loving kindness, breathing out, letting it flow to the rest of your body. Do this for three or four cycles of breath.

4. **Notice how you feel.**

   Take note of the sensations you are experiencing in your chest, whether it feels open or closed, relaxed or tight, heavy or light.

5. **Smile gently.**

6. **Smile as you gently move your focus and awareness to your heart.**

   Smile in your heart. Acknowledge your heart and all that it does for you as you smile, breathing in and out for another five cycles of breath. Continue to breathe slowly and gently shift your focus and awareness to your lungs, smile to your lungs, and acknowledge your lungs and all that they do for you.

7. **Move your focus to another body part, smiling and acknowledging each organ, muscle, bone, blood vessel, or red blood cell.**

8. **Expand your focus to your entire body and smile to and in your body.**

   Notice that your entire body is smiling and breathing as one.

9. **Sit quietly and notice how you feel, perhaps in gratitude of your brilliant body.**

Posing in Child's Pose

Child's pose is a simple yoga technique that can be extremely relaxing and nourishing. It helps you to connect with yourself and the earth like a child might as you let go and breathe slowly, in and out. The pose benefits your physical and mental health as it stretches your spine, hips, thigh muscles, and ankles, while relieving any tension you may be holding in your neck, back, shoulders, or legs. It helps calm the mind, improves circulation, and gets you to breathe slowly.

Here is how you do it:

1. **Sit your buttocks on your heels on the floor, with the aim of having your big toes touch one another.**

   Preferably, sit on a matt, rug or on the grass where it is soft. Try to keep your knees in line with your hips.

2. **Inhale deeply as you reach your arms upward.**

3. **As you exhale, reach forward, and lay your forehead down on the floor, so that your torso is resting against your thighs.**

4. **Inhale and exhale and rest in this pose for at least 30 seconds or as long as you like.**

TIP

There are several variations to this pose. The key is that you don't feel like you are straining, especially your neck. You can place a towel under your shins, a pillow or towel under your belly, or a pillow or block to prop your head up.

Centering and Grounding

The aim of this exercise is to practice a mindfulness meditation out in nature, whereby you engage all your senses to appreciate nature, while employing non-judgmental awareness and appreciation for the connection you have with nature. The practice helps you feel more centered and grounded, which is often much needed when you feel overwhelmed and drained. Try to do any of the following to enjoy the outdoors:

>> Take yourself to a place in nature that you love. It may be a forest, an open field, a beach, or even your garden.

>> You may choose to stand still, sit comfortably, or lie down, as long as you are comfortable.

>> When you are comfortable, close your eyes.

>> Notice the feel of the air on the skin of your face.

>> Notice the feel of the air as it fills your nostrils and then your lungs.

>> Notice the sounds of nature around you. Is there a bird singing? Are the leaves moving in the breeze?

>> Notice the connection your breath brings to you with the air, the breeze, or the sounds.

>> Notice the feel of the earth beneath your body, supporting you.

>> Touch the ground if you can. Sweep the earth with your fingers and hands. What do you notice or feel?

>> Appreciate that farmers till the earth and it is where your nurturance comes from. Appreciate the support the earth provides you and anything else that comes to mind.

>> You may choose now to garden mindfully, walk mindfully, or continue sitting or lying down using all your senses to appreciate your connection to heaven and earth — listening, noticing, looking, feeling, tasting, being.

Digging in the Dirt

Did you know that gardeners are less depressed and anxious, and they feel a stronger sense of connection to something greater, or sense of spirituality? Gardening can be physically demanding, and according to the Centers for Disease Control (CDC), is a form of exercise. The benefits don't stop there. Digging in the dirt means you are outside, in nature, and if you are gardening, you are truly connecting with nature and its rhythm and flow. You are attuned to when the sun shines and when it is raining; when it is time to till the soil and when it is time to harvest. You may rake leaves, shovel, dig, or pull weeds, patiently caring for your garden, knowing you will one day be able to witness the fruits (vegetables, herbs, or flowers) of your labor.

Relaxing Your Muscles Progressively

You can use the connection with your body to soothe the mind by focusing on a body part, tensing it, and then relaxing it. The technique is called progressive muscle relaxation (PMR), and it is extremely effective in lowering stress levels, helps you achieve a better sense of calm and ease, improves sleep, and alleviates body aches. With PMR, you start by first tensing a particular muscle group like the forehead or neck for several seconds and then allow those same muscles to relax for about 30 seconds, mindfully noticing how you feel. When you relieve stress in your muscles, you also release tension in the mind.

1. **Find a comfortable place and position to sit or lie down.**

2. **Close your eyes and focus on your breathing.**

   Slowly inhale through your nose and exhale through your mouth for three cycles of breath.

3. **Squeeze your forehead as tightly as you can and hold it for ten seconds.**

   Notice the tension in your forehead.

4. **Slowly relax your forehead and notice how you feel.**

   Perhaps you can notice the tension leaving your forehead.

5. **Repeat the sequence.**

6. **Tighten your eyes, squeezing them shut for five to ten seconds.**

   Notice the buildup of tension.

7. **Slowly relax the muscles around the eyes, noting how you feel.**

8. **Repeat the sequence.**

9. **Continue tensing and releasing the muscles of your face, neck, shoulders, back, abdomen, arms, hands, legs, and feet.**

   All the while, notice how you feel.

   Avoid tensing the muscles in any area of your body where you're injured or in pain.

Dancing, with or without Abandon

If exercise can help reduce stress and help you find ease, imagine what dancing with abandon can do! How do you think our ancestors let off stress? When you dance, feel-good neurotransmitters and hormones like endorphins and oxytocin are released while stress hormone levels drop. When you move, especially in sync to music, nerve pathways are created in your brain, which not only helps you coordinate your movements, but also helps improve your memory, mood, and cognition. You may feel too burned out to dance, but evidence shows that dance can relieve anxiety and depression and boost your focus and concentration. Even if you're uncoordinated, you will likely benefit from turning on your favorite music and doing a jig or two.

Chapter **17**

Ten Tips to Foster Flourishing at Work

Your ability to flourish at work is very much influenced by whether you feel appreciated, supported personally and materially, get to use your strengths, feel a sense of autonomy, are given opportunities for growth and learning, are able to feel connected and collaborative, and have a semblance of balance in your life between when you *do* and when you get to *be*. Though you don't have control over some factors when it comes to your workplace, you do have control over others. This chapter offers ten tips to help you foster flourishing at work.

Starting the Day with "Me Time"

Face it, once your day gets going, it's usually about taking care of everyone and everything else other than you. If you don't make yourself a priority, no one else will. Even if it seems that you wake up too early as it is, consider setting your alarm to wake you up at least 15 minutes early (preferably more). Let those 15 minutes be your "me time." It is sacred time meant only for you to luxuriate in bed, mindfully sip your tea or coffee as you stare out the window, meditate, or listen to or read inspirational messages. You may go for a mindful walk and be mindful in everything you do, listening to your body or the sounds coming from outside, or being present with your breath as it moves in and out. It's important that you don't look at your emails or phone messages. Rather, imagine that the day hasn't started yet. This is your space in between *being* and *doing,* and a time to set the stage for how you want to feel and what you want to accomplish the rest of the day.

Taking Time Off to Unplug

In today's modern and hectic world, we are rarely "unplugged," and the constant barrage of emails and notifications and the need to monitor your phone and inbox have likely contributed to your burnout more than you may realize. Without taking time off to unplug and disconnect, you invariably might find yourself "on" 24/7, available at any time, even when you are supposed to be sleeping.

To heal burnout, it's necessary that you take time off for yourself to decompress, recharge, and renew. This means being able to unplug every now and then. Aim to create a schedule for when you will be "on" and when you will be "off" and stick to it. You can create time slots in the schedule for checking your emails or doing work during your "off" hours. For instance, you may choose to designate all time after dinner as your "off" time but block 30 minutes to check emails or complete a bit of work. Same goes for the weekend, so that you ensure you have built-in time for rest, to be truly "off," fully present, and participating in your life. Look at your schedule and figure out days or even just afternoons that you can take off completely to detach, relax, and re-center, including taking a vacation or mini-breaks. Enjoy hobbies or fun activities, spend time with people you enjoy being with, or even just get more sleep.

Developing Your Strengths

When you get to use your strengths at work, you are more likely to be able to foster flourishing. Whether you fill out an online questionnaire or work closely with a coach or counselor, you want to figure out your strengths — the activities and abilities you excel in — which support you to feel accomplished. Take time every week to reassess your work to question whether you are being supported to leverage your strengths and what you may need to better achieve your goals. As you go through your workday, observe with open interest and nonjudgment how you may be employing your strengths and if not, how you can do so. Perhaps you would like to improve your strengths or figure out how to strengthen your weaknesses. Is there a course you would like to take or something you want to learn that can improve your knowledge and skills? As growth and learning also foster flourishing, it benefits you to look into courses or opportunities that may be provided by your organization or community that can serve to enhance your knowledge and build your strengths.

Aim to let go of projects and activities that don't play to your strengths, if possible, and delegate them to people who can manage the tasks instead. Though delegating can lighten your workload, it can also increase it if you don't assign tasks to the right people or if you don't communicate your needs clearly. This is where knowing yourself, your value, and your strengths comes in handy. You want to think of delegation not as a way to pass the buck, if you will, but rather as a way to build trust and show respect to someone else because you believe in their ability to help and contribute, and ultimately, play to their strengths.

Enlivening Curiosity

When you're exhausted or feeling depleted, it can be difficult to see much outside of your own circle of misery and the never-ending to-do list. Even when exhausted though, you can aim to flip the switch within yourself and decide to view the world like a young child so that everything is new and interesting. Choose to be in a state of wonder, including when things go awry or when you find yourself feeling frustrated. Being curious supports you to let go of fear around making mistakes, can diminish feelings of overwhelm, and ignites the desire to learn and grow.

Make it a habit to keep a notebook with you so that you can jot down observations and insights. Regularly ask questions to find out more about yourself, others, or the way something works and why. Look for opportunities for growth. Can you learn something new, test out a new theory, discover a way to get better at something, or understand it at a deeper level? Can you put yourself in someone else's shoes and find out more about how they might feel or view a situation? How curious it might be!

Strengthening Your Team of Support

The more you feel that you belong to part of a team that supports you, the better you can flourish. At work, your colleagues can offer advice, assist you in projects, be sources of emotional support, and be mentors in helping you manage uncertainty or difficult situations. A stronger support network at work can nourish career development, help you get promotions, and foster better work engagement and communication among your co-workers or customers. Give some time to considering what sort of support you may want or need from others and how you can be of support to someone else. Make a concerted effort to set time aside to get to know your colleagues, asking them questions about themselves and their goals. Ask for help and be open to gaining new perspectives. Ensure you do something every day to nurture an existing relationship. Take time to chat with a colleague during breaks and make time to meet up outside of work, if appropriate.

Getting Organized

Look at your schedule. Where can you insert breaks? Look at your projects. How can they be split up into smaller goals that can be more easily managed? Look at your list of tasks. Track your time so that you can begin the process of setting boundaries and priorities. Which tasks can be delegated to other people who may be better equipped? Set manageable goals and clear boundaries on your time so that you are aiming to achieve smaller and more doable goals in a time frame that suits you. Estimate how much time each small goal will likely take and add a few hours or a day to give yourself some wiggle room. Prioritize which goals need to be done first and mark your calendar for when you plan on attacking each goal.

Ask yourself whether something really matters and how important it is before you throw yourself into a project. Figure out whether the project is something you have time for, given your current schedule and commitments. Take note of whether the project or activity is going to fuel you or drain you. If it is going to drain you, either don't do it or set limits as to when you will do it. Make sure you set limits for work hours and create a clear separation between your work life and home life, as well as "me time."

Bringing Mindfulness into Your Work

Bringing meditation, especially mindfulness, into your work life helps you reduce stress levels, regulate your emotions, improve your communication skills, focus better, have greater insight, and enhance your performance. The beauty of mindfulness is that you don't need to take time out of your busy life to do it. Rather, you can bring it right into everything you do. You don't need to take a chunk of time out to sit quietly in a lotus position and meditate, though doing so would greatly benefit you if you do find the time. You can bring mindfulness into how you eat, speak, read through emails, or breathe.

Look at your schedule and intentionally create short breaks, even if a break is only a minute long, to do a breath focus, mindfully stretch, or do a mindful check-in with yourself, noting how and what you feel, labeling it and perhaps inquiring as to why you may be feeling a certain way. In this way, you practice listening to your body's signals and attune to your needs.

Embracing Failures as Opportunities

Failing at something or experiencing a setback does not define you or determine your worth. It can, of course, be upsetting and frustrating. It's okay to have a little pity party for a few minutes or more. Get it out of your system, though, because being stuck in negative feelings and identifying with your failures as defining you as a failure are not helpful if you want to flourish. Instead, embrace your failures and setbacks, perceiving them as opportunities to grow and learn, to do things a little differently, or to decide that it is time to take a break and reexamine your goals, priorities, or ideas.

Choose to see opportunities everywhere, *especially* in setbacks. Seek meaning. What is there to learn? What can you do differently? Is this the right path? Seeking meaning does not mean you decide that everything happens for a reason, but rather, you look for reason when things happen. Take a pause, have compassion for yourself, rebalance yourself, and give yourself time to shift your perspective so that you can gain new insight into your situation. Do your research, and when you are ready, get back at it, drawing out a new plan with newfound goals and strategies.

Outsmarting Negative Bias

When you can shift into a more optimistic and compassionate viewpoint, you are more likely to find meaning and growth in stressful experiences. It can improve your performance as well as your ability to gain insight, set boundaries and priorities, and access positive emotions and motives. This may seem like a difficult task when you feel overwhelmed and burned out. The trick is to know that you have it in you to outsmart your own negative bias.

You can outsmart your negative bias by regularly practicing gratitude, being compassionate toward yourself, and cataloguing your accomplishments and wins, either in your journal or in your mind. Be mindful with your words. Speak to yourself like you would a dear friend, at all times if possible, and notice mindfully and compassionately when you don't. Catch yourself when you put yourself down by making a statement that is negative toward yourself or reflects a negative limited belief. Find ways to reframe your words so that they motivate you rather than knock you down. Redirect your focus to something positive that celebrates your accomplishments, something you feel grateful for, or ways you feel lucky so that you can connect with positive emotions and thoughts and improve your sense of well-being and self-value.

Thinking with Your Whole Brain

Accessing any of your brain when you feel burned out can be challenging. But it's possible to use a variety of tools that enable you to use your whole brain, which can help you feel more organized and creative. One tool I find to be helpful is the mind map. Mind mapping is a practice developed by Tony Buzan in the 1960s and is meant to help you organize your ideas, plans, goals, or thoughts and essentially stimulates you to use your whole brain. It involves generating ideas and placing them down on paper, but also using color, free association, and feelings, as they are expressed with drawings or colors. These are guidelines for mind mapping:

1. **Start with a symbol or picture that represents your topic in the center of your page.**

   This allows your mind to open to a full 360 degrees of association. Symbols and pictures are also more stimulating and easier to remember than just words alone.

2. **Write down key words that will act as "information-rich nuggets."**

   These will enable you to recall and do creative association.

3. **Connect the words with lines that radiate from your central image.**

   This helps you see how the image and words relate to one another.

4. **Always print your key words.**

   This makes them easier to read and remember.

5. **Print only one key word per line.**

   This forces you to find the most appropriate word that will cover all or as many associations as you may need.

6. **Print the key words on the radiating lines so that the length of the word is the same length as the line.**

   This enables maximum clarity and encourages you to use your space economically.

7. **Use colors, pictures, dimensions, and codes, which allow for greater association and emphasis.**

   Highlighting and using color helps your memory, stimulates ideas and associations, and helps you prioritize what is most important and what is secondary.

REMEMBER

You can pretty much use mind mapping for everything — from summarizing a chapter to thinking about retirement, problem-solving an issue at the office, or planning a vacation or dinner with friends. You may find the process helps you get a better view of a given situation, organize your thoughts, and lay out a clearer action plan ahead. You can even mind map your path for flourishing!

Index

A

Academy of Management Review, "Crafting a Job: Revisioning Employees as Active Crafters of Their Job" (Wrzesnieski and Dutton), 245

acceptance, 154, 176–177, 239–240

accomplishments, 252, 255–256

acedia, 29

activity, extremes of, as potential source of burnout, 74

acute stress, 34–35

adrenal glands, 36

adrenaline, 34, 36, 151

advancement, opportunity for, as possible reason to choose job, 106

agreeableness, as A in OCEAN, 71

all-or-nothing thinking, 127

alternate nostril breathing, 284–285

American Medical Association (AMA)

  on percent of physicians experiencing symptoms of serious burnout, 31

  STEPS Forward platform, 126

American Psychological Association, on thought or cognitive distortions, 127

American Psychologist, "Promoting and Protecting Mental Health as Flourishing: A Complementary Strategy for Improving National Mental Health" (Keyes), 251–252

anger, costs of unexplored anger, 220

Anger: Wisdom for Cooling the Flames (Nhat Hanh), 185

Angie (pediatrician), when caring is wearing, 50

anhedonia, 178

anxiety, burnout as often associated with, 36–37

appreciation and joy (*Mudita*), 158

appreciation exercise, 287–288

archetypes, 123

Aristotle, 275

Armando (Amazon driver), how burnout feels on the inside, 11–12

aspirational crafting, 249–250

audio tracks, 3

autonomy, boosting of, 247–248

awareness, 140–141, 150. *See also* self-awareness

awe, 173, 210, 252, 253, 265–266

B

bad feelings/bad days, as differentiated from burnout, 11

balance, strategies for adding of into your life, 199

beginner's mind, as one of seven essential attitudes, 154

being present, 24, 52, 142, 153, 178

being unable to prioritize and organize tasks effectively, as personality profile that puts people at risk of burnout, 70

beliefs, challenging yours, 127–128

belonging, allowing time for, 209–213. *See also* connections

Berg, Justin (academic), 244

Bifidobacterium, 199

Big Five factors of personality (OCEAN), 70–71

"Big Quit"/"Great Resignation," 103, 104–105

Bikram yoga, 286

body. *See* physical body

body scan, 144–145

body-mind complex, 194

boundaries, setting of, 86, 94, 132, 242–243, 245, 296, 297

brain

  benefits of plasticity of, 192

  gastrointestinal (GI) tract as "second brain," 198

  thinking with your whole brain, 298

break, taking of, 132

breathing
  alternate nostril breathing, 284–285
  as changing with stress, 95
  difficulties with as symptom of burnout, 35
  focusing on, 145–146
  importance of, 54
  mini appreciation breath break, 115
  reflecting on beauty of, 54
  taking mindful breath, 95–96
Brown, Stuart, 208
Bryant, Fred (author), 178
Buddha, 150, 157, 169
burnout
  awakening your senses to reality of, 140–142
  as badge of honor, 42
  by boredom, 18–19, 77, 88
  causes of, 65–82
  checking your level of, 20–25
  chronic and insidious nature of, 47–48
  coining of term, 8
  as commonplace, 41–42
  complexity of, 10–12, 80, 82
  demographics of people who get burned out,
    31–33
  digging in to how you got to, 85–87
  examining your relationship with, 83–102
  explaining of with Four Factor Model, 79–82
  exploring scope and impact of, 27–44
  financial costs of, 40–41
  first-aid for, 23
  "flavors" of, 17–20, 77, 88
  history of, 29, 46
  how it affects the individual, 33–39
  how it feels on the inside, 11–12
  impact of on organizations, 39–44
  insidious effects of culture of, 41
  jobs that put you at risk of, 31–32
  moral injury as distinguished from, 43
  by neglect, 19, 77, 88
  as not the "new normal," 46–50
  observing your own pathway to, 48–49
  only way out of as through it, 7, 44, 55

physiological signs of, 36
physiology of, 34
prevalence of, 30–31
psychological effects of, 36–37
signs of, 12–17
social impact of, 37–38
by socialization, 19–20, 77, 88
sources of, 66–75
as step 4 in looking out for signs of, 14
symptoms of, 35–36
by volume, 17–18, 77, 88
what it is, 8–9
what it is not, 9–10
wisdom of paying attention to, 44

C

Calm (app), 154
calm, establishing of, 94–95
Cambridge Dictionary, definition of humor, 57
cardiovascular disease, as symptom of
    burnout, 35
care
  as building flourishing communities, 268–269
  culture of care, 267–280
  knowing you are worthy of receiving it, 129
career, assessing yours, 111–113
caregiver, caring for, 125–126
Caregiver archetype, 123–124
caring, setting example for, 270–271
Cassian, John (monk and theologian), 29
catastrophizing, 128–129
centering exercise, 288–289
Centers for Disease Control (CDC), 289
change
  acceptance of what you can and can't
    change, 143
  cultivating a safe and brave inner space for,
    175–192
  exploring other options for (aspirational
    crafting), 249–250
  finding the will and way for, 176–185
  getting into a place of acceptance for, 239–240

Harvard Business Review
  article on changes in workplace, 110–111
  report on healthcare costs of burnout, 40
Harzer, Claudia (psychologist), 260
Hatha yoga, 286
having hard time saying "no," as personality
    profile that puts people at risk of burnout, 70
headache, as symptom of burnout, 35
healthcare
  burnout as common occurrence in, 121
  caring for caregivers, 125–126
  challenge of burnout in, 120–124
  it's not you; it's a flawed system, 124–126
  US spending on, 124
  when caring people make mistakes, 125
heart's desire, connecting with, 110
hedonia, 275
help and support
  being willing to accept, 130–136
  fostering team of support, 131
  having difficulty asking for support or help, as
    personality profile that puts people at risk of
    burnout, 70
  importance of social support, 211
  lack of, in Four Factor Model, 79, 80
  nourishing relationships and seeking trusted
    support, 261–264
  shifting your approach to work by helping
    yourself, 132–133
  strengthening your team of support, 295–296
Hendriks, Martjin, 275
Henry Ford Health System, "Getting Rid of Stupid
    Stuff" program, 126
here and now stone (practice), 155
high workload, in Four Factor Model, 79
history
  acknowledging yours can be fruitful, 68
  as factor affecting burnout, 24, 67–69
  tracing path of your life for clues, 69
Ho, Henry C. Y., 268
Holt-Lunstad, Julian, 211
honeymoon phase, 13
Ho'oponopono ("make things right") (practice), 230

Huckman, Robert (researcher), 131
humanity, as one of six virtues, 260
humor, 57, 58
hydration, 200, 204
hypothalamic-pituitary-adrenal (HPA) axis, 35

I

"I Am a Miracle" (exercise), 173, 174
icons, explained, 3
identity, as factor affecting burnout, 24
Indeed, study of people experiencing burnout, 30
individuals, impact of burnout on, 33–39
ineffectiveness, 16–17
infrastructure
  cultivating of one that supports your life force,
    193–213
  self-assessing yours, 213
inner critic, 33, 58, 185–191
Insight Timer (app), 154
Instagram, challenges of, 27
intention, setting of, 102
International Journal of Environmental Research,
    "Flourishing in the Workplace: A One-Year
    Prospective Study on the Effects of Perceived
    Organizational Support and Psychological
    Capital" (Ho and Chan), 268
intrinsic motivation, 209
intrinsic values, 114
Iyengar yoga, 286

J

job crafting, 72, 244–245
job description, reviewing of, 106–107
jobs
  balancing your passion with reality of, 109
  deciding whether you and your job are a good
    fit, 103–118
  do you and your job have good chemistry?
    104–111
  figuring out what changed, 110–111
  getting crafty with yours, 244–245
  optimizing the one you have, 246–247

potential sources of burnout inherent in any job, 74–75

understanding what yours demands of you beyond the job description, 107–108

when yours doesn't fit, 114–118

why did you choose yours? 105

Journal of General Internal Medicine, survey of healthcare workers and first responders, 121

Jung, Carl (psychiatrist), 123

just like me (practice), 161–162

justice, as one of six virtues, 261

K

Kabat-Zinn, Jon (founder of MBSR), 152, 153

Karuna (compassion), 158

Keyes, Corey L. M. (researcher), 251–252

kindness, 58–59, 157–174

knowing where you are, before charting a course, 141–142

Koenig, Harold G. (author), 134, 212

Kripalu yoga, 286

Kriyas (breathwork and poses), 286

Kropp, Brian, 110

Kundalini yoga, 286

Kuo, Ming, 208

L

Lactobacillus, 199

Lazarus, Richard, 147

learned helplessness, 14

letting go, as one of seven essential attitudes, 154

life circumstances, changes in, as impacting sources of burnout, 75

life experiences exercise, 80, 81

life force, cultivating infrastructure that supports yours, 193–213

lifestyle values, 114

lighter side, of managing burnout, 57–58

lightness through radical acceptance, as later stage of self-compassion progress, 169

Littman-Ovadia, Hadassa (researcher), 260

location, as possible reason to choose job, 106

loneliness, 28–33, 215

Love Pyramid, 210–211

The Love Response (Selhub), 210

Loving Kindness Meditation (LKM), 158–160, 212–213

loving kindness, meeting suffering of burnout with, 168–172

Lydia (attorney), as feeling ineffective, 16–17

M

magnification, 128

Malcolm, as having feelings of depersonalization, 15–16

Maloney, Deirdre (author), 107–108

management, as possible reason to choose job, 106

Maslach, Christina (social psychologist), 29, 108

Maslach Burnout Inventory, 22, 29

masterfulness, 255–256

May, Gerald G. (psychiatrist), 183

Mayo Clinic, on percent of physicians reluctant to seek mental health treatment, 123

MBSR (Mindfulness Based Stress Reduction program), 152

McKinsey & Company, on people who said they were "living their purpose," 278

McRae, Emily Rose, 110

"me time," starting the day with, 293–294

meaning

building sense of to foster flourishing, 278–279

connecting with, 237–238

extracting more, 249

looking for, 132

as M in PERMA model, 252

making of, burnout as obstacle to, 38–39

milking situations for, including at work, 264–265

mismatch in, 73–74

seeking of when there seems to be none, 87, 90, 93

ways to enhance, 255

organizations, impact of burnout on, 39–44

overgeneralization, 128

overidentifying with job or passion, as personality profile that puts people at risk of burnout, 70

overload, as burnout by volume, 17–18, 77, 88

overpleasing, as burnout by socialization, 19–20, 77, 88

overweight, as factor that puts people at risk of burnout, 33

oxycodone, 122

oxytocin, 216, 219, 290

P

parasympathetic nervous system (PNS), 95

passion, 85–86, 91, 109

patience
cultivating of, 55, 142–143
as one of seven essential attitudes, 153
plotting a personal strategy with, 241–243

patterns, anticipation of, 243

pausing, 53, 150, 206, 207

paying attention, value of, 24

people pleaser, as personality profile that puts people at risk of burnout, 32–33, 70, 88, 90

perfectionist, as personality profile that puts people at risk of burnout, 33, 70, 88, 89–90

PERMA model, 252, 254, 255, 259, 272

persistence, 142–143

personal strategy, plotting one with patience, 241–243

personal timeline, 48–49

personality
Big Five factors of, 70–71
connecting your profile to burnout, 72
defined, 69
as factor affecting burnout, 24, 69–72
in Four Factor Model, 79, 80
knowing yours, 70–72
profiles that put you at risk of burnout, 32–33
self-assessment on, 88–89

personality tests, 70, 71

personalization, 128

Peterson, Christopher, 259

Pew Research Center, on "Big Quit"/"Great Resignation," 103

physical body
brilliance of, 194
minding yours, 143
as one of Four Foundations of Mindfulness, 150
scanning of, 144–145
smiling to yours, 287–288
taking care of yours, 52–53
use of to ease your mind, 283–291
as your constant companion, 144–146

physical exercise
building of into your life, 203–204
doing what you love with people you love, 204
enhancement of, 283–284
examples of, 284
focusing on fitness in, 204
lack of as behavior that puts people at risk of burnout, 33
rationale for, 201–202
rest and recovery time in, 204
tapping into mindful movement to heal burnout, 204–209
when you feel burned out, 203

physical timeline, 49

physical vitality, 258–259

physician, as job that puts people at risk of burnout, 31, 121

Pisano, Gary (researcher), 131

pitfalls, anticipation of, 243–244

play deprivation, 208

playing, as not just for kids, 208–209

PMR (progressive muscle relaxation), 290

PNS (parasympathetic nervous system), 95

police officer, as job that puts people at risk of burnout, 31–32

positive emotions, 60–61

positive emotions, examples of, 252–253

positive identity, cultivating of in workplace, 273

post-traumatic stress disorder (PTSD), in workplace, 43

power, recognizing yours, 59–60

The Power of Now (Tolle), 140

practices

  compassion with equanimity, 223–224

  connecting to flourishing, 256–257

  focusing on the breath, 145

  giving and receiving compassion, 217–218

  here and now stone, 155

  Ho'oponopono ("make things right") forgiveness prayer, 230

  just like me, 161–162

  listening deeply, 226–227

  Loving Kindness Meditation (LKM), 158–160

  mindfulness in action, 149–150

  pocket practices to get started with self-compassion, 172–174

  scanning the body, 144–145

  self-compassion break for burnout, 166–168

  spiritual practice/spirituality, 133–134, 212–213

  uncovering your core values, 180–183

  where are my feet? 154–155, 205

prebiotics, 199

prestige, as possible reason to choose job, 106

prioritizing, based on data, 98

private suffering, mismatch of public persona with, 28

prize, keeping your eye on, 60, 116

probiotics, 199

Proctor, Kim-Elisha (executive coach and teacher), 42

progressive muscle relaxation (PMR), 290

"Promoting and Protecting Mental Health as Flourishing: A Complementary Strategy for Improving National Mental Health" (Keyes), 251–252

Providence (healthcare system), "No One Cares Alone" program, 126

PTSD (post-traumatic stress disorder), in workplace, 43

public persona, mismatch of with private suffering, 28

purpose

  building sense of to foster flourishing, 278–279

  connecting with, 237–238

  mismatch in, 73–74

"Purpose of Life Predicts Better Emotional Recovery from Negative Stimuli" (Stacey et al.), 278

Q

Qi (Chi), 194–196

Qi Gong ("Energy Work"), 196, 204

quick fixes, no quick fix to burnout, 7, 51–52, 66

R

reacting, versus responding (mindfulness in action), 148–152

recognition, as component of "Three R" approach, 13, 94

recognition, lack of, in Four Factor Model, 79

reintegration, as one of five R's of restorative justice, 225, 229–230

relationship crafting, 246

relationship timeline, 49

relationships

  characteristics of quality ones/healthy ones, 211, 222

  having healthy connections in, 254–255

  managing difficult ones, 219–224

  mending your relationship with yourself, 224–225

  nourishing relationships and seeking trusted support, 261–264

  as one of five R's of restorative justice, 255, 256

  as R in PERMA model, 252

  with your job, 104–111

releasing, 53

relief, possibility of, 51–52

"Religion, Spirituality, and Health: The Research and Clinical Implications" (Koenig), 134

repair, as one of five R's of restorative justice, 225, 228–229

resilience, 13, 233–250, 258

Resilience For Dummies (Selhub), 234

resources, unlocking of from within, 271–272

respect, as one of five R's of restorative justice, 225, 226–227 responsibility, as one of five R's of restorative justice, 225, 227–228

rest and recovery time, in physical exercise, 204

restabilize, as component of "Three R" approach, 13

restorative justice, five R's of, 225–226

retail worker, as job that puts people at risk of burnout, 32

A Return to Love (Williamson), 59

reward, as organization risk factor that can lead to burnout, 108

Roberts, Laura (academic), 273

Rogers, Carl (psychologist), 177

Ruch, Willibald (psychologist), 260

Ruiz, Don Miguel, 269–270

Rumi (poet), 171–172

Ryan, Richard M. (neuroscientist), 209

S

salary, as possible reason to choose job, 105

Savoring: A New Model of Positive Experience (Bryant and Veroff), 178

savoring the moment, cultivating capacity for, 178–179

Schaefer, Stacey M. (researcher), 264, 278

school principal, as job that puts people at risk of burnout, 31

security, as possible reason to choose job, 106

Self Compassion Test, 165

Self Love, 210

self-acceptance, 140, 171

self-assessment, 87–94, 99, 213

self-awareness, 124, 139, 140, 195, 258, 271

self-blame, 24, 67, 111, 177

self-care, 14, 23, 50, 52, 55, 56, 80, 86, 90, 92, 98, 99, 118, 122, 123, 125, 130, 132, 135–136, 192, 193, 225, 241, 268, 271

"self-care holiday," 52

self-compassion, 23, 58–59, 67, 98, 102, 115, 140, 153, 157, 160, 162–174, 184, 189, 192, 211, 217, 226, 228, 236–237, 238, 239–240, 241, 243, 255, 258, 265, 273

self-confidence, 67, 68, 202

self-critical words, 67

self-discovery, 224, 225

self-doubt, 14, 16, 68, 98, 114, 151, 152, 171, 238, 272, 273, 274

self-efficacy, 201, 210

self-esteem, 164, 201, 210, 283

self-flagellation, 67, 69

self-forgiveness, 96, 153, 164

self-image, 67, 202, 204

self-kindness, 23, 157, 158, 167

self-love, 169, 211–212, 225

self-medicating, 10, 122–123, 135

self-nurturance, 211

self-pity, 160, 165

self-value, 80, 158, 192, 235–236, 238, 240, 241, 242, 255, 256, 270, 273, 298

Seligman, Martin, 251, 252, 253, 255, 259

senses, awakening of to reality of burnout, 140–142

serotonin, 95, 198, 201, 219, 283

seven essential attitudes, in building mindfulness platform, 153–154

sexual problems, as symptom of burnout, 35

shame, shifting away from, to opportunity, 84

shame/blame game, 84

Shanafelt, Tait D., 213

Shinrin-Yoku ("forest bathing"), 208

silver linings, finding of in burnout, 184–185

situational burnout, 14

skills
  as factor affecting burnout, 24
  as possible reason to choose job, 106

sleep, guidelines for, 205–206

sleep disruption, as symptom of burnout, 35

slow walk, benefits of, 205

slowing down, strategies for, 199–200

smiling to your body (exercise), 287–288

SNS (sympathetic nervous system), 95

So Good They Can't Ignore You (Newport), 109

social isolation, 215

Social Love, 210

social media, challenges of, 27

About the Author

Dr. Eva Selhub, or Dr. Eva as her clients like to call her, has been practicing and teaching mind-body medicine and methods to tap into our innate ability to be resilient for over 25 years. She is the founder of Resilience Experts, LLC, a company that provides inspirational and informative coaching and consulting specializing in helping individuals and corporations alike to avoid burnout, and achieve optimal wellness, resilience, innovation, and leadership. Her goal: Keep people out of the hospitals, out of burnout, and fully engaged and thriving in life, even in the face of adversity!

Dr. Eva is an internationally recognized expert, physician, speaker, and executive leadership and performance coach, and a consultant in the fields of stress, resilience, and corporate wellness. As an author, speaker, and coach, she uses her powerful gift to translate complex information into practical and usable knowledge that any individual can access. Dr. Eva has previously authored five other books, including *The Love Response, Your Brain on Nature, Your Health Destiny, The Stress Management Handbook, and Resilience for Dummies.* She has been published in medical journals and featured in national publications including *The New York Times, USA Today, Self, Shape, Fitness,* and *Journal of Women's Health* and has appeared on radio and television in connection with her work, including *The Dr. Oz Show.*

Dr. Eva served as an instructor of medicine at Harvard Medical School and as a clinical associate of the world-renowned Benson Henry Institute for Mind-Body Medicine at the Massachusetts General Hospital for close to 20 years, serving as their medical director for six of those years. Dr. Eva offers unique programs for individuals and companies that promote executive health and organizational well-being. She combines her clinical expertise and years of scientific research in neuroplasticity and stress with an in-depth practical study of meditation, spirituality, exercise physiology, and nutrition. Dr. Eva's method of teaching is energizing, personal, insightful, compassionate, and straight to the point. She doesn't mess around, yet she does it with love! She brings in humor along with personal experiences that move her audiences while also enabling them to tap into their own personal journeys, making the learning experience memorable and effective. She gives them the realistic picture behind statistical figures and scientific findings, while blending in optimism, mixed with great storytelling and actionable ideas to latch onto.

For more information on Dr. Eva's workshops, coaching, and consulting, visit her websites at www.drselhub.com and www.drselhubcorporate.com.

Dedication

This book is dedicated to my family, including my parents Jacob and Shirley, siblings and sister in-law, Julie, Eliya, and Laura, and my niece and nephew, Maia and Ezra. It is also being dedicated to my soul family, Lisa Ross and Dorsey Schulman. They fill my heart with love and inspiration, have been my steady support through my own trials and tribulations, and are my "reason why."

Author's Acknowledgments

I'd like to express my appreciation to Tracy Boggier and Tim Gallan along with the entire Wiley team for the clear direction and editing. I am honored to have been given the opportunity to dive more deeply into burnout and be able to share my knowledge and experience. Thank you also to Dr. Steve Hickman for his beautifully written chapters that moved me to want to continue writing this book. I would also like to thank all the colleagues and teachers who have supported and guided me along the way to enable me to step out of "medicine" and explore other facets of life, business, and spirituality. Thanks to all the great writers, meditation teachers, and fearless thought leaders whose work has inspired and informed this book. Lastly, thank you to my family, dear friends, and all of my patients and clients who have taught me how to teach, learn, and grow.

Publisher's Acknowledgments

Acquisitions Editor: Tracy Boggier

Development Editor: Tim Gallan

Copy Editor: Christine Pingleton

Technical Editor: Joseph P. Bush, Ph.D.

Production Editor: Magesh Elangovan

Cover Image:
© Vitezslav Vylicil/Adobe Stock Photos

Leverage the power

Dummies is the global leader in the reference category and one of the most trusted and highly regarded brands in the world. No longer just focused on books, customers now have access to the dummies content they need in the format they want. Together we'll craft a solution that engages your customers, stands out from the competition, and helps you meet your goals.

Advertising & Sponsorships

Connect with an engaged audience on a powerful multimedia site, and position your message alongside expert how-to content. Dummies.com is a one-stop shop for free, online information and know-how curated by a team of experts.

- Targeted ads
- Video
- Email Marketing
- Microsites
- Sweepstakes sponsorship

20 MILLION PAGE VIEWS EVERY SINGLE MONTH

15 MILLION UNIQUE VISITORS PER MONTH

43% OF ALL VISITORS ACCESS THE SITE VIA THEIR MOBILE DEVICES

700,000 NEWSLETTER SUBSCRIPTIONS TO THE INBOXES OF

300,000 UNIQUE INDIVIDUALS EVERY WEEK

# of dummies

Custom Publishing

Reach a global audience in any language by creating a solution that will differentiate you from competitors, amplify your message, and encourage customers to make a buying decision.

- Apps
- Books
- eBooks
- Video
- Audio
- Webinars

Brand Licensing & Content

Leverage the strength of the world's most popular reference brand to reach new audiences and channels of distribution.

For more information, visit dummies.com/biz

PERSONAL ENRICHMENT

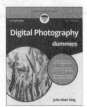

9781119187790	9781119179030	9781119293354	9781119293347	9781119310068	9781119235606
USA $26.00	USA $21.99	USA $24.99	USA $22.99	USA $22.99	USA $24.99
CAN $31.99	CAN $25.99	CAN $29.99	CAN $27.99	CAN $27.99	CAN $29.99
UK £19.99	UK £16.99	UK £17.99	UK £16.99	UK £16.99	UK £17.99

9781119251163	9781119235491	9781119279952	9781119283133	9781119287117	9781119130246
USA $24.99	USA $26.99	USA $24.99	USA $24.99	USA $24.99	USA $22.99
CAN $29.99	CAN $31.99	CAN $29.99	CAN $29.99	CAN $29.99	CAN $27.99
UK £17.99	UK £19.99	UK £17.99	UK £17.99	UK £16.99	UK £16.99

PROFESSIONAL DEVELOPMENT

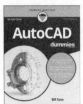

9781119311041	9781119255796	9781119293439	9781119281467	9781119280651	9781119251132	9781119310563
USA $24.99	USA $39.99	USA $26.99	USA $26.99	USA $29.99	USA $24.99	USA $34.00
CAN $29.99	CAN $47.99	CAN $31.99	CAN $31.99	CAN $35.99	CAN $29.99	CAN $41.99
UK £17.99	UK £27.99	UK £19.99	UK £19.99	UK £21.99	UK £17.99	UK £24.99

9781119181705	9781119263593	9781119257769	9781119293477	9781119265313	9781119239314	9781119293323
USA $29.99	USA $26.99	USA $29.99	USA $26.99	USA $24.99	USA $29.99	USA $29.99
CAN $35.99	CAN $31.99	CAN $35.99	CAN $31.99	CAN $29.99	CAN $35.99	CAN $35.99
UK £21.99	UK £19.99	UK £21.99	UK £19.99	UK £17.99	UK £21.99	UK £21.99

dummies.com

dummies®
A Wiley Brand